CAROLINE
AND
CHARLOTTE

CAROLINE
AND
CHARLOTTE

REGENCY SCANDALS
1795–1821

ALISON PLOWDEN

SUTTON PUBLISHING

This book was first published in 1989 by
Sidgwick & Jackson Limited.

This new paperback edition first published in 2005 by
Sutton Publishing Limited · Phoenix Mill
Thrupp · Stroud · Gloucestershire · GL5 2BU

British Library Cataloguing in Publication Data.
A catalogue record for this book is available from the British
Library.

ISBN 0 7509 4173 1

Typeset in 11/12.5pt Photina.
Typesetting and origination by
Sutton Publishing Limited.
Printed and bound in Great Britain by
J.H. Haynes & Co. Ltd., Sparkford.

Contents

Chronology

1762
12 August   Birth of George Prince of Wales, later Prince Regent and George IV

1768
17 May   Birth of Princess Caroline of Brunswick-Wolfenbüttel

1795
8 April   Marriage of the Prince of Wales and Princess Caroline

1796
7 January   Birth of Princess Charlotte of Wales

1797
August   Separation of the Prince and Princess of Wales

1806
May–July   The Delicate Investigation
October   The Death of the Duke of Brunswick

1811
6 February   The Prince of Wales is sworn in as Regent

1813
March   Death of the Duchess of Brunswick

1814
16 June   Princess Charlotte breaks off her 'engagement' to the Prince of Orange
12 July   Runs off to join her mother in Bayswater but is forced to return to Carlton House
August   The Princess of Wales sails for the Continent

1816
2 May   Princess Charlotte marries Prince Leopold of
                           Saxe-Coburg-Gotha

1817
6 November   Princess Charlotte dies in childbirth

1820
January   Death of George III and accession of Prince
                           Regent as George IV
6 June   Queen Caroline arrives back in London
17 August   The 'trial' of Queen Caroline opens in the House
                           of Lords
10 November   The case against her is dropped

1821
20 July   The queen is refused entry to Westminster Abbey
                           for the King's coronation
7 August   Death of Queen Caroline

1830
26 June   Death of George IV

ONE

With All My Heart I'll Marry . . .

Says the King to the Prince, 'You know you are deeply in debt, Sir;
A wife you must take – 'tis vain to bounce and fret, Sir,
You'd better send to Germany to fetch some pretty cousin,
There Highnesses Serene you may have by the dozen,

And you shall marry
Your Cousin – Cousin Cary.'

The Prince replied, 'Good Father, if you'll but find the money,
I'll take whom you please, and she shall be my Honey;
There's Caroline of Brunswick will give her pretty hand,
If you'll but pay my debts, I'll take her at command,

And with all my heart I'll marry
My Cousin – Cousin Cary.'

'Should I pay your debts', the King said, 'I should be much to blame, Sir;
There's Clarence, and there's York would quickly want the same, Sir;
John Bull will discharge them, you never need to doubt it;
So e'en take your Wife and I'll speak to Pitt about it.

And so you shall marry
Your Cousin, Cousin Cary.'

The morning of Wednesday 1 April 1795 found the naval squadron escorting Caroline of Brunswick to England for her marriage to the Prince of Wales fogbound in the North Sea about eight leagues offshore between Orfordness and Yarmouth. It was not until the early hours of Friday 3 April

– Good Friday – that the weather cleared, and Commodore Jack Payne was able to get the frigate *Jupiter* under way again and sail on down the coast before a brisk east-south-east wind, passing Harwich at eleven o'clock. That night was spent at anchor off the Nore, and on Saturday the flotilla entered the Thames estuary, reaching Gravesend at two in the afternoon. The river banks were lined with spectators, the day was fine and 'the whole prospect most beautiful' – at least according to the account of James Harris, Earl of Malmesbury, on board the *Jupiter*.

Lord Malmesbury, who had had the task of fetching the bride from Germany plus the anxiety of conveying her across a corner of Europe currently under threat of attack by the conquering armies of revolutionary France, was understandably euphoric in anticipation of being able to deliver his charge safely into the arms of her groom, but the long-term prospects for the success of the union were not encouraging.

George Augustus Frederick, Prince of Wales, eldest son and heir apparent of George III, King of England, was thirty-two years old and, on paper at any rate, the most eligible bachelor in the western world. His attitude towards matrimony, however, had always been disappointingly negative. Indeed, some ten years earlier he had sworn that he would never marry. He had 'settled it with Frederick' – Duke of York and his next favourite brother – that Frederick would marry and that the crown would descend to his children. But Frederick's wife had turned out to be barren, and the other princes were now all either comfortably suited with mistresses, or for other reasons unwilling or unable to do their duty by the family. George III's plain sturdy little Queen (she had been Charlotte of Mecklenburg-Strelitz) had survived no fewer than fifteen pregnancies and successfully reared seven sons and five daughters, but the remarkable fact remained that by 1795 there were still no grandchildren – or at least no grandchildren born on the right side of the blanket. It was not, however, concern for the future of the Hanoverian succession which had finally propelled the Prince of Wales towards the altar – it was stern financial necessity.

The scandal of the Prince's debts was an old story. His income from the Civil List, supplemented by the relatively modest revenues of the Duchy of Cornwall, had never been anything like enough to support his ample life-style as a *bon viveur*, aspiring glass of fashion, racing man, connoisseur, collector, and patron of the arts – probably no income ever would have been enough to satisfy the needs of so dedicated and proficient a spender of money and there had been something of a showdown back in 1787. Parliament had then had to be persuaded to settle the most pressing of his Royal Highness's obligations, and his Civil List allowance had been raised by £10,000 to £60,000 a year. But early in 1794 another crisis loomed, as once again the Prince's debts approached a staggering six-figure sum. Ungrateful tradesmen were beginning to refuse his custom, and he was being dunned in the street by his creditors, some of whom went so far as to petition the Prime Minister for relief. Clearly another rescue operation would have to be mounted, but it was equally clear that this time John Bull, as represented by an increasingly unsympathetic House of Commons, would first demand some earnest of reform from the prodigal. That summer, therefore, the Prince of Wales went to see his father and abruptly informed him that he was now ready to enter 'a more creditable line of life', to get married and settle down.

Surprised but pleased, the King stipulated only that his son's wife must be a Protestant and a princess, which inevitably meant a German princess, and offered to send some suitable 'confidential' person on a talent-spotting expedition. But it seemed that the Prince had already made up his mind to throw the handkerchief in the direction of his cousin Caroline of Brunswick-Wolfenbüttel. King George was thought to disapprove of marriages between such close relations – Caroline was his niece – and he continued to urge his son to make 'particular enquiries about her person and manners'. Nevertheless he could not help feeling complimented that his sister's child should have been thus singled out and told William Pitt that she was the person who 'naturally must be most agreeable to me'. The Queen, on the other hand, remained noticeably tight-lipped, telling her son Ernest that she was resolved never to speak about the marriage, 'so that no one should say she had any hand in anything'. She had never cared for Caroline's mother, she went on, but she would make the princess welcome and hoped, though plainly without conviction, that the couple would be happy. It has been suggested that her attitude was due to pique that her own niece, Louise of Mecklenburg-Strelitz, had been passed over. The explanation more probably lies in the fact that Queen Charlotte had heard some very disturbing reports about the Princess Caroline: that her governess had to stick closely to her side at dances in order to prevent her from making an exhibition of herself by having 'indecent conversations' with men; that her parents had forbidden her to speak to anyone at all except her governess; that all amusements had had to be banned because of her unbridled passions and generally 'indecent conduct'.

According to other sources, any of his brothers, or anyone else who had been in Germany recently, could have told the Prince of Wales that the Brunswick princess had the reputation of being 'very loose'; but although he must surely have heard the gossip he appears to have paid no attention. He did not even make any of the usual discreet enquiries regarding the lady's personal appearance, character, and habits. In fact, he seems to have spent considerably less time and trouble over his choice of a wife than he would have done over a pair of boots or a new waistcoat. Nor is it clear why Caroline should have been so immediately and obstinately preferred to every other possible candidate. It later occurred to Lord Malmesbury that she may have been put into the Prince's head by the Duke of Clarence out of spite, 'with a view to plague the Duke and Duchess of York whom he hates . . . well knowing that the Princess Caroline and the Duchess of York dislike each other, and that this match would be particularly unpleasant to her and the Duke'. But if this was so, then the Duke of York gave no hint of any displeasure in his congratulatory note to his elder brother. The princess, he wrote, was 'a very fine girl and in every respect in my opinion a very proper match for you. That you may be completely happy with her, is my most hearty wish.'

On the available evidence it has to be assumed that the Prince of Wales did not greatly care whom he married. Since he was being forced into wedlock for sordid financial reasons alone he seems to have felt that any Protestant princess would do, seizing cynically on the first name which was suggested to him, whether by his brother William or another. Certainly he was impatient to get the whole tiresome business over with as quickly as possible, but such matters were not to be hurried. Although the King had given his consent and notified the Prime Minister of his son's projected engagement by the end of August, it was late autumn before Lord Malmesbury received His Majesty's command formally to ask for the Princess Caroline for the Prince of Wales. His lordship was in Hanover, on his way home after completing a special mission to Berlin, when these instructions arrived in the post, and he needed to make only a short detour to reach the neighbouring Duchy of Brunswick in Lower Saxony on Thursday 20 November. He got a warm welcome, the offer of apartments in the ducal palace, servants, the use of a carriage, and an invitation to dinner from the Duchess, who was 'all good nature', and the Duke, 'as usual civil, but reserved and stiff'.

Malmesbury the veteran diplomat and the Duke of Brunswick, a military man much respected for his qualities of personal courage, were old acquaintances, but the English envoy had not previously encountered the object of his current errand. In 1781 an English schoolboy doing the Grand Tour with his tutor had spent several months in

Brunswick and fallen a little in love with Princess Caroline. Young John Stanley (he later became Lord Stanley of Alderley) saw the princess three or four times a week, but only as a star for ever out of his reach. Caroline at fourteen had been a lively, pretty child with light coloured hair hanging in curls on her neck, with rosebud lips from which it seemed that none but sweet words could flow, and always simply and modestly dressed. 'How well I remember her in a pale blue gown with scarcely a trick of ornament,' an older John Stanley was to recall in sentimental mood.

By the time Lord Malmesbury arrived to ask for her hand, Caroline was twenty-six, an age by which most unmarried women were at their last prayers as the saying went, and appeared 'much embarrassed' – or perhaps still in a mild state of shock – when his lordship was first presented to her. Malmesbury's dispassionately observant eye noted a pretty enough face but 'not expressive of softness – her figure not graceful – fine eyes – good hand – tolerable teeth, but going – fair hair and light eyebrows – short, with what the French call "des épaules impertinentes"'. Despite her initial (and uncharacteristic) display of self-consciousness, the princess was quite obviously vastly happy with her future expectations, and so, equally obviously, was her mama. The Duchess, who chattered incessantly, could talk of nothing else and made no attempt to conceal her astonished delight at the turn events had taken. All the young German princesses had learned English in the hope of becoming Princess of Wales, she told Malmesbury at one of their long gossipy sessions over the card table, but she had always been careful never to put such an idea into Caroline's head, knowing that the King had often expressed his disapproval of the marriages of first cousins. Naturally enough, the Duchess did not mention any of the other possible objections to her daughter becoming Princess of Wales.

Malmesbury's first few days in Brunswick were largely taken up by socializing – dinners, balls, and suppers and paying ceremonial visits to the various members of the ducal family and other local dignitaries. He also found himself called upon to have a series of time-consuming discussions with the Duke, who was being urged to go to Holland to take command of the Allied army which was attempting, not very successfully, to contain the French. This did not give him much opportunity to get to know the Princess Caroline, but on 26 November he noted in his diary that she improved on acquaintance, was gay and cheerful, and seemed to have good sense.

The main part of the mission was being held up by an irritating wait for Malmesbury's full powers and credentials to be sent from London. These came at last on 1 December, and two days later his lordship drove solemnly to court in one of the official ducal carriages to make his public and ceremonial proposal to the Princess Caroline on behalf of the King of England's son. The Duke of Brunswick, although 'rather embarrassed', played his part in the proceedings with proper dignity. The Duchess shed tears, and the princess also appeared 'much affected' but nevertheless bore up well and made her replies in a clear, distinct voice. The troth-plighting ritual was followed by an 'immense dinner' and a reception for the offering of 'compliments of felicitation', at which Caroline was for the first time addressed as Princess of Wales, and the day ended with supper, another huge and elaborate meal. Next morning, Count Feronce, the Brunswick Secretary of State, waited on Malmesbury for the signing of the marriage treaty, which had been drawn up in English and Latin, and presented him with a snuff box from the Duke and a diamond watch from Princess Caroline. The Brunswick end of the formalities were now complete, and it only remained to make the necessary arrangements for the bride's journey to her new home.

On 3 December a messenger had arrived from the Prince of Wales, bearing a copy of his picture and a bundle of letters, including one for Lord Malmesbury urging him in the most vehement terms to set out with the Princess *immediately*. The Prince was eager to avoid any appearance of unnecessary delay, 'bad on every account but particularly so to the public, whose expectations have now been raised for some months . . . besides the suspense, and the naturally unpleasant feelings attendant upon suspense, which I myself must be subject to'. His Royal Highness did not mention the naturally unpleasant feelings attendant upon the fear of an imminent invasion by bum-bailiffs which he must also have been subject to.

It was all very awkward. Caroline, of course, wanted to set out for England at once, and so, for that matter, did Lord Malmesbury; but, as he pointed out in a private letter to the Home Secretary, the Duke of Portland, it was not quite as simple as that. It had to be remembered that he was in Brunswick under the King's orders, and could do nothing without the King's express command. It was just like the Prince of Wales to disregard every consideration but his own convenience and place Malmesbury in this embarrassing predicament 'by conveying to me his wishes, or rather his orders, without having previously communicated with His Majesty's Ministers. . . . If he should be displeased with me for a non-compliance with these wishes', continued his lordship rather plaintively, 'I only have to entreat your Grace to justify me, when any justifications may be necessary. . . . I most heartily join with the Prince in his earnest desire to see the Princess at Carlton House, but sincere and strong as this desire is on my part, I cannot stir from hence but by the King's order.'

Malmesbury had hoped to be able to pay his respects to Portland at Burlington House by Christmas, but Christmas approached, and still no orders came from London regarding the route the travellers were to take. Holland, with the shorter sea crossing, would obviously be preferable in winter, but in the present international political climate the security of the Low Countries could not be guaranteed – a fact which reinforced Malmesbury's determination not to move without authority. However, he assured the Prince of Wales that not an hour would be wasted once it had pleased His Majesty's ministers to inform him to which port he was to conduct the princess, and he went on to write encouragingly of her cheerfulness and good humour, and of his conviction that she meant to devote her life to the study of her husband's happiness.

In truth the ambassador was far from optimistic about Caroline's suitability for the role in which she had been so nonchalantly cast. Since the signing of the marriage treaty the Duke of Brunswick had roused himself from his brooding preoccupation with his own problems for long enough to have a couple of serious talks with Malmesbury about his daughter. 'She is not stupid,' he had said earnestly, 'but she has no judgement', adding that it had always been necessary to keep a very strict eye on her. He was extremely anxious that Caroline should make a success of things in England and wanted to make her realize that her high position would not be simply one of 'amusement and enjoyment; that it had its duties, and those perhaps difficult and hard to fulfil'. The Duke, it seemed, had few illusions about his future son-in-law, appearing 'perfectly aware of the character of the Prince'.

Malmesbury had also been hearing some straight talking from the Duke's resident mistress. Mlle de Hertzfeldt was another old acquaintance, a highly intelligent and agreeable woman of the world, genuinely devoted to her protector and concerned for the welfare of his daughter. Caroline, remarked this percipient onlooker, was not a bad girl at heart, nor had she ever done anything really bad, but she had no tact, no reserve, and absolutely no discretion. She would blurt out the first thing that came into her head – 'with her the word always runs ahead of the thought' – and even in the little court at Brunswick this regrettable habit was inclined to give people the wrong idea. Mlle de Hertzfeldt was frankly very much afraid of the consequences if the princess were to be suddenly let loose on London society – not only would her head be turned by flattery, but the unscrupulous and scheming women who would surround her would be able to manipulate her any way they liked.

The Duke's mistress therefore thought it of the utmost importance that Caroline should be kept out of the limelight, to begin with at least. Then, too, her chances of a happy life in England would depend heavily on her getting on well with her mother-in-law, but unfortunately the Duchess of Brunswick returned Queen Charlotte's dislike and had talked far too openly on the subject. The Duchess, in short, was a silly woman who had never given her daughter the example and guidance she needed, with the result that, while the princess was ill at ease with her father, she felt no proper respect for her mother. In her anxieties, de Hertzfeldt begged Lord Malmesbury to take Caroline in hand himself. 'She will listen to you. She has found that you talk good sense in a pleasant, easy manner, and you will make a far greater impression on her than her father whom she fears too much, or her mother, whom she does not fear at all.' The Duke had also 'earnestly entreated' the ambassador to advise and direct his daughter, to warn her never to show jealousy of, or indeed appear to notice, her husband's inevitable infidelities, not to ask questions, and, above all, 'not to be free in giving opinions of persons and things aloud'.

To be invited to create a silk purse out of this particular sow's ear in the limited time available was a challenge which would have defeated most people from the start, although it is true that no one could have been better qualified for the task than this patient, urbane, smooth-tongued, infinitely worldly wise diplomat, whose long professional career had taken him to all the major courts of Europe, from Madrid to St Petersburg. It is also true that Caroline was pathetically ready to listen, even when Malmesbury, sitting next to her at supper, recommended 'perfect silence on *all* subjects' during her first six months in England. The following evening, again sitting beside her at the supper table, he advised her to avoid familiarity, to have no confidantes, to avoid giving any opinion, to approve but not to admire excessively, on no account to meddle in politics, to be very attentive and respectful to the Queen, and to endeavour to keep on good terms with her.

The princess, her tutor admitted, took all this very well. She wanted to be popular, she said, but supposed rather wistfully that Malmesbury thought her too confiding. An amiable quality, he replied carefully, but not one to be indulged by those in high places without incurring great risk. Popularity was never attained by familiarity. On the contrary, 'it could only belong to respect, and was to be acquired by a just mixture of dignity and affability'. Answering Caroline's flow of questions about life at the English Court, his lordship seized the opportunity to emphasize that while of course he hoped she would enjoy every ease and comfort of domestic happiness in private life, in public she should always appear as Princess of Wales, surrounded by 'all that appareil and etiquette due to her elevated situation'. The King and Queen, he told her, never missed attendance at Divine Service on Sundays, and he urged her to follow their example and do her best to make the Prince do the same.

Lessons continued relentlessly through December, with Malmesbury always trying to set his pupil's mind on 'thinking of the *drawbacks* of her situation', to impress her with the idea that 'those of a very high rank have a price to pay for it, and that the life of a Princess of Wales is not to be one of all pleasure, dissipation, and enjoyment; that the great and conspicuous advantages belonging to it must necessarily be purchased by considerable sacrifices'. His 'eternal theme' to her, as he put it, was '*to think before she speaks, to recollect herself*', to cultivate discretion, reserve, prudence, dignity, and *tact*, and to remember that she could never have too much of these essential attributes of a great princess.

Although Malmesbury honestly admired Caroline's sunny good nature and marvelled at her willingness to accept his criticism and advice in the spirit in which they were offered, his doubts remained. Well disposed and well meaning she might be, but there was so little mental substance, he mused

11

in his diary, no depth or strength of character, and a light and flighty mind. In the hands of a steady and sensible husband she would probably turn out very satisfactorily, but not even the most partial witness would think of applying the adjectives 'steady and sensible' to the Prince of Wales. Caroline herself had told Malmesbury that she knew something of his reputation as a womanizer, that she was prepared on this point and was determined never to appear jealous. However, she did ask some pretty pointed questions about the Countess of Jersey, the Prince's current *chère amie*, and when her spinster aunt, the Abbess of Gandersheim, told her that her husband would certainly deceive her and make her unhappy she showed disquieting signs of uneasiness, despite Malmesbury's efforts to shrug it off as the nonsense of an envious old maid.

There was another awkward moment when the Brunswicks received an anonymous letter, abusing the Prince and 'warning them in the most exaggerated terms against Lady Jersey, who is represented as the worst and most dangerous of profligate women.' To Malmesbury's intense annoyance the Duchess of Brunswick not only showed the letter to her daughter, but discussed its contents freely with all and sundry. Caroline presently showed it to Malmesbury, who dismissed it as the work of 'some disappointed milliner or angry maid-servant and deserving no attention'. Indeed, the princess seemed more distressed by another communication which had just arrived from the King of England, expressing the hope that his niece and daughter-in-law would not have too much vivacity and be content to lead a retired and sedentary life. This was plainly not at all what his niece and daughter-in-law had in mind, and it was rather too noticeable that the hints dropped by the poison pen that Lady Jersey would be ready to lead her instead into a life of promiscuity had not alarmed her as they should. Her parents, however, no doubt remembering the tragedy of their elder daughter, who had died in mysterious circumstances after being unfaithful to her husband, *were* frightened. Mlle de Hertzfeldt renewed her warning that Caroline needed a firm hand – 'il faut la gouverner par la peur, par la terreur même' – and Lord Malmesbury decided the time had come to administer a short sharp shock. 'It was *death* to presume to approach a Princess of Wales,' he told her, 'and no man would be daring enough to think of it. She asked me whether I was in earnest,' he recorded. 'I said such was our law; that anybody who presumed to *love* her was guilty of *high treason*, and punished with *death*, if she was weak enough to listen to him: so also would *she*. This', added Malmesbury, 'startled her', as well it might.

Perhaps fortunately, since everybody's nerves were becoming rather frayed, the long awaited marching orders had now at last – on 26 December – arrived in the postbag from London. The travellers were, after all, to rendezvous with their naval escort at a Dutch port, and, faithful to his promise, Malmesbury wasted no time in getting on the road. The Duchess of Brunswick had reluctantly agreed to accompany her daughter as far as the coast. The Duke, repeatedly recommending Caroline to Malmesbury's care, urged him to be a second father to her.

The weather had turned bitterly cold, and when the party reached Osnabruck on the afternoon of New Year's Day 1795 they were greeted by a courier bearing the disquieting news that the French had crossed the frontier into Holland. In spite of later reports that they had been driven back by the British expeditionary force under General Dundas, Lord Malmesbury was taking no chances. As he told the Prince of Wales, he could only act as if he were travelling with his own wife and children. The frost was now so severe that the Dutch could not open the sluices, their traditional defence against invasion, and it would also very likely prevent Commodore Payne from bringing his squadron into the Scheldt estuary. Malmesbury believed Holland to be in the most imminent danger and wrote to the Foreign Secretary,

Lord Grenville: 'It would be blameable in the extreme were I to conduct the Princess into that country at such a moment, and without the certainty of having a fleet to convey her out of it. . . . My duty', he added, with the air of one stating a hitherto unsuspected truth, 'is to arrive *safe*, and not to sacrifice this circumstance to the wish of arriving *soon*.'

Osnabruck was crowded with starving refugees from revolutionary France, and while he waited for more news of the fighting from army headquarters Malmesbury tried to organize some relief for them. 'I persuade the Princess Caroline to be munificent,' he wrote. 'She disposed to be but not knowing *how* to set about it.' Once the idea had been put into her head, though, she readily gave ten louis 'of her own accord' to an *émigré* child – and then quite spoilt the effect by trying to press a handful of double louis on Malmesbury himself when he complimented her on the value of the Brunswick coinage. 'Cela ne me fait rien,' she cried. 'Je ne m'en soucie pas. Je vous prie de les prendre.' It seemed she was incapable of discriminating between *giving* as a benevolence, and flinging money away like a child. 'She thought that the act of getting rid of the money and not seeming to care about it constituted the merit.' Malmesbury took a deep breath and tried patiently to explain what real benevolence was, recommending it as a quality that would, if rightly used, make her more friends and give her more genuine satisfaction than anything else. This whole concept, he was sorry to see, was quite new to her, but he thought 'she felt the truth of it'.

There were, however, times when he despaired. 'Princess Caroline very gauche at cards – speaks without thinking – gets too easy – calls the ladies (she never saw) "Mon coeur, ma chère, ma petite." I notice this, and reprove it strongly.' The Princess, for the first time, seemed inclined to take umbrage, which Malmesbury affected not to notice. His lordship was also beginning to have trouble with the Duchess, who was understandably not enjoying being dragged round the ice-cold countryside in the dead of winter and the middle of a war. She wanted urgently to go home to her cosy routine and her beloved card table, but this Malmesbury could not allow. The Princess of Wales must on no account be left unchaperoned until she was safely surrounded by reliable English ladies. If she were taken by the French, moaned the Duchess, her brother the King would be very angry. No doubt he would be very sorry, replied Malmesbury, but 'your Royal Highness must *not* leave your daughter till she is in the hands of her attendants'. Quite early in his career the Earl of Malmesbury, then plain Mr Harris, a young *chargé d'affaires* in Madrid, had taken so firm a line with the Spanish government that he had successfully thwarted a threatened invasion of the Falkland Islands almost single-handed. He was now more than a match for the unhappy Duchess of Brunswick. 'She argues,' he noted, 'but I will not give way, and *she* does.'

After a week at Osnabruck there were signs of a thaw, setting in, letters from The Hague reported all apparently quiet, and Malmesbury decided to try and press on. On 9 January the travellers reached Delden, just over the Dutch border, but about four leagues beyond the town they were met with more bad news. The French had crossed the river Waal in strength, heavy fighting was going on, and Malmesbury was advised '*on no account to come into Holland*'. That night was spent uncomfortably at an inn at Delden with an artillery barrage in progress 'at no great distance', and in the morning Malmesbury hurried his charges away to Osnabruck again. Caroline took this latest set-back with her usual cheerfulness, though she 'seemed sorry not to go on towards the fleet'. Unlike her mama, she was enjoying the adventure and declared she was not afraid of cannon or the French. Indeed, she took pride in boasting that as a Brunswicker she was not afraid of anything – *ein Braunschweiger darf alles* – and Malmesbury admitted that she certainly appeared to have inherited her father's physical courage, but as he wanted mental decision, so she lacked any sound understanding or steadiness. She was, in short, a creature of impulse, far too easily caught and distracted by superficial impressions, loving to talk, to gossip and giggle and whisper girlish confidences, making 'missish friendships that last twenty-four hours'. She possessed 'some natural but no acquired morality, and no strong innate notions of its value and necessity; warm feelings and nothing to counterbalance them; great good humour and much good nature – no appearance of caprice – rather quick and *vive*, but not a grain of rancour'.

While jotting down this character sketch of the princess in his diary, Malmesbury was considering his next move. Holland was now out of the question – before the end of the month it would be completely overrun. They would therefore have to embark from the north German port of Stade, and that meant waiting until the mouth of the Elbe was free from ice. Meanwhile they could not stay at Osnabruck, for one thing it was too close to the front and would very likely soon be occupied by the retreating army. But Malmesbury was determined not to let Caroline go back to Brunswick, where she would undoubtedly revert to all her bad old ways of 'familiarity and easy intimacy' among her former cronies. Instead, he decided to make for Hanover. In that uncommonly correct and decorous annexe of the English court the future Princess of Wales would be accorded every last detail of the formal respect due to her exalted rank and have a chance to grow accustomed to it. In fact, the more he thought about it, the more his lordship began to feel that this enforced delay might be a blessing in disguise, giving Caroline a much needed dry-run – a period of preparation during which to acquire the habit of 'proper, princely behaviour', so that by the time she did finally arrive in England it might have become almost natural to her. He tried to explain this to his pupil in another long, serious talk, warning her that she would be judged in England by the impression she made at Hanover, urging her to make a special effort to please the older people there, recommending the exercise of 'great attention and reserve', and, as always, 'preaching circumspection'.

The journey from Osnabruck turned into a nightmare of discomfort. The cold was intense, worse than anything Malmesbury had ever experienced anywhere out of Russia. The unfortunate servants, perched on the outside of the carriages, were frozen solid. Inside, the Duchess was 'benumbed' and, as a result, increasingly peevish. Even after their arrival at Hanover she went on complaining about the cold in what Malmesbury considered a quite vulgar fashion, was troublesome about choosing her apartments in the palace, difficult about holding a regular Court day, which Malmesbury insisted upon, mean about tipping, and generally behaved in a thoroughly disagreeable and ill-mannered way. Malmesbury often had occasion to deprecate and reprove Caroline's disrespectful attitude towards her mother, but he could hardly be surprised by it.

During the six weeks or so which were to be spent in Hanover his lordship persisted in his attempt to conduct a one-man finishing school, despite frequent attacks of discouragement. 'Princess Caroline very *missish* at supper . . . Princess too childish and over-merry at supper.' It seemed impossible to cure her of the habit of *tutoy*ing people she hardly knew and calling them 'ma chère' or 'mon coeur', or of her unashamed curiosity – 'a silly pride of finding out everything' – especially about other people's love affairs, which led her at times to make 'the most improper remarks and conversation'. This was something which Malmesbury, foreseeing only too clearly the sort of social chaos it would create in London, made the most determined effort to correct.

Caroline continued to listen patiently to his lectures, though on one occasion she did admit that she would not have put up with them from anyone else, but unfortunately they only seemed to make a very temporary impression, so that Malmesbury began to believe that she was incapable of any strong or lasting feelings, her mind being so incorrigibly shallow and frivolous, her heart so 'very, *very* light'. By the same token, her good humour might be unfailing and praiseworthy, but her sense of humour was often unacceptably earthy. For example, when she had to have a tooth drawn she apparently thought it funny to send it to Malmesbury by her page. 'Nasty and indelicate,' he noted vexedly. And while on the subject of delicacy . . .

'Argument with the Princess about toilette,' runs the entry in his lordship's diary for 18 February. 'She piques herself on dressing quick; I disapprove this. She maintains her point.' Suppressing a shudder, Malmesbury had a quiet word with Madame Busche, Caroline's dresser, asking her to explain that the Prince of Wales was very fastidious in his tastes and would expect his wife to pay the most careful attention to personal daintiness – something which the princess was apt to neglect to the point where she became positively offensive. On the following day she appeared 'well washed *all over*' – she must, presumably, have told him this herself – but Malmesbury kept up the pressure.

Early in March he was recording that he had had another conversation with the Princess Caroline, endeavouring, as far as was possible for a *man*, 'to inculcate the necessity of great and nice attention to every part of the dress, as well as to what was hid as to what was seen'. He knew, he added, although he does not say how, that her underclothes and stockings were coarse and cheap and never washed or changed often enough, and went on to reflect sadly on how amazingly her mother – although an Englishwoman with no excuse for not knowing better – had neglected her education in this vital department. In fact, the English had never enjoyed an especially good reputation for cleanliness, but things were changing, at least among the *haut ton*, where the Prince of Wales's friend, that immensely influential model of sartorial elegance George 'Beau' Brummel, was setting a fashion for meticulous grooming and high standards of personal hygiene for both sexes.

In the middle of March, Malmesbury received a welcome reinforcement with the arrival of the Hon. Mrs Harcourt, wife of General William Harcourt who had succeeded the Duke of York as Commander-in-Chief of the British forces in Holland, currently being routed by the French. The Harcourt family, of Nuneham Courtenay near Oxford, were old and trusted friends of the King and Queen. Mrs Harcourt, who had been with her husband at army headquarters now established at Osnabruck, had had a premonition that, being as it were on the spot, she might be asked to chaperon Caroline to England, considering 'the difficulty attending any lady's coming over at this time to fetch the Princess'. Not that she was overjoyed at the prospect. 'I am always wretchedly ill at sea. How I am to stand such a voyage at such a season I know not.' She was already suffering from an inflammation of the eyes and face and apart from that had absolutely nothing suitable to wear. 'I know not what I shall do for clothes. . . . I have none with me, and as to money we are really ruined.'

But there was, of course, no question of refusing a royal request of this nature, and after an unpleasant journey – after such a severe winter the roads were more than usually bad, with the carriages up to the axles in mud and slush left by the melting snow – Mrs Harcourt, still moaning gently, reached Hanover on 16 March. Like a good courtier, she at once professed herself delighted with the princess, who was so very good natured that it seemed impossible she should not succeed. Mrs Harcourt was sure the Prince would love her, she was so affectionate and her desire to please so very engaging. 'She is all openness of heart, and has not a shadow of pride.'

Lord Malmesbury, with his more intimate knowledge of the princess, remained unconvinced, but when the suggestion came up that he should stay in Germany on official business instead of accompanying her to England, Caroline burst into tears and spoke to him with such apparently genuine 'kindness and feeling' that he was quite touched. In fact, despite the exasperation she had so often caused him, there is no doubt that his lordship had developed a reluctant fondness for this great boisterous, over-friendly, slatternly creature who, he very much feared, was destined for nothing but disappointment and disaster. For her part, Caroline had come to depend heavily on Malmesbury as her guru and father-figure. On at least one occasion she had expressed a hope that he would accept a position in her household – though she was afraid he would not consider it good enough for him – and had several times declared it would be a comfort to have him near her. She was sure no one else would ever give her such good and honest advice.

But the whole strange little interlude was now coming ineluctably to an end. Early in March letters had arrived from England to say that a naval escort was on its way to the Elbe; on the 24th the travellers left Hanover for Stade and at seven o'clock on the evening of Saturday 28 March they went on board the *Jupiter* off Cuxhaven to be greeted by a fifty-gun royal salute which was echoed by the rest of the fleet. 'Very fine evening, and fine sight,' observed Malmesbury with satisfaction. The sea was smooth, the wind in the south-east, the weather charming, and everyone consequently in a good temper. Caroline, who most likely had never seen the sea before, much less been on it, was thrilled. 'The Princess delighted with the ships, and the officers greatly pleased with her manners and good humour.' Indeed, despite Mrs Harcourt's forebodings, the voyage went off perfectly. 'The weather began to be fine the day we left Hanover; the wind was fair, the sea as smooth as glass, accommodation good, society agreeable, and the whole . . . like a party of pleasure.'

For Caroline that week spent at sea was a bubble of pure enchantment – perhaps the first, and certainly the last, time of unclouded happiness she was ever to know. 'The Princess's sweet temper and affability of manner has charmed and delighted everyone,' wrote Mrs Harcourt, 'and all the officers of the ship declare they should have had more trouble with any London lady than Her Royal Highness has given. She is always contented, and always in good humour; and shows such pleasant, unaffected joy at the idea of her prospect in life, that it does one's heart good to see anybody so happy.' It seems, though, that there were some people on board the *Jupiter* who viewed Caroline's prospects rather more realistically than poor sentimental Mrs Harcourt, or the innocent princess herself. In fact, some people, 'knowing the discomforts she would have to contend with', were sorry to see her so elated and tried tactfully to bring her down to earth a little. But Caroline would not have her bubble burst – not yet, anyway. Was she not going to be married to the finest and handsomest prince in the world, and live in the most desirable country in Europe? Of course she was happy, ecstatically so. How could she be otherwise? Lord Malmesbury, who had been with Jack Payne catching up on the latest gossip about the finest handsomest prince in the world and the Countess of Jersey, could have told her.

Things started to go sour from the moment Caroline first set foot on the soil of the most desirable country in Europe. At eight o'clock on the morning of Easter Sunday the travellers transferred from the *Jupiter* to the royal yacht *Augusta* for the final stage of the journey up-river from Gravesend to Greenwich, arriving at noon after a 'pleasant and prosperous sail' only to find that the royal carriages and ceremonial escort of the Prince of Wales's Light Dragoon Guards had not yet put in an appearance. There followed an embarrassing hiatus of at least an hour, during which the princess and her party were entertained by the attentive but flustered Governor of the Hospital for Seamen and his two sisters. Caroline was much intrigued by the Greenwich pensioners, who had streamed out of the chapel before morning service was half over, 'forsaking the pulpit' in their eagerness to catch a glimpse of the distinguished visitors, and as she bowed and smiled from a window of the Governor's house she was moved to enquire if every Englishman was missing an arm or a leg. So much for all

Lord Malmesbury's homilies on tact and discretion and thinking before one spoke!

When the official reception committee did at last turn up it included the Countess of Jersey, newly appointed lady of the bedchamber to the Princess of Wales. It was Lady Jersey, so Malmesbury heard, who had caused the delay in the first place by simply not being ready, and her ladyship at once began to make her presence disagreeably felt by criticizing Caroline's dress in terms which led Malmesbury to speak to her quite sharply. Mrs Harcourt had taken great pains over the princess's toilette that morning, and she was wearing white muslin over a blue satin slip, which sounds both pretty and suitable – echoes of that 'pale blue gown with scarcely a trick of ornament' which had once so charmed young John Stanley. Lady Jersey, however, had come prepared with an elaborate robe of white satin and insisted that Caroline must change into it before setting out for London. The princess's measurements had, of course, been sent to London so that a trousseau could be ordered for her, but in the circumstances it seems only too probable that the white satin was not calculated to flatter her dumpy little figure.

More trouble threatened over the seating arrangements in the carriages. Lady Jersey having the effrontery to say that as riding backwards always made her ill, she hoped she would be allowed to sit *forwards* – that is, next to the princess. This was strictly against etiquette, and although the easily bullied Mrs Harcourt would have conceded the point, Lord Malmesbury most certainly would not. Fixing her ladyship with a fishy eye, he remarked that she should never have accepted a situation as lady-in-waiting if riding backwards in a coach disagreed with her. If she was *really* likely to be sick, then she had better travel with himself and Lord Claremont, leaving Mrs Harcourt and Mrs Harvey Aston (the other bedchamber lady) to accompany the princess. This, he noted with grim satisfaction, settled the business. Lady Jersey sat sulkily beside Mrs Harcourt with her back to the horses, and no more was heard about feeling sick.

According to Malmesbury, there was little sign of popular interest or applause on the road to London, but the report in *The Times* speaks of 'Westminster Bridge and all the avenues leading to the Park and the Palace' being crowded with spectators and carriages, and of the Princess bowing and smiling 'with the greatest good nature'. The princess was finally deposited at St James's at about three o'clock and taken up to the Duke of Cumberland's vacant apartments overlooking Cleveland Row. Here a crowd was waiting to 'huzza', and she at once appeared at the open window to curtsy and smile in response. These pleasantries, which continued 'for some minutes', were brought to an abrupt end by the arrival of the Prince of Wales from Carlton House; and, no one else being in the room, it was left to Lord Malmesbury to perform the introductions. We have his own succinct account of this famous first encounter between bride and groom.

> She very properly . . . attempted to kneel to him. He raised her (gracefully enough), and embraced her, said barely one word, turned round, retired to a distant part of the apartment, and calling me to him, said 'Harris, I am not well; pray get me a glass of brandy.' I said, 'Sir, had you not better have a glass of water?' – upon which he, much out of humour, said with an oath, 'No; I will go directly to the Queen', and away he went . . .

– leaving behind him a situation which had jolted even Malmesbury out of his customary unshakable poise. As for Caroline, she was not surprisingly, stunned, exclaiming 'Mon Dieu! est ce que le Prince est toujours comme cela? Je le trouve très gros, et nullement aussi beau que son portrait.' This too, was not surprising. Two years later the Prince of Wales was to turn the scales at 17 stone, and already the marks of good living and self-indulgence were only too apparent on his large, florid countenance. Malmesbury managed to stutter something about his Royal Highness being naturally 'a good deal affected and flurried at this first interview', which must have sounded unconvincing even to him. Certainly it did not convince Caroline, who showed an alarming disposition to make further criticisms, and Malmesbury was only rescued from his embarrassment by a timely summons from the King.

Exactly why the Prince reacted so violently to the first sight of his bride has never been satisfactorily explained. Contrary to the usual assumption, her physical appearance cannot have come as any very great shock. In view of the close connections which existed between England and Germany – especially Hanover and Brunswick – he must already have had a pretty clear idea of what she looked like. True she was no beauty, and would have compared particularly badly with the graceful, assured elegance of Lady Jersey, but Caroline was no freak. In her twenties she still possessed a certain blowsy blonde attraction – Horace Walpole told Miss Berry within days of her arrival that, although she was a bit on the plump side and used too much rouge, 'everybody speaks most favourably of her face as being most pleasing'. The press reports, too, were generally favourable, remarking on her expressive eyes, good teeth and complexion, and beautiful hand and arm, while *The Times* declared magisterially that she might properly be deemed 'a very pretty woman'. The Prince of Wales may not have wanted to marry his 'Cousin Cary', but he had had long enough to get used to the idea; and, although she was later to give him cause enough for ill will, it is hard to find any excuse for his treatment of her on that first afternoon, or any explanation apart from sheer petulant bad temper.

Dinner that evening, which was hosted by the vice-chamberlain and attended by all those who had been detailed to escort the Princess of Wales to London, set the seal on a disastrous day. Caroline, needless to say, was by no means the first royal bride to find herself expected to make up a threesome with her husband's mistress, and perhaps if Lady Jersey had not been so obviously intent on putting her down, the Prince less openly uncivil, she might have been able to accept the situation with at least a show of indifference. But as things were, her fighting spirit had been roused, and the poor girl reacted to humiliation and disappointment in the only way she knew – by trying to hit back. It was brave, but it was a fatal mistake. 'I was far from satisfied with the Princess's behaviour,' wrote a deeply mortified Lord Malmesbury; 'it was flippant, rattling, affecting raillery and wit.' Worse still, she would persist in 'throwing out coarse vulgar hints' about Lady Jersey, who sat by demurely and triumphantly mute, watching the newcomer make a fool of herself in front of the Prince, who was 'evidently disgusted' by his fiancée's 'giddy manners' and pathetic attempts to be clever and sarcastic. Indeed, in Malmesbury's opinion, this unfortunate dinner party served to fix his initial dislike, which was soon to flower into 'positive hatred'.

The marriage had to go ahead, of course. It was far too late now to cancel arrangements made months in advance and, in any case, impossible to withdraw without creating a catastrophic scandal and loss of face on both sides. The ceremony was scheduled for the evening of Wednesday 8 April and would take place in the presence of the King and Queen and 'all the persons of elevated rank in the kingdom' at the Chapel Royal, St James's. Although it was not an occasion which the general public were invited to share, some buildings in the vicinity had been illuminated in its honour, and on the following day *The Times* and the *Morning Chronicle* were able to inform their readers that the bridal gown had been made of white silver tissue, richly trimmed with silver, and ornamented with a profusion of jewels. The Princess had also worn a coronet and a royal robe of crimson velvet bordered with ermine. Her four bridesmaids, the Ladies Mary Osborn, Charlotte Spencer, Caroline Villiers, and Charlotte Legge, all the daughters of dukes or earls, had been dressed alike in white satin over white crepe slips embellished with stripes of silver foil and spangles, and on their heads bandeaux of spangled crêpe and silver laurel leaves, topped by three large white ostrich feathers.

The chapel was suffocatingly hot and crowded, but the bride showed no sign of nervousness, appearing to be in the best of spirits and chattering away to the Duke of Clarence who escorted her up the aisle. The groom, on the other hand, 'looked like death' and, as Lord Malmesbury put it, 'had manifestly had recourse to wine or spirits'. The Duke of Bedford saw him swallow several stiff brandies, and by the time he arrived at the altar he had reached that state sometimes described as 'tired and emotional' – fuddled, weepy, and so unsteady on his legs that his two ducal groomsmen, Bedford and Roxburghe, had their work cut out to keep him upright. This was bad enough, and nor was the service itself without its embarrassing moments. For when the Archbichop of Canterbury, John Moore, came to the words relating to 'any person knowing of a lawful impediment' he laid down his book and looked very earnestly for a second or two at the King as well as at the royal groom, who was 'much affected and shed tears'.

With the possible exception of the bride, few people present in the Chapel Royal can have failed to grasp the significance of Dr Moore's meaning glances. Few people present can have been unaware of the persistent and well-grounded reports that some ten years earlier the royal groom had gone through a form of marriage with Maria Fitzherbert, a respectable widowed lady who had since been his most regular companion, but whose principles had prevented her from agreeing to share his bed without benefit of clergy. Although rumours of this 'marriage', performed behind locked doors in Mrs Fitzherbert's drawing-room by the Reverend Johnes Knight in December 1785, were always vehemently denied by the Prince and his friends – the fact that Mrs Fitzherbert was a devout Roman Catholic made the matter even more sensitive – its existence had become a pretty open secret in court and political circles. (Describing Caroline's arrival in London to Miss Berry, Horace Walpole had observed facetiously that it was not thought Mrs Fitzherbert would forbid the banns.) Under the terms of the Royal Marriages Act it would, of course, have been judged invalid in the eyes of the law, but – quite apart from the unholy scandal which would have been caused – the Church might have experienced a good deal of difficulty in side-stepping the obstacle of a pre-contract freely entered into before witnesses by consenting adults and blessed by an Anglican priest. The Archbishop's hesitation is, therefore, understandable, and he further emphasized his qualms of conscience by twice repeating the passage in which the Prince engaged 'to live from that time in nuptial fidelity with his consort'. Even as the vows were being spoken, though, it was noticed that HRH was 'perpetually looking at his favourite Lady Jersey'. The Duke of Leeds, walking immediately in front of the bridal couple in the procession from the chapel, could not help remarking how little conversation passed between them, and 'the coolness and indifference apparent in the manner of the Prince towards his amiable bride', still nodding and smiling like a mechanical toy. 'What an odd wedding,' commented Lady Maria Stuart, who was present at the Drawing-Room which followed.

Although still obviously unhappy, the Prince sobered up sufficiently to respond to the formal congratulations offered at the reception held in the council chamber at St James's, and to appear 'very civil and gracious' to the distinguished guests. The royal family then retired to the Queen's quarters at nearby Buckingham House, where a splendid supper had been provided, so that it was approaching midnight before bride and groom finally reached Carlton House – by which time, according to the bride, the groom had ceased to take any interest in the proceedings. 'Judge', she said bitterly to one of her ladies-in-waiting some years later, 'judge what it was to have a drunken husband on one's wedding day, and one who passed the greatest part of his bridal night under the grate, where he fell, and where I left him.'

Caroline's disillusion had been rapid and complete. Certainly it was hard to 'conceive or foresee any comfort' from a connection in which Lord Malmesbury was also already lamenting having taken any share.

TWO

Separation In High Life

My abhorrence of her is such . . . that I shudder at the very thoughts of sitting at the same table with her, or even of being under the same roof.
                                        The Prince of Wales, June 1796

Oh! mine God, what I have suffered! Luckily I had a spirit, or I never should have outlived it.
                    The Princess of Wales to Charlotte Campbell, December 1810

A separation on mere disagreement of temper is repugnant to all the laws that govern any State which professes a reverence for religion and morality.
                                        The Lord Chancellor, January 1798

On the day after the royal wedding a whole coachful of wedding-cake drove away from Carlton House – a large piece parcelled up and sealed with the Prince's seal being sent to all their attendants 'with their R. H.'s compliments'. There was a good deal of other traffic in and out of the Prince of Wales's London residence that Thursday. The Queen went to breakfast and Lord Malmesbury to dinner. The bridegroom was observed going out for a solitary morning ride, and all those who had been honoured with invitations to the wedding Drawing-Room were expected to call to enquire after the bride's health – a custom which Lady Maria Stuart thought extraordinary, and rather indelicate. She went, of course, but not until the evening, and was informed her Royal Highness was *very well* and at dinner.

The weekend was spent at Windsor, where, as Mrs Selina Wilson told her friend Mrs Stapleton, 'all was gala'. The Prince still appeared to be sulking (or nursing his wedding hangover), for he escorted his bride neither to church at St George's on the Sunday morning nor at the promenade on the Castle Terrace afterwards – the contemporary equivalent of a royal walkabout. But, according to Mrs Wilson, the King made up this deficiency by handing the Princess of Wales everywhere himself, 'and looking at her with so much delight as must impart pleasure of itself to all who wish him well'. It is also nice to know that one member at least of Caroline's new family was showing her some elementary courtesy. Mr Wilson thought her 'genteel' and even 'very pretty', with an exquisitely fine complexion. His wife added that he thought she looked happy and that 'the gaping multitude seemed pleased with her whole demeanour'.

If Caroline did indeed look happy it says much for the durability of her famous good nature, though she may have been temporarily cheered by the King's attentions and the obvious approval of the Windsor crowd. The rest of the 'honeymoon' however, was an unmitigated disaster. The newly-weds spent some weeks at Kempshot Park, a rented house near Basingstoke, where, as the Princess later told Lord Minto, there was no other woman present but Lady Jersey, while the men of the party were all 'very blackguard companions of the Prince's, who were constantly drunk and filthy, sleeping and snoring in boots on the sofas'. The scene was, she said, more like Shakespeare's Prince Hal carousing at the Boar's Head tavern than any of her preconceived notions of how a prince and a gentleman should behave. The conversational tone had been suited to the rest, and 'the whole resembled a bad brothel much more than a palace'.

Caroline was never above exaggerating to make a good story, but it is true enough that Lady Jersey was constantly present during the early months of her marriage, and the Prince's male cronies were a notoriously hard-drinking set.

Nor can there be any reasonable doubt that this was a miserable time for her. One thing, though, had been accomplished. By the time the couple moved down to Brighton in June the Princess of Wales was pregnant, and the Prince wrote to his mother on the 26th that the sea air seemed to agree with her, as, in spite of the shockingly bad weather they were having, she was 'in the best health and spirits possible, excepting at moments a little degree of sickness which is the necessary attendant upon her situation'. According to Caroline's own account, she had been astonished to find herself 'wid child' and had at first refused to believe it. She and the Prince had only lived as man and wife for two or three weeks at most, and, if Lord Minto understood her mysterious 'hums and haws' correctly, she had thought him incapable.

The Princess's pregnancy gave her an undeniable additional importance and status in the royal family, and the correspondence between the Prince, his mother and his sister Elizabeth that summer contains frequent references to the matter – antenatal advice, anxious enquiries, and good wishes. But although Princess Elizabeth clung to the hope that Caroline would settle down and 'turn out a very comfortable little wife', it was by now all too obvious that there was never going to be anything 'comfortable' about the union of this calamitously ill-assorted pair.

The Prince of Wales's taste always ran to older women (Lady Jersey was in her forties and a grandmother), to mature, sophisticated, stylish women, experienced in the arts of pleasing. Everything about the uncouth, hoydenish Caroline grated unbearably on his tender sensibilities, and, of course, everything she said and did made things worse. Admittedly she must often have been extremely tiresome and silly – tossing at him (her own expression) the letters she had brought from the petty German courts, saying, 'There, that's to prove I'm not an imposter!'; giving back pert answers when she would have done much better to have held her tongue; making would-be funny remarks and only succeeding in being vulgar. She was, in short, acting like an insecure child trying desperately to attract attention from the adult world, and her husband's cold disapproval and obvious withdrawal served only to goad her into still more outrageous acts of naughtiness. Lord Malmesbury, dining at Carlton House some three weeks after the marriage, was shocked and saddened by her light and even improper conduct, but when the Prince reproached him for not having sent any advance warning from Brunswick, his lordship felt bound to point out that he had not been given any discretionary powers. On the contrary, his instructions had been positively limited to asking for the Princess Caroline in marriage *and nothing more.* The fact that the Princess was proving to be just as unsuitable as he and the other prophets of gloom in Brunswick had privately foreseen certainly gave him no satisfaction, and now he had to suffer the injustice of the Prince's resentment, for Malmesbury could see it had 'left a rankle in his mind'.

But any lingering 'rankle' against Lord Malmesbury counted for nothing in comparison with HRH's resentment over the shabby way Parliament had treated him. As promised, as soon as the wedding was over, the Prime Minister had raised the matter of his financial position in the Commons, and had suggested that, as a married man, the Prince should be granted a rise of £65,000 a year from the Civil List – thus bringing his total annual income up to £138,000. Out of this, the government proposed to deduct £25,000 a year to 'service' his debts, and Mr Pitt further suggested that the £13,000 represented by the Duchy of Cornwall revenues should be set aside to form a sinking-fund which would eventually pay off the principal. However, when it was revealed that the debt now amounted to a horrifying £630,000 – all incurred since the settlement of 1787 – the mood of the House turned distinctly nasty. For the Opposition, Charles (later Lord) Grey demanded that the royal increase should be £40,000 not £65,000, while other leading Whigs, including Fox and Sheridan, favoured a plan for selling off the Duchy of Cornwall or some other Crown estates in order to settle the whole rather disgraceful mess without more ado.

Unfortunately for the Prince, the year of his marriage had coincided with a period of widespread political unrest, with revolutionary Jacobin societies holding defiant mass meetings in the capital, and acute economic distress in rural areas. Seventeen ninety-five was the year of the notorious Speeenhamland decision, when the Newbury magistrates were forced into using the parish poor rate to make up their farm labourers' wages to an agreed minimum level, based on the price of a standard gallon loaf. This rudimentary system of supplementary benefit was quickly adopted by other local authorities, but after a failed harvest and the worst winter in living memory there were food riots in several southern towns that summer. Against this background, the Commons' reluctance to provide outdoor relief for an incorrigibly spendthrift and untrustworthy member of the royal family was not exactly surprising, but the King had committed himself to support the ministerial proposals and felt he could not, in honour, back down. It therefore looked as if Pitt would have to resign – until the Prince was persuaded to end the deadlock by agreeing to accept a drastically revised scheme, putting the whole of the £65,000 increase, plus his Duchy revenues, under the control of a panel of commissioners who would use it to pay off his creditors, and try to ensure that a similar situation did not arise again. This got the government out of an embarrassing predicament, but left the Prince himself worse off than ever, since he now had to support a wife out of an income which had actually been reduced in real terms. His mother felt the Princess ought to be able to manage on an allowance of £4,000 a year for clothes, charities, and incidental expenses, but as Parliament had apparently specified that she should have £5,000, the

Prince decided to place this amount in the hands of two trustees to be doled out as pin-money, and further arranged to allow her £7,000 or £8,000 a year to pay the wages of the establishment he considered she must retain to 'support her rank'. This establishment was, however, to be kept to a minimum. He had ostentatiously reduced his own household and also planned to dismiss Caroline's 'useless' maids of honour as part of the stringent economy campaign forced on him through 'the infamous deceit of Pitt'.

None of this improved his temper, his sense of grievance, or his attitude towards his wife, and marital relations had already degenerated into barely veiled hostility – a 'wrangling couple who could scarcely keep up in public the face of conjugal decorum'. 'Quand à nous,' the Prince wrote bitterly to his mother at the end of September, 'we go on tolerably well, très [?]nnement [ennement?], aussi méchante aussi médisante et aussi menteuse que jamais' (very discordant, as wicked, as slanderous, and as untruthful as ever). All the same, for the sake of their unborn child, some public semblance of conjugal decorum had to be maintained, even though Lady Jersey was still a member of the household (no question of saving on *her* salary) and, so rumour had it, missed no opportunity of putting the Princess out of countenance. The Duke of Wellington, repository of all the royal family's secrets, later declared that it was Lady Jersey who had made the Brunswick match in order to bring down Mrs Fitzherbert – a far more dangerous rival to her ascendancy than poor Caroline would ever be. Mrs Fitzherbert, for her part, had not forbidden the banns. Instead she had retired to the country, where she was currently biding her time in dignified silence.

Caroline's baby was expected early in the New Year, and the Queen had already begun to interview staff for the nursery. Lady Dashwood, wife of one of the gentlemen of the King's privy chamber and herself lady of the bedchamber and close friend of Princess Elizabeth, was chosen to be Governess of the new establishment; and on 15 August, just before leaving for the annual family holiday at Weymouth, the Queen saw Dr Michael Underwood, the obstetrician or 'man-midwife' as such practitioners were still sometimes rather contemptuously described by the old-fashioned. They had a long conversation, reported Her Majesty in a letter to the Prince of Wales, 'and agreed almost upon every point relating to the qualities requisite for a good nurse'. Dr Underwood had not yet received any applications from candidates for this important post, but promised to pass on details of any which might reach him without delay. He also recommended that if the Princess 'should feel too full' she might find it beneficial to be blooded. This operation was not, however, to be undertaken without the advice of a physician, 'particularly as nobody about her at present is in the least acquainted with her constitution'.

The Queen continued to be exercised over the choice of a nurse – that is, of course, a wet nurse – who must be not only perfectly healthy and scrupulously clean in both her person and habits, but good-tempered, sober, discreet, and in all respects of irreproachable moral character. By early November a short list of three women in the appropriate stages of pregnancy was under consideration – Mrs Bower or Bowers of Brighton, another lady who was 'the wife of a chymist . . . of very reputable parents, well brought-up, and a very proper person for the honour she aspires to', and a Mrs Smith, who seems to have been the favourite. Dr Underwood had seen and approved her. He had also inspected her elder child, but not the second which was reported to be fourteen months old, 'very large headed, and so fat that it cannot walk' – this apparently being regarded as something of a tribute to its mother's prowess as a provider. As well as this, Mrs Smith had the advantage of being the youngest of the three candidates and for that reason if no other was the Queen's preferred choice, 'as the youngest milk is always the best'. The only question was, would she be ready to answer the summons when it came? She expected to be delivered by mid-December; but, wrote the Queen, 'should it so happen as it frequently does that she should go beyond her time about 10 days or a fortnight, she may in all likelihood not be fit to come when she is wanted'. The best advice Her Majesty could give, and based on her own considerable experience, was that Mrs Smith should be engaged, but that both the other ladies should be seen, and 'the one which is the most proper be told to keep herself in readiness, in case the one latest brought to bed should not answer'. In the event, it was Mrs Bowers who won the coveted honour, so presumably Mrs Smith had indeed been out in her reckoning.

Having disposed of the question of wet-nurses, Queen Charlotte, in a long letter to her son, went on to drop a hint about what she called the 'childbed linin', advising that the Princess should be told to order it immediately because 'it takes a great deal of trouble to make such a quantity in a short time'. She also urged that a monthly nurse be engaged without delay, since the good ones were always in great demand, and added that she hoped Lord Cholmondeley (the Wales's lord chamberlain) had ordered the cradle. 'Tell him I, as an experienced woman in such matters, say it should be without rockers to it.'

The Queen did not want to appear meddlesome, but there was one other matter which Dr Underwood was anxious should be mentioned; this was 'that he thinks the Princess should come to town sooner than you intend'. As a woman of experience in such matters, Her Majesty thought this a reasonable request, especially in the case of a first child, for 'if any little uneasy feelings should alarm the Princess at a place where she had not those about her who she wishes to employ, it might perhaps occasion a great deal of unnecessary fright'. The Queen did not like her daughter-in-law any more – in fact liked her rather less – than she had expected to, but just now it was important that she be cherished and protected from unnecessary alarms.

Caroline did not, however, show any signs of suffering

from little uneasy feelings and when she and the Prince arrived back in London at the end of November she appeared to be blooming. Lady Dashwood was standing by at Nero's Hotel, ready to move into Carlton House at a moment's notice, the baby linen and the rockerless cradle were also presumably ready in good time, and everything continued to go smoothly. At the beginning of January, Lady Dashwood sent word to her friend Princess Elizabeth that she thought all 'would (or rather) might be soon over', and the Princess wrote to her brother from Windsor on the 4th:

> You may easily imagine what a constant state of anxiety we have been in; whenever the door opens we are in expectation of good news and when at Frogmore the house bell makes me jump and fly to the window in hopes of being the person to bring the news of this happy event to mama who thinks much of you, for we are sure that you are upon the *high fidgets* walking about the room, pulling your fingers and very anxious.

The family at Windsor had to wait another three days for news of the happy event which came in a brief note from the Prince of Wales, dated Carlton House, 9.45 a.m., 7 January 1796. 'The Princess,' he wrote to his mother,

> after a terrible hard labour for above twelve hours, is this instant brought to bed of an *immense girl*, and I assure you notwithstanding we might have wish'd for a boy, I receive her with all the affection possible, and bow with due defference [*sic*] and resignation to the decrees of Povidence . . . Pray have the goodness to apologize to my dear sisters for my not writing to them, but I am so fatigued that I can only sign myself . . . [etc.].

He also informed the King in rather more formal terms that 'the Princess is just brought to bed of a daughter, and thank

God both the mother and child are quite well and likely to continue so. The Princess has had a very severe time indeed, having been upwards of twelve hours in constant labour. I hope your Majesty will forgive my saying anything more at present.'

The Prince was, in fact, quite worn out, having gone two whole nights without sleep. He had been present at the birth, along with his uncle the Duke of Gloucester, the Archbishop of Canterbury, the Lord Chancellor, the Lord President of the Council, and various other dignitaries who had been summoned to attend as official witnesses at this 'interesting and important occasion', and he was now more than ready to take to his bed himself.

On the following day the *Morning Chronicle*, announcing the safe arrival of the newest member of the royal family, could not resist drawing attention to the fact that 'the Prince and Princess of Wales have been nine months married this day'. The gates of Carlton House had been thronged all the previous morning with the carriages of the nobility and gentry calling to enquire for the Princess; but, said the *Chronicle* 'it may save our fashionable readers the trouble of immediately appearing in person to know that no names will be taken down till after two o'clock this day'. On Monday the 11th it was given out that the hours of enquiry after mother and child would be from two to four o'clock in the afternoon, between which times members of the public, that is 'all respectable persons of both sexes', would be admitted to an ante-chamber and served with wine, cake, and caudle. This last was a warm drink of thin gruel, sweetened, spiced, and mixed with ale or wine, considered particularly suitable for post-parturient women and commonly also served to their visitors.

As the fashionable and respectable world flocked to pay its respects in proper form at Carlton House, within the family circle there was much relief and some genuine pleasure. The Queen begged her congratulations, 'and a kiss to the young lady'. Princess Elizabeth added heartfelt wishes that 'every blessing and happiness may attend my (already) dear little niece', and the King was delighted. He had no regrets that the baby was a girl – indeed, he had always hoped it would be. 'You are both young', he wrote to his son on 7 January, 'and I trust will have many children, and this newcomer will equally call for the protection of its parents and consequently be a bond of additional union.'

'The dear King', reported Princess Elizabeth two days later, 'talks of nothing but his grandchild, drank her health at dinner and went into the Equerries room and made them drink it in a bumper.' The Queen had by this time been up to town to take her first look at her granddaughter. 'My accounts of her beauty', she declared, 'make every lady curious to see her'. Plans were being made for a ceremonial visit by the King and princesses.

But while mother and child continued to do well, and congratulations and good wishes flowed in from family and friends, the baby's father suffered a sudden and mysterious emotional *crise*. He wrote quite calmly to his mother on the afternoon of 9 January, reporting that the Princess (Caroline) had had a good night and was generally as well as could be expected. The following day, in a state of intense nervous excitement bordering on hysteria, he was making his will. In this extraordinary, disjointed, rambling, and repetitive document, over three thousand words long scribbled out in his own hand, the Prince bequeathed all his wordly property 'of every description, denomination and sort' to his 'beloved and adored Maria Fitzherbert', the wife of his heart and soul, his only true and real wife in the eyes of Heaven and dearer to him, even millions of times dearer, than the earthly life he was expecting (so he said) to resign at any moment.

As to his new-born daughter, he left her in the sole custody, care, and management of the King his father, the Queen, and thereafter his various brothers and sisters. 'This I have been so far induced to be explicit upon,' he continued, meaning that the mother of his child, call'd the Princess of Wales, should in *no way either be concern'd in the education or care of the child, or have possession of her person*, for though I forgive her the falsehood and treachery of her conduct towards me, *still the convincing and repeated proofs I have received of her entire want of judgement and of feeling, make me deem it incumbent upon me and a duty, both as a parent and a man, to prevent by all means possible the child's falling into such improper and bad hands as hers.*

A page or two further on the dutiful parent remembered that the jewels which 'she who is call'd the Princess of Wales wears *are mine, having been bought with my own money*, and therefore those every one and the whole of them I bequeathe to my infant daughter as her own property, and to her who is call'd the Princess of Wales I leave one shilling'.

Although the Prince of Wales, vain, touchy, hypersensitive to ridicule, and possessing an unrivalled talent for self-dramatization, habitually operated on a short emotional fuse, exactly what had provoked this particular outburst remains unclear. It can only be assumed that someone had picked this moment of all others to pass on one of Caroline's choicer indiscretions relating to his supposed sexual inadequacy. But whatever the truth of the matter, the war on the domestic front was now about to enter a new and altogether more actively rancorous phase.

Before the end of January the Prince and his mother had decided that Lady Dashwood, whose constitution was delicate, must be given an assistant, and the Queen 'ventured to make enquiries' about a Miss Garth, a young lady in her early twenties, brought up 'in a very plain and solid way', and seeming to have all the necessary qualifications of common sense, docility, and modesty. Her appearance was neat, clean, and not 'befeathered', her manners were pleasing, and she showed no signs of any unbecoming inclination to put herself forward or 'get into the great world'. For his part, the Prince was only too ready to trust his mother's judgement in such matters and leave 'the whole and entire management' of them in her hands. Frances Garth was accordingly engaged as sub-governess, but HRH begged that the Queen would undertake to '*put her upon her guard* before ever she puts her foot in the house' and ensure that she clearly understood she would be responsible to him and Lady Dashwood alone 'for everything going on perfectly correctly'.

There was to be no deviation from the rules laid down by the Prince for the day-to-day running of the nursery. Apart from the ladies of the royal household, no outsiders were to be admitted; and as a precaution against the possible spread of infection, there was to be absolutely no intercourse between the nursery staff and the rest of the servants or tradespeople. Mrs Bower was allowed to have three or four friends in to see her on one evening a week, but they were not to stay later than ten o'clock, and none of the other servants in the house were to be of the party. Mrs Bower's meals were to be served at regular times – breakfast at eight thirty, dinner at two, tea at six, and supper at nine. Everyone was to be in bed by eleven and rise early. Either Lady Dashwood or Miss Garth was to be on duty or on call at all times, and one or other of them, together with a Mr Hownham (presumably a footman-cum-security guard) must always be available to escort their charge on her daily airings in the gardens of Carlton House. The infant princess was to be moved into Lady Dashwood's room when the nursery was being cleaned, but must on no account be kept sleeping out of her cradle or out of the nursery after 3 p.m.

There appears to have been no attempt to stop 'her who is call'd the Princess of Wales' from seeing her daughter. On the contrary, the rules allowed for a daily visit to her rooms, which was as often as most upper-class mothers were in the habit of seeing their infants. But at the same time it is clear that there was never even a pretence of consulting her wishes over the ordering of the nursery establishment, and arrangements for the christening went ahead without reference to her, the Queen sending a 'christening suit' trimmed with family lace and a special cradle, also lace trimmed. Caroline was, though, present at the ceremony, which took place on Thursday 11 February in the Great Drawing-Room at St James's Palace. Here the baby was baptized by the same Archbishop of Canterbury who had married her parents ten months previously and given the names Charlotte Augusta after her grandmothers, who were also godmothers – Princess Mary standing proxy for the Duchess of Brunswick.

Of all family occasions a christening should be one of the most joyful, and to the outward eye this christening – with the first representative of the long-awaited new generation thriving in her nest of silk and lace, a young mother whose demonstrable fecundity gave every promise of male heirs to come, and a father who had at last entered the holy estate of lawful matrimony and provided for the Protestant Succession – this christening certainly seemed to give the circle of doting aunts and proud grandparents a legitimate (in every sense) excuse for rejoicing. So it was especially mortifying that the event should have coincided with the moment when it was no longer possible to ignore or conceal the impending breakdown of relations between the baby's parents. In fact, gossip about the 'indecent neglect and contempt' with which the Prince of Wales treated his wife had been circulating for some time in the London clubs and salons, and stories that he had stripped her rooms of furniture and taken back his wedding-present jewellery to give to his mistress naturally lost nothing in the retelling. 'The numberless reports and anecdotes of his manner of behaving to the Princess are no doubt in part invented, and in part much exaggerated,' wrote Lord Glenbervie, himself a noted gossipmonger. 'But if the twentieth part of them have any foundation, that is sufficient to fix the highest degree of blame on his conduct.'

No doubt some of the talk *was* exaggerated, but equally there could be no denying that Caroline was being ostentatiously cold-shouldered by her husband and his family. 'She drives always alone,' wrote the lawyer Charles Abbot in his diary, 'sees no company but old people put on her list by the Queen, Lady Jersey, etc. She goes nowhere but airings in Hyde Park. The Prince uses her unpardonably.'

'She is, I am afraid, a most unhappy woman,' recorded another sympathizer. 'Her lively spirits which she brought over with her are all gone, and they say the melancholy and anxiety in her countenance is quite affecting.'

Years later Caroline told a member of her household staff that she would rather die than have to go through those early months in England again. 'Sooner or later we must all die; but to live a life of wretchedness twice over – oh! mine God, no!' Immured in the alien and intimidating grandeur of Carlton House, with no kindred spirits to chat to and few if any inner resources to fall back on, of course she was depressed, lonely, and bored to tears. She was also growing increasingly resentful. It was unfortunate that she had failed to make friends with her mother-in-law – as Mlle Hertzfeldt had predicted, that might well have made all the difference to her situation – but it was doubly unfortunate that the Queen and Lady Jersey should have been cronies. Against such a formidable alliance Caroline was powerless and knew it. 'I am surrounded by miserable, evil minds and everything I do is put in a bad light,' she wrote to a friend in Germany. She disliked the Queen, the 'old Begum' or 'old Snuffy', but regarded Lady Jersey as the real enemy. 'I hate her and I know she feels the same towards me.'

Certainly the Countess appears to have made no attempt to conceal her malice, of which there had been a notable example the previous summer. Caroline had given a packet of her letters to a clergyman, a Dr Randolph, who was planning a visit to Brunswick. Illness, however, caused his journey to be postponed, and he was asked to return the letters to the

Princess of Wales. This, declared Dr Randolph, he duly did, taking them in person to Charing Cross to catch the Brighton mail and addressing them care of Lady Jersey, then in waiting at the Pavilion. According to Lady Jersey, the package never arrived; but according to a story later leaked to the press, her ladyship had not only received the missing letters but opened and read them and, finding they contained indiscreet references to 'old Snuffy', had seized the opportunity to stir up trouble for the Princess with her in-laws.

Around the middle of April 1796 the Princess decided she had had enough of Lady Jersey. Since she hardly ever saw her husband these days and never saw him alone, she was, as she put it, obliged to have recourse to her pen and say what she wished in a few sentences. Literary composition did not come easily to Caroline – in fact, her father had admitted rather shamefacedly to Lord Malmesbury that she was barely literate – and she was certainly not up to English composition. She therefore addressed the Prince in ill-spelt, characteristically slovenly French, but her meaning was unmistakable. Beneath the piteous complaints of the wronged and neglected wife, 'the mother of your child', finding herself in the disagreeable and embarrassing position of having to spend 'all the long day' shut up in the company of a person she could neither like nor esteem and who was her husband's mistress, there lay a declaration of war.

The Prince replied promptly and in English which he knew she could understand, even if she could not write. He was astonished by her insinuations that she was being forced to spend her time with Lady Jersey, and deeply shocked by the indecorous' epithet she had applied to one of his oldest and most valued friends. In any case, she had at least half a dozen other ladies in her 'family', any one of whom she could summon to keep her company whenever she liked. If, as he rather suspected, Caroline was contemplating some sort of campaign to win public sympathy, then he advised her to think very carefully where such a course might lead. 'We have unfortunately been oblig'd to acknowledge to each other that we cannot find happiness in our union,' he went on. 'Circumstances of character and education . . . render that impossible. It then only remains that we should make the situation as little uncomfortable to each other as its nature will allow.' For his part, he would do his best to ensure that his wife enjoyed every gratification which custom, etiquette, and his own, most unjust pecuniary difficulties allowed. However, he warned, any attempt by her to set up a contrary interest would most effectually counteract these wishes for her comfort. 'Let me therefore beg of you to make the best of a situation unfortunate *for us both*' – something which would certainly not be achieved by '*wantonly* creating or magnifying uncomfortable circumstances'.

But Caroline was not going to be silenced as easily as that. She replied by dragging up various revealing remarks made by the Prince regarding 'Lady Jerser' at 'Breyten', although she apologized if she had given offence by describing the lady in question as his mistress, and went on to deny absolutely any thought of trying to make a party for herself in England. The very idea was ridiculous. She had always admired Queen Charlotte, she said, for her wise avoidance of anything whch smacked of political intrigue and had wished, like Her Majesty, to find happiness in a tranquil domestic life. Alas for such hopes! But she did not despair of one day being able to earn her husband's esteem, and his affection would also, of course, be very precious. For the moment, however, she dared ask for no other recognition than that owing to the mother of his child.

Unimpressed by these lofty sentiments, the Prince retorted that if Caroline admired his mother so much, she had better seek to follow the Queen's example of wifely virtue by studying to promote his comfort, which was not to be effected by 'irritating insinuations or fretful complaints' or, for that matter, by spreading the tale of their private differences round the family. The fact that she had shown his letters to the Duke of Gloucester would do no harm, because the Duke was too concerned for the credit of the family to talk to outsiders; but no appeal, even within the family circle, could be made with any degree of propriety. HRH sincerely hoped that 'this painful contest' could now be considered at an end.

It could not. Caroline wanted to know why, if it was all right for her to copy the Queen, she should not beg the Prince to copy the King's 'steady and correct' conjugal example? As for her so-called 'appeal' to the Duke of Gloucester, who was her uncle as well as the Prince's and whom she had always regarded as a second father, surely that was very natural, situated as she was alone in 'this immense country?' Less understandable, in her opinion, was the fact that her husband had chosen to complain about her to her old friend Lord Malmesbury, whom she had scarcely seen since her arrival in England, and had made all sorts of very unfair and untrue allegations about her. It was perfectly true that the Prince had been discussing his marital problems with Lord Malmesbury and had even gone so far as to express his desire for a separation. This conversation had taken place in the strictest confidence, and Malmesbury, the most discreet of men, swore that he had not said a word to a soul, but obviously someone had been talking out of turn.

The Prince was by now 'tired to death of this silly altercation' and was proposing that, since, through no fault of their own, nature had made them incompatible, he and Caroline should abandon any further pretence of married life, though he could see no reason why they should not continue their intercourse 'upon a civil and friendly footing'. 'Intercourse' was perhaps an unfortunate choice of word in the circumstances. At any rate Caroline wanted the terms of this 'civil and friendly' relationship defined in writing. More specifically, she wanted an unequivocal undertaking that her husband would never again seek the exercise of his conjugal rights. There was no difficulty about that. 'Even in the event of any accident happening to my daughter, which I trust Providence in its mercy will avert,' he wrote on 30 April, 'I shall not infringe the terms of the restriction by proposing, at any period, a connection of a more particular nature. . . . I shall now,' he concluded optimistically, 'finally close this disagreeable correspondence.'

Again, it was not to be as easy as that. To her husband's unspeakable irritation, Caroline was still not satisfied. She did not consider it had been made sufficiently clear that it was he, not she, who had made the first move towards a separation and she therefore felt she owed it to herself to inform the King, as her sovereign and father-in-law, of what had passed, to throw herself at his feet and beg for his future guidance and protection. The Prince of Wales was appalled at what appeared to be nothing more than a frivolous desire to make 'general mischief and noise' and also, so he told his mother on 7 May, 'both shock'd and hurt to death' that the king should be plagued with his affairs. In the family at large there was consternation. The Princess Elizabeth expressed herself as 'most sincerely grieved' on her beloved brother's account. The Queen promised to use her good offices with the King, if he should choose to confide in her, but was 'fully persuaded he will be against any open rupture'. The Duke of Gloucester hoped that a reconciliation might be effected by 'the fatherly interposition of the King', and the Duke of Clarence, while privately sympathizing with his brother's predicament, told a friend that he thought the Prince was behaving very foolishly in his treatment of his wife.

The King's reaction, as predicted, was one of disapproval. 'You seem to look on your disunion with the Princess as merely of a private nature,' he told his son in a letter dated 12 June. On the contrary, 'as Heir Apparent of the Crown your marriage is a public act, wherein the Kingdom is concerned. . . . The public must be informed of the whole business, and being already certainly not prejudiced in your favour, the auspices in the first outset would not be promising.'

The public had, in fact, already been informed of the existence of 'the rumour of a SEPARATION IN HIGH LIFE' by

an item in *The Times* on Tuesday 24 May, and it had already
been made clear where public sympathy lay. When Caroline
appeared at the Opera on the following Saturday 'the house
seemed as if electrified by her presence, and before she could
take her seat, every hand was lifted to greet her with the
loudest plaudits. The gentlemen jumped on the benches and
waved their hats, crying out *Huzza*! If, continued the *Times*
report, 'the Princess will only afford the public a few more
opportunities of testifying their respect for suffering virtue, we
think it will bring more than one person to a proper reflection.'

The *Morning Chronicle* took the same line, declaring that
everyone pitied *her* and execrated *him*. The *True Briton* also
expressed its respectful concern for the Princess, an 'amiable
and accomplished personage who has been the object of so
much unmerited ill treatment', and thought she would be lost
to those feelings of sensibility which she was well known to
possess, if she did not heartily despise Lady J—. As to the
gentleman concerned: 'we are afraid he is incorrigible – a total
disregard to the opinions of the world seems to mark every
part of his conduct'. The *True Briton* hoped that 'the public
will have too much sense of their own duty in return to
disregard him' and went on: 'we have long looked upon his
conduct as favouring the cause of Jacobinism and democracy
in this country more than all the speeches of HORNE TOOKE,
or all the labours of the *Corresponding Society*'. *The Times*, too,
saw grave constitutional danger ahead if the heir apparent
were permitted to continue his present way of life unchecked:

> When the high pesonages in the most exalted ranks of
> society, discard all the respect they owe to themselves;
> when they stoop to the most disgraceful connexions and
> above all their vices, disorders and imprudence raise just
> apprehensions for the welfare of the State . . . it is then
> that the liberty of the Press ought to resume its dignity
> and denounce and point out to the public opinion him
> whom public justice cannot attaint.

The target of these attacks was by now almost beside himself with annoyance over the injustice of it all. To the Prince of Wales his wife had become a positive *fiend*, a very monster of iniquity, 'the vilest wretch this world was ever curs'd with,' bent on destroying him and the whole royal family. He was revolted as much by her entire want of principle as by her 'personal nastiness'. The very thought of being under the same roof with her gave him the shudders, and as for sitting at table with her – he would rather see toads and vipers crawling over his victuals.

While the Prince avoided London and any danger of encountering the Princess, Caroline perforce remained at Carlton House, resolutely attending Court functions – she was present at a Drawing-Room on 16 June – and sometimes taking baby Charlotte for carriage airings in the Park, an activity which she quickly discovered to be an unfailing popularity-winner. On 13 June the Prince's erstwhile crony, the Opposition leader Charles James Fox, was re-elected to the Westminster constituency. As Fox's supporters bore him in triumph along Pall Mall towards Devonshire House, *The Times* reported that 'as the procession passed by Carlton House the mob expressed a wish to see the infant Princess, in consequence of which the sash of one of the upper windows was held up, and the Royal child shown to the populace, who gave three cheers'. Not content with using his 'poor little girl' as an instrument in her campaign against him, the 'much injured father' was outraged to hear that Caroline had gone to congratulate Mr Fox in person. Surely, he wrote, in one of the many long and anguished letters addressed to his mother during this period, surely the King must now see her in her true colours, 'how false, how mischievous, how treacherous she is and at the same time how much she may be, and actually is made the tool not only of private views, but of party, and even of the worst of parties at this moment, the democratick'.

The King, however, remained stubbornly unconvinced,

clinging to the belief that any indiscretions or mistakes committed by his niece were to be ascribed to her inexperience and lack of sympathetic husbandly guidance. The fact of the matter was, of course, that so long as 'Lady J—' held on to her position in the Princess's household, Caroline would continue to figure as a wronged wife and unhappy mother and thus be assured of the support of the nation's moral majority. The more worldly wise members of the royal family such as the Duke of York could see the force of this, and Caroline herself was making it clear that there would be no healing the domestic breach while 'Lady Jerser' or 'Jersery' (there must surely have been an element of perversity in these misspellings) remained on the staff at Carlton House.

By the end of June the Prince had finally been persuaded to agree that his wife should no longer be expected to employ his mistress or admit her to her 'private society'. Lady Jersey resigned on the 29th, after writing the Princess a rude letter which *The Times* described as 'one of the most disrespectful we ever recollect to have read'. But the *Morning Chronicle* confidently informed its readers that the 'unhappy difference' which had for some time existed between the Prince and Princess of Wales was now 'perfectly settled' and trusted that 'the interest that has been manifested in favour of the decencies of life will make the household of the Prince, like that of his royal father, an example to his country'.

The Prince's royal father certainly hoped this would be the case, and Caroline, at the behest of the Queen, wrote a dutiful letter to her husband asking for a reconciliation. As far as she was concerned, their 'misunderstanding' no longer existed; if he would do her the honour of seeking her company, she would do her best to make it agreeable. If she had ever displeased him in the past, she hoped he would be generous enough to forgive her.

But the Prince's enforced surrender to the pressure of public opinion in the matter of Lady Jersey's resignation had not disposed him to feel either generous or forgiving. On the contrary, he remained unshaken in his conviction that his wife was deliberately trying to humiliate him before the world by spreading the most vile and damaging slanders about him, and that she and her friends – or rather those who were using her as a tool – were behind the attacks currently being made on him in the public prints. His only response to her proffered olive-branch, therefore, was to put in a token appearance at Carlton House, where his coldly formal behaviour seemed to indicate no more than a desire never to see her again. 'As soon as dinner was over,' reported Lady Stafford, one of Caroline's supporters, 'he went to Lady Jersey. He protests he will never go to the Opera with the Princess and is entirely directed by Lady Jersey. This is called a reconciliation!'

There was, of course, no question of anything approaching a genuine reconciliation. Lady Jersey might have flounced out of Carlton House but she had only flounced as far as the house next door, where the Prince installed her with her husband, (explaining long-windedly to his mother that Lord Jersey, who was still his Master of the Horse, really could not be expected constantly to make the arduous journey to and from Grosvenor Square), and so far from severing his connections with her ladyship, he proceeded to spend most of the summer in her company. She was his guest at another rented estate, Critchell House near Wimborne in Dorset, and in September they were together at the seaside resort of Bognor.

But while HRH saw no good reason why he should not follow his inclinations and his mistress round the south of England with all the freedom of his bachelor days, he was outraged when his wife expressed a desire to spend a short holiday in East Anglia with his friends and employees Lord and Lady Cholmondeley. Indeed, he professed to be quite shocked at the 'novelty' of the idea of a Princess of Wales travelling about on her own, attended only by ladies. Certainly he had never heard of his grandmother, the late Princess Dowager, 'scampering over England in this kind of way'. It was all quite unsuitable and improper. Rather more to the point, as he wrote to the Queen, it would be setting a dangerous precedent, affording Caroline an opportunity of showing herself off in the country and of 'repeating her tricks, especially as she still persists in the line of conduct she so artfully and maliciously has adopted of endeavouring to draw popularity to herself at my expense, and at the expense [*sic*] of the whole family'. He therefore had felt no hesitation in giving the proposal his 'most decided negative'.

The Prince was also annoyed to discover that his wife had been enlarging her social circle, inviting company to dinner composed of others besides her household and making unauthorised additions to the official list of persons eligible to be asked to evening parties at Carlton House. Caroline accepted the veto on her visit to the Cholmondeleys philosophically, although she was disappointed. The more so, she wrote, because she understood it had been agreed that she should enjoy uninterrupted 'those innocent pleasures consistant [*sic*] with my rank'. She proved a good deal less amenable over the matter of the friends she was allowed to entertain, and this argument rumbled on into the autumn of 1797. The Prince then told Lord Cholmondeley that, while he was and ever had been ready to indulge the Princess in such amusements as he deemed consistent with her dignity and also as far as his financial embarrassments – still a very sore point – would permit, 'Yet while she remains under my roof the rules I have laid down are unalterable and *must* be adhered to. With respect to the disappointments which the Princess says she has met with since she came into this country,' he continued, 'I believe, my dear friend, you well remember that they cannot have exceeded mine.'

It was a 'threadworn subject', and HRH wanted to hear no more of it, but Caroline came back with a demand for a ruling from the King. If His Majesty would choose 'either to send his sentiments in writing, or to speak them to her, she should be ready to obey his commands'. However, even when the King had been persuaded to write a memorandum giving it as his opinion that the Princess of Wales could not properly receive any society 'but such as the Prince approved of', the Princess announced her intention of confronting her husband and having it out with him, once and for all.

Greatly alarmed, the Prince insisted on the presence of Lord Cholmondeley to act both as witness and bodyguard, but the encounter, which took place in Caroline's rooms at Carlton House on the afternoon of 5 December, was brief and bloodless. According to the Prince's own account, the Princess, speaking in French, had immediately burst out: 'Monsieur, Monsieur il ne s'agit point d'explication du tout.' It was useless to go over the old battleground again, and she had only two words to say. During the two and a half years she had lived in his house he had never treated her either as his wife, as the mother of his child, or as Princess of Wales, and she wished to give notice that as of this moment she had nothing more to say to him and no longer regarded herself as subject to his orders or his 'rules' – this last hated word being pronounced in English. Having delivered herself of what was no doubt a well-rehearsed speech, the Princess paused for breath, and the Prince enquired coldly, also in French:

'Is that all, Madame, all that you have to say to me?'

'Yes,' said Caroline.

The Prince then bowed and withdrew. 'Thus ended the interview, he told his father, and with it the marriage.

Caroline's *démarche* had been made possible by the fact that by this time she was, for all practical purposes, living apart from her husband. Yet the King still refused to sanction a formal separation on the grounds of a 'mere disagreement of temper' – especially when it was only too obvious that all the consequent public obloquy would fall on the already dangerously unpopular Prince of Wales.

The Princess had been well advised by, among others, Lord Thurlow, a former Lord Chancellor now in opposition. And in the judgement of the present Chancellor, no blame would be imputed to her by 'all sober and religious persons whose loyalty is upheld by their confidence in the virtues of your Majesty's character to which under God the stability of the British Government . . . is chiefly to be ascribed.' To these good people Caroline would appear not as a woman 'desirous of a separation for her own personal satisfaction' but rather as one 'submitting with much grief and concern at her own unhappiness' to her husband's wishes in the matter. It seemed that no serious misunderstanding could have arisen 'had it not been for that unhappy distaste the Prince has been too apt to explain, and upon which it is impossible to reason'. It was not even as if the alliance had been forced on HRH 'for reasons of state'. On the contrary, he had entered into it by his own free choice, and 'every consideration of duty and of interest condemn his aversion to it'. It was, therefore, continued Lord Loughborough impressively, of the utmost importance to preserve at least 'the outward appearance of cohabitation' and 'suppress all idea of a publick separation as incompatible with the religion, laws and Government' of a properly conducted Christian country.

The government's reluctance to risk such a potentially destatbilizing scandal within the royal family was understandable – especially at a time when, as the Lord Chancellor felt in duty bound to point out, the 'general indisposition' towards the Prince of Wales had grown so strong that it must not, in the interests of 'publick safety', be given any additional impetus. There was, though, a recognition of the fact that some concessions would have to be made to ease the domestic tensions at Carlton House, where the Prince was complaining bitterly that he was being forced to submit to the sort of wifely defiance which no ordinary husband would be expected to put up with, and prevented from exerting his natural authority for fear of exciting an unjust public outcry. The King had therefore agreed that his daughter-in-law might take a house somewhere in the country to be used as a temporary unofficial residence – a holiday home and escape-hatch – and in August 1797 she had rented the Old Rectory in the village of Charlton near Blackheath.

The Old Rectory, though finely situated with a wide view of the Essex marshes, was a modest enough place, but to Caroline it represented freedom, emancipation, and relief from intolerable strain. 'I was free,' she later told Lady Charlotte Bury. 'I left Carlton House and went to Charlton. Oh! how happy I was! Everybody blamed me, but I never repented me of dis step. Oh! mine God what I have suffered! Luckily I had a spirit, or I never should have outlived it.'

'Poor Princess!' commented Lady Charlotte, recording these artless confidences in her diary, 'she was an ill-treated woman, but a very wrong-headed one. Had she remained quietly at Carlton House and conducted herself with silent dignity, how different might have been her lot!'

Lady Charlotte, writing with the benefit of hindsight, may well have been correct in this assumption, but silent dignity had never been one of Caroline's strong points. However valiantly she had set herself to outface a campaign of petty and spiteful persecution, hers was not the sort of gritty patient courage which can sit out any storm and weather it in the end. A creature governed by impulse and instinct, she was a classic case of the heart ruling the head. 'Oh, mine God!' she told Charlotte Bury in another burst of confidence, 'I could be the slave of a man I love; but one whom I love not, and who did not love me, impossible – c'est autre chose.' Now, after two years of disillusionment, boredom, and frustration, she had been given an opportunity to escape from the domination of a man she had come frankly to loathe and despise, and she simply took it without hesitation – without thought of the price which would eventually have to be paid.

THREE

The Delicate Investigation

The Princess of Wales has told me that she got a bed-fellow whenever she could, that nothing was more wholesome . . . that she did what she liked, went where she liked, and had what bed-fellow she liked, and the Prince paid for all.

. . . her Royal Highness the Princess of Wales told me she was with child . . . and that if she was discovered she would give the Prince of Wales the credit.

Extracts from the statements of Charlotte Douglas, June 1806 and
December 1805

We are happy to declare to your Majesty our perfect conviction that there is no foundation whatever for believing that the child now with the Princess is the child of Her Royal Highness.

Report of the Commission of Inquiry on the charges brought by the
Prince of Wales against the Princess his wife, 14 July 1806

When Caroline bowled away from Carlton House in August 1797 she left her daughter behind. There had, of course, never been any question of taking the little girl out of her father's custody – under the English legal system in any dispute between husband and wife a father's rights over his children remained absolute whatever the circumstances – but despite the acrimony which surrounded their parting, the Prince was still allowing the Princess more or less unrestricted access.

Although Caroline was later to develop a bizarre craze for collecting babies, she showed no signs of eccentricity in her attitude towards her own baby, appearing as a normally concerned and affectionate mother in so far as she was allowed to be. 'I was upstairs when my dear little Charlotte was undress'd and stay'd till she was in bed and the dear little Angle [sic] was remarcable well,' she had once written to Lady Dashwood during one of the governess's frequent absences on sick-leave, and went on: 'I am much obliged to you for your great attention to her and hope you will not return at eight o'clock if it is not convenient to yourself as I am quite capable with my Ladys so I can go upstairs if anything should be the matter and then I will lett you know.'

Fully aware of the propaganda value of motherhood, Caroline's advisers had always encouraged her to show herself in public with her child as often as possible, and although some members of the royal family might speak disapprovingly of 'the weakness of the mother in making a plaything of the child', both parents were predictably to make use of her as a weapon of war. In his letters to the King the Prince of Wales referred movingly to his 'poor little girl' about whose future education and upbringing he must, as 'a father, 'feel the greatest anxiety'; while for her part Caroline missed few opportunities of stressing her maternal status and urging her errant husband to remember the duty he owed to the child who would suffer all her life from her parents' disunion.

The eighteen-month-old Charlotte, however, was less immediately affected by her parents' disunion than she had been by changes in the nursery establishment made necessary by the death of Helen Dashwood in October 1796. The position of governess was temporarily filled by Miss Goldsworthy, once governess to the princesses and known in the family as Gouly, who was lent by the Queen until January 1797, when the appointment of the Dowager Countess of Elgin as governess to the Princess Charlotte was announced in the *London Gazette*. Lady Elgin – her charge christened her 'Eggy' – was already in her late fifties, which seems a little old for such a demanding job, but she was a kind, sensible, tactful body, and Charlotte flourished in her care.

Six months later another sub-governess was added to the strength. Miss Hayman, described by Charlotte Bury as 'a fine and rare specimen of English character' (though she came apparently from a Welsh family), blunt-spoken, high-principled, 'but tender in heart', arrived at Carlton House on 1 June, and her correspondence contains the earliest first-hand description of Charlotte by an outsider. 'The merriest little thing I ever saw – pepper-hot too: if contradicted she kicks her little feet about in a great rage, but the cry ends in a laugh before you well know which it is.'

Charlotte 'showed all her treasures, and played all her little antics' for the entertainment of this latest member of her court, and the Prince of Wales was also prepared to lavish on the governesses some of that famous charm which had been so notably lacking in his other domestic dealings. After expressing the hope that Miss Hayman would be 'tolerably comfortable' under his roof and not find the restrictions of nursery life too irksome, he turned to Lady Elgin and said, 'It is an additional pleasure to me that Miss Hayman is one of my own countrywomen,' and taking them both by the hand, added, 'You are both my countrywomen: my two first titles are Welsh and Scotch.' Honest Miss Hayman was quite overcome by so much condescension. 'Never had anyone such captivating manners,' she wrote. 'I could have sat down and cried that he is not all that he ought to be – sometimes it is impossible to think his heart is not naturally good.'

The Princess of Wales was equally gracious to the new governess, coming into the nursery to see her and asking if she did not think baby Charlotte was 'wonderfully like' the Prince. She stayed for about half an hour, chose some lace for frocks, and was 'most kind'. Next day, the Princess, who had taken one of her impulsive fancies to the cheerful, good-natured Miss Hayman, came in again for a chat, and when Lady Elgin tried to put a stop to too much fraternization by saying repressively, 'Miss Hayman must now kiss Her Royal Highness's hand', Caroline, who was quite impervious to hints, only exclaimed, 'Oh, we will shake hands', and began a long gossiping conversation about novels.

Three days after her arrival Miss Hayman had to escort her charge to Buckingham House, or the Queen's House as it was more often known, to see the King on his birthday. Since the Prince of Wales was present, the Princess was not, but otherwise the whole family was assembled. The King took the baby from her nurse, which caused a threatened outcry. 'However,' recorded Miss Hayman, 'she soon recovered her good-humour and played with her grandpapa on the carpet a long while. All seem to doat [*sic*] on her, and even the Prince played with her . . . and she seemed to know him from the rest extremely well.'

This was intelligent as well as tactful, for in general Charlotte saw very little of her papa. The Prince never visited the nursery wing these days – presumably for fear of running into his wife. According to Miss Hayman, his time for seeing the child was when dressing or at breakfast, but sometimes a week or more would go by without his sending for her, and the sub-governess often did not know whether he was at home or not. There could be no such doubt about the Princess. Approachable as ever, she had herself shown Miss Hayman round the empty splendours (many of them still unpaid for) of Carlton House, pulling up the dust covers 'like an old housekeeper', as she said. It was all very sumptuous, but Caroline dismissed it as 'useless' – even the bedrooms were too grand for any sensible person to sleep in. Certainly it could in no way be described as a family house. As the practical Miss Hayman commented, so many of the rooms were for show that it seemed fortunate the Princess had no more children, as there would have been nowhere to put them.

After her departure for Charlton, Caroline still made regular trips up to town and continued to single out Miss Hayman for flattering marks of attention. However, the governess soon discovered that it was not possible to keep on good terms with both her employers; and on 7 November, Lord Minto wrote to his wife: 'Miss Hayman . . . has just been dismissed by the Prince because, being uncommonly agreeable and sensible, the Princess liked her company.' The Princess was not, as it happened, destined to be deprived of her friend's company for long, for Miss Hayman entered her service as her 'privy purse' or book-keeper/accountant, and since, as well as her other agreeable qualities, she was an accomplished musician, she made a welcome addition to the household at Charlton.

Caroline also saw as much as she probably wanted of her little girl, who came with her governess on regular visits. Indeed, a house at Blackheath, Shrewsbury Lodge, was taken for several weeks every summer for the young princess and her entourage. Charlotte was fast growing into a sturdy, energetic toddler, and there are a number of engaging glimpses of her during these brief, unclouded baby years – trotting about on a leading-string held by Lady Elgin; blowing kisses and 'doing the popular' to the crowds in St James's Park on the King's birthday, tearing her cap in her eagerness to show Miss Hayman how Mr Canning took off his hat to her as he rode past Carlton House; being 'cruelly bit' by fleas at Weymouth in the summer of 1797; behaving like an angel and showing the greatest pleasure when her grandparents gave her a very large rocking-horse; and delighting her relations at Windsor in December 1798 by her spirited rendition of that well-known patriotic number 'Hearts of Oak'.

Charlotte's mama had by this time left the Old Rectory and established herself in another rented house, later described by a foreign visitor as a modest mansion, 'not so large as that of a petty German baron'. Montague House, which belonged to the Duchess of Buccleuch, was actually an elegant, smallish, late seventeenth-century country house, lying just outside the boundary wall of Greenwich Park and set in a particularly attractive garden. Lord Minto remarked that the

Princess had done up her new home and made a number of improvements since getting a longer lease on it, and indeed it suited her so well that she was to stay there for the next sixteen years. Lord Minto, a frequent visitor to Blackheath at this period, also had several opportunities to observe Caroline with her daughter, reporting that the two of them seemed to be on the best of terms, romping together on the carpet, the Princess of Wales down on her hands and knees. He was impressed by Charlotte, now rising three, who danced while the ladies played the piano and sang 'God Save the King' and 'Hearts of Oak', which seems to have been her favourite party piece. Minto, wishing his own girls were so accomplished, thought her a 'fine, thriving child, very lively, intelligent and pleasant', and added that although 'excessively fond of romp and play, she is remarkably good and governable. One day', he wrote to his wife, 'she had been a little naughty, however, and they were reprimanding her. Amongst the rest, Miss Garth said to her, "Now you have been so very naughty I don't know what we must do to you." The little girl answered crying and quite penitently, "You must *soot* me" – meaning, shoot her, but they let her off rather cheaper.'

It was now more than a year since the Prince and Princess of Wales had separated. There had been no sign so far of any *rapprochement* taking place between them, but at the end of 1798 the Prince did make one apparently serious attempt to open negotiations – inviting his estranged wife to dinner at Carlton House and even, it seems, suggesting she should return to live there for the winter. His motives for this rather surprising move remain obscure, although they were perhaps not unconnected with the fact that, having at last disengaged himself from Lady Jersey's toils, HRH was doing his best to persuade Mrs Fitzherbert to agree to resume their former relationship and may have hoped to increase his chances of success by using the prospect of a reconciliation with his other wife to divert public attention. Caroline certainly suspected some kind of trap, but in any case had no intention of ever again putting herself in the position of having to submit to the oppressive restrictions imposed by Carlton House. She was, she announced defiantly, a very determined person when she had once formed an opinion, and on this point 'her resolution was fixed'.

Lord Minto thought she was wrong and told her so, begging her to 'reflect seriously on any step she might take if similar overtures were renewed'. Caroline, however, resisted all attempts to persuade her to reconsider her position. She knew that Minto would think her 'a very wicked woman', but he did not know and could not imagine all the circumstances. He might otherwise agree with her, she told him with great earnestness. His lordship, who had already been made the embarrassed recipient of some startlingly frank royal confidences, conceded that the contempt and horror which the Princess felt for her husband were, in fact, 'justifiable'. Nevertheless, as a responsible legal adviser, he considered himself in duty bound to persist in urging the necessity of not refusing any further offers of reconciliation, while at the same time admitting that he thought any experimental resumption of marital relations would be doomed to failure – given the characters and obstinacy of both parties. He also thought that Caroline would end the loser, in so far as the blame for failure would most probably be laid at her door, 'on grounds sufficiently plausible to deprive her of the sympathy and interest which at present accompanies her retirement'. In the event, the Prince's offer was not renewed, and after a good deal of heart-searching Mrs Fitzherbert returned to him, though she told a friend that they were living 'like brother and sister'. Caroline is said to have welcomed this development. She always maintained that Maria Fitzherbert, 'an excellent woman', should be regarded as the Prince's lawful wife; and besides, if he was happily suited, he would be more likely to leave her in peace to enjoy her freedom.

In 1798 she was still very much enjoying this freedom. In addition to her annual £5,000 pin-money from the Exchequer, the Prince was making her an allowance of £12,000 a year, and although this never seemed quite enough for her needs it enabled her to maintain herself and her mini-Court in pretty tolerable comfort and style. As well as a vice-chamberlain, a privy purse, and mistress of the robes she was able to call on the services of two ladies of the bedchamber and three bedchamber women (who took it in turns to come into waiting). Then there was her devoted page, Thomas Stikeman, while below stairs the staff included a butler, a chef, half a dozen maids, two boys, a porter, various other assorted menials both male and female, and a gardener. It seems probable that the gardener at Montague House had extra help, for a German tourist visiting the Princess of Wales in her rural retreat wrote admiringly of the neat flower borders and large, well-cultivated vegetable plot where, so his hostess informed him, she 'endeavoured to acquire the honourable name of a farmer' and did not disdain to supplement her income by selling her produce in the London markets.

Like most ladies of the period, Caroline sought to fill her days by dabbling in a variety of artistic pursuits, practising her music (with more enthusiasm than skill, according to Charlotte Bury), and trying her hand at painting, sketching, and modelling in clay – she attempted a portrait bust of her daughter and several of her acquaintances. The German, Herr Campe, also describes a form of 'mosaic work' undertaken by the industrious royal artist. This appears to have been a method of decorating the reverse side of a sheet of ground glass with a design of pressed dried flowers, or creating an inlaid effect with a number of contrasting *faux marbres* finishes and using the result as a table-top.

When gardening, music, novel reading, and fancy work palled, the Princess entertained her friends. Freed now from the tyranny of her mother-in-law's 'lists' of approved names, she was able to indulge both her natural inquisitiveness and her taste for socializing to the full. 'She has a system of seeing all remarkable persons,' observed Lord Glenbervie. The guests invited to Montague House were drawn indiscriminately from the worlds of the arts and sciences, from politics, the law, and the armed services, so that Lord Byron and Walter Scott, the painter Sir Thomas Lawrence, and Admiral Sir Sidney Smith mingled with George Canning, Charles Grey, Henry Dundas, and the great Mr Pitt himself under the Princess of Wales's hospitable roof.

Society took the road to Blackheath motivated in part by curiosity and a desire to annoy the Prince of Wales, but sometimes also with a certain amount of trepidation. 'You will be glad to know that I am alive and *well* after yesterday,' Lady Caroline Stuart-Wortley wrote to her mama. In fact, dinner had been very pleasant and not at all alarming. Lady Caroline had met a great many people she knew, and the Princess had quite gone out of her way to be friendly.

The Princess possessed neither the inclination nor the intellectual equipment necessary to create a literary or political salon – her tastes ran more to games like 'musical magic', charades, or forfeits – but her parties were nearly always amusing, and when she chose to make the effort, she could be a charming and thoughtful hostess. 'I never saw any person, not royal or royal, who understood so well how to perform the honours at their own table as the Princess,' commented one of her guests. Another remarked on her talent for combining the dignity of her position with an unaffected and natural ease.

But this was Caroline on a good day, and visitors to Black heath never quite knew whether to expect an evening of civilized conversation, a boisterous game of blind man's buff, or a wild conga danced through the house and grounds, or whether they would find the Princess in a confidential mood ready to hold the unwary with a glittering eye and a long-winded recital of her grievances against the royal family. Another of her more disconcerting habits was to disappear with one of her gentlemen friends, leaving the rest of the company to entertain themselves and, of course, speculate on what the missing couple were getting up to. On one such occasion the Princess of Wales and her current companion were absent for several hours. This was beyond a joke, and the other guests, neglected, hungry, and cross, were audibly disinclined to take a charitable view. But when faithful Miss Hayman tried to point out that such behaviour was liable to be misunderstood by English society and to provoke unkind comment, Caroline took offence. The docile young woman who had once begged Lord Malmesbury to tell her freely of her faults now 'neither desired nor liked' advice, however well intentioned. Her private life, she indicated, was her own affair, and as for society, it could mind its own business.

After her husband's brutal and public rejection it was very understandable that Caroline should wish to demonstrate, both to herself and the world at large, that other men could find her desirable. After his visit to Blackheath early in the new century, Herr Campe wrote tactfully of 'the lovely princess' – polite convention, then as now, demanding that all princesses be described as 'lovely'. This Caroline certainly was not, but despite her bad figure and the ungainly effect created by a too short neck and over-large head, she was still, in her late twenties and early thirties, by no means entirely without physical attraction. Miss Hayman, seeing her dressed for a Drawing-Room in the summer of 1797, had thought her 'very pretty'; and Lady Charlotte Bury, recalling the days before her employer had grown coarse and bold and bloated, gives her credit for having been a pretty woman, mentioning her fine blonde hair, fair complexion, deep-set eyes. She could also, of course, be very good company, at any rate in small doses and when not in one of her exaggerated moods of bravado or self-pity.

Gossip about her relationships with men started almost as soon as she moved into Montague House. The rising young politician George Canning and Sir Thomas Lawrence, who had been commissioned by the King to paint the Princess of Wales and her daughter, were both widely believed to be her lovers. Nor were they the only ones. In 1801 and again in

1802 rumours that she was pregnant circulated freely. Caroline herself appeared quite unconcerned by this sort of talk and made no attempt to modify her life-style, but in 1805 the consequences of what often appears to have been a calculated rejection of every accepted standard of propriety began at last to catch up with her.

Perhaps the most surprising thing is that it had taken so long, but constantly recurring scandals over the moral, financial, and other associated shortcomings of the Prince of Wales and his brothers had already done so much harm to the royal family's image that officialdom naturally recoiled from the prospect of yet more bad publicity. However, when gossip about the Princess of Wales turned into detailed and circumstantial accusations, the government was forced into taking notice.

This particular commotion had its origins in another of Caroline's unsuitable friendships, this time with one of her neighbours at Blackheath. Early in the spring of 1801 Sir John Douglas, his wife Charlotte, and their infant daughter had moved into a rented house on the Common, nice and handy for Chatham for Sir John, a lieutenant-colonel in the Royal Marines. He had also recently been appointed groom of the bedchamber to one of the royal dukes, but this impressive-sounding position was more noted for social cachet than monetary reward, and the Douglases were chronically hard up. So, when their old friend Admiral Sir Sidney Smith turned up on their doorstep that summer looking for a convenient *pied-à-terre* out of the fog-polluted air of London, they were only too pleased to let him have one of their spare rooms as a paying guest. The Admiral soon found his way over to Montague House, where he joined the cosy circle of gentlemen surrounding the Princess of Wales and, according to gossip, the even cosier circle of her regular bed-mates. Gossip also made him Charlotte Douglas's lover, but whether this was true or not he succeeded in rousing Caroline's curiosity about the lady, and, being Caroline, she promptly set out to satisfy it.

One cold November day, with snow lying on the ground, Lady Douglas was sitting with a friend in her parlour overlooking the heath when she became aware of two ladies 'pacing up and down before the house, and sometimes stopping, as if desirous of opening the gate in the iron railing to come in'. One of these ladies was presently introduced as Miss Hayman; the other, dressed 'elegantly' but with startling unsuitability in a lilac satin pelisse and primrose-yellow half-boots, was easily recognizable as the Princess of Wales. Unsure about the rules of etiquette to be followed in such circumstances, Lady Douglas went to the window and made a curtsy, which was immediately acknowledged by a friendly nod from outside. Urged on by her friend, who said, 'You should go out; her Royal Highness wants to come in out of the snow', her ladyship went to the front door and found that Caroline needed no encouragement. She came bustling up, all smiles and exclaiming: 'I believe you are Lady Douglas, and you have a very beautiful child; I should like to see it.'

Lady Douglas, however, was obliged to explain that she would regretfully have to forgo the honour of presenting her little girl, since the baby and the rest of the family were spending the cold weather in London, and she herself had only come down to Blackheath for a brief visit. But of course she held the gate open and begged the distinguished strangers to step inside, and Caroline came and sat talking and laughing in the parlour for more than an hour. At last, after expressing her pleasure 'at having found me out and made herself known', she shook hands and went away. A week or so later the Douglases received an invitation to dine at Montague House, and from then on the two ladies were constantly in one another's company.

'The Princess became so extravagantly fond of me, that however flattering it might be, it certainly was very troublesome', declared Charlotte Douglas afterwards, when it had all gone sour. The Princess, she went on, would push past my servant, and run upstairs to my bedchamber, kiss me, take me in her arms, and tell me I was beautiful, saying she had never loved any woman so much; that she would regulate my dress, for she delighted in setting off a pretty woman; and such high-flown compliments that women are never used to pay to each other. . . . She would exclaim, Oh! believe me, you are quite beautiful, different from almost any Englishwoman; your arms are fine beyond imagination, your bust is very good, and your eyes, Oh, I never saw such eyes – all other women who have dark eyes look fierce, but yours are nothing but softness and sweetness.

Apparently she went on like this all the time, even in front of other people, much to Lady Douglas's embarrassment. The Douglases, for their part, quickly realized that her Royal Highness was 'a very singular and very indiscreet woman' and resolved always to be very careful and guarded in their dealings with her. However *she* might forget her exalted station – and she forgot it all the time – *they* never for a moment lost sight of her being the wife of the heir apparent.

In March 1802 Caroline begged her dear Lady Douglas to come and spend a fortnight at Montague House and help her out by acting as a temporary lady-in-waiting. She could have her own suite of rooms and bring her little girl and a maid, and, of course, Sir John could come and see her whenever he liked. After some show of reluctance her ladyship agreed to this proposition and during her stay attended the Princess to the theatre on two or three occasions and at a couple of dinner engagements. She was, however, increasingly surprised and shocked by the general tone of Caroline's conversation, which she found to be 'very loose' and not at all what she had been accustomed to hear; some of it, in fact, she did not even care to repeat to her husband. Her Royal Highness seemed to be without education or talent or any desire to improve herself. At times one could only suppose that she was 'a good deal disordered in her senses'.

But in spite of her vulgarity, her lack of education or talent, her capricious temper, and even her unprincipled attempts to use her friend as cover – saying with many significant looks to people who criticized her intimacy with Sidney Smith that, on the contrary, the Admiral came to the house to see Lady Douglas – Lady Douglas made no effort to end their peculiar attachment, and after she returned to her own home the same 'apparent friendship' continued as before. Caroline would often walk over the Heath for long confidential chats, and one evening in May or June, according to Lady Douglas's recollection, she arrived announcing that she had been in 'a great agitation' and urging her dear Lady Douglas to guess what had happened to her. Finally, after much guessing and giggling and sly references to cravings for ale and fried onions, the Princess said: 'Well, I'll tell; I am with child and the child came to life when I was breakfasting with Lady Willoughby. The milk flowed up into my breast so fast that it came through my muslin gown, and I was obliged to pretend that I had spilt something and go upstairs to wipe my gown with a napkin.' She hoped the child would be a boy, she went on, and 'if it was discovered she would give the Prince of Wales the credit of being the father, for she had slept two nights at Carlton House within the year', but she thought she would be able to manage very well and seemed remarkably unconcerned. In reply to her friend's anxious questions, she pointed out that she was already known to be in the habit of taking in poor people's children who were brought to her door in baskets and would use that method of smuggling her own safely out of the way. As for her appearance on occasions when she had to meet the royal family, that was easy. She knew how to manage her dress and, by padding herself more and more behind, could arrange it so that no one would notice anything amiss.

To what extent Caroline expected or intended this whole farrago of nonsense to be taken seriously is impossible to say, but it is not very likely that Charlotte Douglas, a shrewd and experienced matron who was herself just then in the seventh month of pregnancy, ever really believed that the Princess of Wales was 'with child' in 1802, although it suited her to pretend to do so. Caroline, she recalled later, had sat beside her on the sofa one day, and put her hand on her stomach and said, laughing: 'Well, here we sit like Mary and Elizabeth in the Bible!' She was determined to be present at her friend's lying-in 'from the beginning to the end', and would bring a bottle of port wine and a tambourine to make merry. Understandably unenthused by the prospect, Lady Douglas was equally determined to keep her out, if possible without offending her. But tact was wasted on Caroline, who had about as much sensitivity as a charging rhinoceros. Lady Douglas was brought to bed on 23 July, and despite locked doors and other diversionary tactics, the Princess succeeded in finding her way in, elbowed the nurse aside, insisted on taking the child from the doctor, and so confused him that, although an old and experienced practitioner, he quite forgot to give his patient the customary restorative draught. Luckily she was not 'subject to faint away', but her ladyship still thought it a very strange omission where life was at stake and found the Princess's behaviour more indicative of curiosity than concern for her friend's welfare.

Baby Douglas, another girl and 'a remarkable large fine child', also survived her unconventional royal reception without mishap. Inevitably she was to be named Caroline, the Princess standing godmother. At the christening party she sat on the floor – 'a thing she was very fond of doing' – in the Douglases' parlour and declared the occasion to be 'the pleasantest lively affair she had ever known'. She herself appeared to be in tearing high spirits, eating an amazing supper of chicken and potted lamprey (a sort of eel) served together on the same plate and staying until after two o'clock in the morning, all the time making deliberately intriguing references to the 'secret' she and Lady Douglas shared and which, thought her hostess, she was really bursting to reveal.

Her Royal Highness's 'civilities' continued throughout the rest of the summer. Lady Douglas was constantly being urged to bring her children to Montague House. She was breast-feeding, but when she would have modestly retired to suckle the baby, Caroline made her stay and do it with her in the drawing-room. At other times the Princess would come across the Heath accompanied by one or other of her ladies and sit nursing her little god-daughter for hours together. Then, some time in the autumn, again according to Charlotte Douglas, Caroline quarrelled with Sir Sidney Smith. This made for awkwardness, since the Admiral was still lodging with the Douglases. 'She therefore became shy of us all, and we saw little of her.' But at the end of October, Lady Douglas met her coming out of church, dressed in an all-enveloping cloak and carrying a large muff. She looked ill and appeared 'morose', and Lady Douglas surmised that she must be very near her time.

The next development in the saga was a note from Caroline warning her friends not to call on her until further notice, because the servants were afraid that some of the foundling children might be carrying the measles. Nothing more was heard, and the Douglases went down to Gloucestershire for Christmas without seeing her again. When they returned to Blackheath towards the end of January 1803, Lady Douglas, who would not have been human if she had not been acutely curious, wasted no time in going to pay her duty to the Princess and found her with an infant asleep on the sofa. At first Caroline seemed 'confused' and uncertain whether to be 'rude or kind'. Finally, however, she decided on the latter and uncovered the child, saying: 'Here is the little boy. I had him two days after I saw you last; is not it a nice little child?' Her words, as Lady Douglas later deposed, being such as 'clearly imported' that it was her own child. She also said: 'We gave it a little milk at first, but it was too much for me and now we breed it by hand, and it does very well.' Lady Douglas thought the Princess would have said more, but she was unfortunately inhibited by the presence of one of her ladies,

Mrs Fitzgerald. Indeed, it seems to have been Mrs Fitzgerald who did most of the talking, telling Lady Douglas how the baby had been brought in by a poor woman from Deptford whose husband had left her, and that it had been a very poor, ill-looking little thing but now, with all the care it was getting, it was growing to be very pretty.

Certainly the child, whose name was William, was getting plenty of attention. The Princess of Wales's drawing-room that morning was strewn with all the rather messy paraphernalia associated with a young baby – spoons, plates, and feeding boats covered the tables, while clothes and nappies hung to air in front of the fire 'literally in the style of a common nursery'. Lady Douglas, whose 'entertainment' now consisted of sitting by to see the infant fed and fussed over and changed, noticed with some incredulity that the Princess was always 'particularly tenacious' of performing this part of the ceremony herself, tossing the soiled napkins on to the elegant marble hearth regardless of her company.

Although the Douglases continued to be invited to Montague House from time to time, the old cosy habits of intimacy were plainly at an end now that Caroline had baby William to lavish her devotion on. So, when Sir John received a letter expressing his General's wish that he should transfer himself down to Portsmouth, he and his wife – according to his wife – welcomed this opportunity of escaping from embarrassing social situation at Blackheath. The Princess seemed equally glad to see them go, coming over for the first time in months to say goodbye to Sir John, who was going on ahead of his family, staying for four hours, and quite overpowering them all with kindness now that they were leaving. However, when Lady Douglas, on the eve of her own departure, went with her little girls to bid a last farewell to her one-time bosom friend, she was treated with scant civility, and the children were left to shiver in the cold hallway by an insolent footman. Her angry complaints were barely attended to. After the most cursory apology Caroline rushed out of the room, coming back to thrust a small box into the outraged mother's hands and exclaim carelessly, 'God bless you, my dear Lady Douglas. Goodbye.' Her ladyship tried to return the gift – it turned out to be a gold necklace – which she regarded as little more than an insult, being thrown at her as it were and in such unpleasant circumstances. But the Princess had turned away, pointedly ignoring her, and Charlotte Douglas was left to make the most dignified exit she could manage from a house where once she had been petted, courted, and almost 'idolized'. Unable to resist a glance over her shoulder, she saw Caroline looking out 'to see if she had fairly got rid of me' and heard her laughing 'immoderately' with one of her companions.

Caroline had made a potentially dangerous enemy by this foolish and quite unnecessarily offensive behaviour, but even so the episode might have ended in no more than ill feeling had not Augustus, Duke of Sussex, decided to return to England in the late summer of 1804. Sir John Douglas still held the position of equerry to his Royal Highness, and although the job had never yet yielded any salary and did not look like doing so now – Sussex, the sixth and next to youngest of the King's surviving sons, was suffering from an acute attack of the family complaint of insolvency, having come home 'without a single shilling in his pocket' – his reappearance gave the Douglases all the excuse they needed to return to London and civilization. Naturally they took an early opportunity of driving out to Blackheath to renew their acquaintance with old friends and, naturally, left cards on the Princess of Wales, if only 'for the sake of appearances'. The reaction from Montague House was swift and ungentle. Lady Douglas received a curt note, written at the Princess's command by one of the ladies-in-waiting, informing her that her visit had been unwelcome and requesting her not to repeat it.

Accustomed though she was to Caroline's capricious temper, this still came as quite a shock to Charlotte Douglas. What she found especially wounding was the use of a lady-in-waiting as intermediary, bearing in mind how insistent the Princess had always been in the past that her friend was never to communicate through her ladies but *always* directly to *herself.*

On reflection, Lady Douglas thought she could make a shrewd guess at what had prompted so crude and cruel a dismissal. Caroline had never expected the Duke of Sussex to return to England. She had also counted on Lady Douglas, who alone knew all her guilty secrets, being safely settled two hundred miles away in Devonshire for the foreseeable future. Now, not only were the Douglases back in town, but Sir John was actually in attendance on the Duke at Carlton House itself, where he might at any moment have the honour of being made known to the Prince of Wales. The Princess's *fear* and *rage* had therefore got the better of every prudent consideration.

Whether this was so or not; whether, as she later affirmed, she believed that Lady Douglas had been betraying her confidence; or whether she was just bored by her former friends, irritated by their persistence, and thinking to choke them off for good, Caroline had made another serious mistake in tactics. Although scarcely the black-hearted villains sometimes depicted by her apologists, the Douglases were not overburdened with scruples. They were, in short, on the make – typical enough examples of the breed which attaches itself limpet-like to the periphery of any royal circle in the hope of social or financial gain. Charlotte Douglas, in particular, was an ambitious woman, and there is not much doubt that she would have gone on swallowing her pride for as long as there seemed the slightest chance of profiting from her connection with the Princess of Wales. She was, however, just as capable of turning nasty and now, remembering all the ammunition so thoughtfully provided by the Princess herself, felt in a strong enough position to try the effect of a little genteel blackmail. She therefore wrote to her Royal Highness in a strain of highly injured innocence. She had always behaved towards the Princess with the respect her exalted station demanded and even when secrets had been forced upon her had kept them most honourably. But she would not lie under the unjust imputation of having done wrong. Rather than do so she proposed to furnish her husband and friends with a full and circumstantial account of everything which had passed since the day when the Princess had arrived uninvited on her doorstep to seek out her acquaintance, and leave them to judge who was telling the truth.

Caroline's response to this preliminary shot across her bows must surely have exceeded Lady Douglas's wildest dreams. Taking leave not merely of her senses but of every last vestige of self-control, she proceeded to send two vulgarly abusive 'anonymous' letters through the twopenny post, calling her ladyship all kinds of names, such as 'impudent, *silly, wretched, ungrateful* and illiteral' (meaning illiterate) and also accusing her of having told everybody that the Princess was the mother of the 'Deptford child'. The letters were followed up by two drawings 'of a most indecent nature', again sent through the public post, and representing Lady Douglas *in flagrante delicto* with Sir Sidney Smith.

There seems never to have been any real dispute that these extraordinary effusions were the work of that 'restless, mischievous person the Princess of Wales'. According to Lady Douglas, anyone who had ever heard her speak would have instantly recognized her style – both letters were plainly written by a foreigner and a very ill-educated one at that. As for the drawings, they too were done by her own hand, and the words on them were in her handwriting – the Douglases and Sidney Smith were all prepared to swear to that without a moment's hesitation. And if further proof were needed, at least one of the covers had been sealed with the Princess's own seal.

Caroline had now, of course, put herself hopelessly in the wrong. Sir John and Lady Douglas and Sir Sidney Smith could justly demand explanations and apologies and they at once formally requested an audience with her Royal Highness. Her Royal Highness, realizing that she had overstepped the mark, went into retreat – 'much indisposed' and unable to see anyone – while hurriedly summoning her brother-in-law Edward, Duke of Kent, with whom she had always been on friendly terms, to extricate her from this latest scrape.

The Duke of Kent, fourth in line of seniority in the royal brotherhood and a natural born busybody, came bustling importantly to the rescue, only too pleased to be invited to interfere. He was not personally acquainted with the Douglases, but he knew Sidney Smith and through him proceeded to exert pressure on Sir John and his lady to agree, at least for the time being, to forgo their very natural desire for satisfaction, pointing out that if the matter were to become public it would greatly distress the King and be injurious to his health, especially in view of the delicate state of his nerves. It was certainly a disgraceful affair – abominable even – but if the Douglases would be generous enough to try and forget what had happened Kent promised to speak seriously to the Princess of Wales, to impress her with a sense of her folly and its potentially dangerous consequences. In the end, placated by an invitation to dine at Kensington Palace, John Douglas rather reluctantly undertook to bury his 'private calamity' for the sake of His Majesty's peace of mind and the public good, but at the same time he reserved 'a full right' to bring the subject forward again should he feel it justified and when 'it was not likely to disturb the repose of the country'.

There, for the moment, the matter rested, but of course there was never any realistic possibility of being able to keep so titillating a piece of scandal permanently under wraps – too many people already knew or had guessed the reasons which lay behind Caroline's quarrel with her erstwhile cronies. Caroline was later to claim that the campaign of character assassination mounted against her in the London clubs and drawing-rooms during the spring and summer of 1805 had been master-minded by the Douglases and originated in the malicious imagination of Lady Douglas. Lady Douglas claimed, with equal conviction, that it was the Princess herself who precipitated the crisis by 'a fresh torrent of outrage' intended to undermine her own and her husband's good name and which Sir John quite naturally regarded as releasing him from his former undertaking to 'remain quiet *if left unmolested*'. He therefore laid the whole matter before the Duke of Sussex, in order, explained his wife, that with the assistance of his amiable patron he might 'acquaint the Royal Family of the manner the Princess of Wales was proceeding in' and seek the protection of the King and the heir apparent. The heir apparent, as that member of the royal family most immediately concerned, at once demanded a full and detailed account of the Douglases' association with his estranged wife and in particular 'commanded them to be very circumstantial in their detail respecting all they may know relative to the child the Princess of Wales affected to adopt'. Thus it was that during the winter of 1805–6, while the rest of the country was still preoccupied in coming to terms with the epic news of the great naval victory recently gained at Trafalgar and the concomitant tragedy of Lord Nelson's death, Sir John Douglas and his lady were to be found closeted with Colonel McMahon, the Prince of Wales's confidential secretary and, some said, pimp, with his close friend Lord Moira, or with the lawyers in King's Bench Walk, dredging up every last little thing they could recall about their friendship with the Princess.

These question-and-answer sessions – at one of them the Prince of Wales himself came and sat beside Lady Douglas, scribbling copious notes of her replies – continued on into the spring, and the picture of Caroline now being exposed to the light of public day was not a pretty one. The Douglas version portrayed a woman whose temper was 'so tyrannical, capricious and furious' that no man on earth could be expected to put up with it; an offensively crude, coarse, ill-bred woman who found amusement either by insulting her guests (she had once called Lady Douglas a liar in the middle of a dinner party and deliberately reduced her to tears at a time when she was far advanced in pregnancy), or else by embarrassing the company to death by insulting and ridiculing the royal family: they were ugly and ill made and had 'plum-pudding faces'; the Duke of Cambridge looked like a sergeant 'and so vulgar with his ears full of powder'; the Duke of Kent was a disagreeable man and not to be trusted; and so on.

But this was not the half of it. After hinting that the Princess had displayed unnatural, that is lesbian tendencies, Lady Douglas went on to accuse her Royal Highness of being an immoral woman who brazenly flaunted her promiscuity, an adulteress who boasted that 'she got a bed-fellow whenever she could'; that her husband was 'the most complaisant man in the world' that she did what she liked, went where she liked, and had what bed-fellow she liked and the Prince paid for all'. Add to this her alleged 'confession' about her pregnancy, the appearance of the mysterious 'Deptford child' at Montague House, plus her alleged readiness to foist the paternity of her bastard on to the heir apparent, and the matter ceased to be an affair of mere spiteful tittle-tattle. As the Lord Chancellor observed, if the cuckolded husband had been a common man, Caroline could have slept with the Devil and no great harm done, but 'the Prince of Wales has no right to risk his Daughter's Crown and his Brothers' claims' – such accusations once made 'must be examined into'. As soon as the Prime Minister heard about them he very properly declared that he had no choice but to inform the King without delay.

The King still retained a soft spot for his wayward niece – indeed, his attentions to her had further soured the never exactly cordial relations between father and eldest son. Even now, if it had been a question of just one attachment, even if there was a child, His Majesty would, he said, have tried to screen her if it could have been done with safety to the Crown. But faced with so much evidence of such apparently careless profligacy there was nothing he could do, and the King therefore authorized the setting up of a Commission empowered to 'enquire into the truth of certain written declarations touching the conduct of Her Royal Highness the Princess of Wales'.

William Pitt had died at the end of January 1806, and a few days later a new coalition government, optimistically christened 'the Ministry of All the Talents' and headed by William Wyndham, Lord Grenville, leader of the convervative Whigs, came into office. The committee of Privy Councillors appointed at the end of May to carry out what became known unofficially as 'the Delicate Investigation' into the Princess of Wales's morals was therefore composed of Grenville, as Prime Minister, Earl Spencer, the New Home Secretary, the Lord Chancellor Thomas Erskine and the Lord Chief Justice, with the Solicitor-General, Sir Samuel Romilly, in attendance.

This impressive array of talent began its task by interviewing a succession of footmen, pages, housemaids, laundresses, and others behind closed doors at Number 10 Downing Street. But, as might be expected in the circumstances, the evidence thus extracted proved vague, contradictory, and often second- or even third-hand. Robert Bidgood deposed that in the year 1802 Sir Sidney Smith had been hanging around Montague House at all hours of the day and night, and seemed able to come and go without observing the formality of ringing the front door bell. Bidgood's wife Sarah added that the coffee-woman, Frances Lloyd, had told her that Mary Wilson the housemaid had once seen the Princess and Sir Sidney in 'such an indecent situation' that she had fainted from the shock, and a footman, William Cole, swore he had once found them together on a sofa in 'so familiar a posture as to alarm him very much'. On the other hand, Samuel Roberts, another footman, never remembered seeing Sir Sidney alone with the Princess, and Caroline's own page, Thomas Stikeman, while admitting that the Admiral *had* sometimes been alone with Her Royal Highness, sometimes as late as eleven o'clock at night, and *had* sat on the same sofa with her, he, Stikeman, had never known there was anything 'questionable' about their friendship, or noticed anything other than the 'lively vivacity' and familiarity with which the Princess treated all her gentlemen visitors.

Among Caroline's other gentlemen visitors, Thomas Lawrence, the artist, was mentioned as having slept several nights at Montague House when he was painting the Princess's portrait and, according to William Cole, had sat up alone with her very late at night after the other ladies had retired. Another gentleman whose frequent presence became 'a subject of conversation' among the servants was Captain Thomas Manby RN, commander of the frigate *Africaine*. Frances Lloyd had seen the Princess of Wales in the garden with a man she believed to be Manby at six o'clock one morning in 1803 when the household was staying at Ramsgate and Captain Manby's ship was anchored in the Downs. Robert Bidgood had seen him and Caroline kissing each other on the lips, and when the Princess went to stay at Southend in May 1804 he suspected that the Captain often slept in the house. Frances Lloyd told William Cole about 'delightful doings' with the Captain at Southend, but Thomas Stikeman, although made uneasy by Manby's coming so often and staying so late, loyally denied any suggestion of an improper familiarity between them, and so did Charlotte Sander. Mrs Lisle, one of the regular ladies-in-waiting, agreed that the Princess certainly seemed to prefer the Captain's company to that of her female acquaintance, but she had behaved towards him 'only as any woman would who likes flirting'. Harriet Fitzgerald, who had come to live with Caroline in 1801, as 'a friend and companion' and had been at Southend with her, had no recollection of Captain Manby's ever sleeping in the Princess's house, nor did she know of Sidney Smith ever having been alone with her.

Over the matter of Caroline's alleged pregnancy in 1802 and the paternity of the Deptford child, opinion below stairs was again divided. Frances Lloyd thought the Princess had 'looked as if she was with child' but also remembered the baby, said to have been about four months old, being brought to Montague House by its mother, who had cried and said she could not afford to keep it. Betty Townley, the laundress who did the Montague House washing, testified that she had once noticed the linen to be more stained than usual and was of the opinion that this 'was from a miscarriage, the linen had the appearance of a miscarriage. . . . There were fine damask napkins, and some of them marked with a little red crown in the corner.' She, too, remembered the arrival of the Deptford child and used to do its washing. Other people recalled either hearing rumours that the Princess of Wales was pregnant, or thinking that she looked pregnant. William Cole observed that she had grown 'very large' in the summer of 1802, and then 'in the latter end of the same year she appeared to be grown thin'. Thomas Stikeman had never supposed, from looking at her Royal Highness, that she was with child, but, he went on, 'from her shape it is difficult to judge when she is with child. When she was with child of the Princess Charlotte I should not have known it when she was far advanced in her time, if I had not been told it.' On a less subjective level, all those in a position to know the facts – Caroline's dresser, the housemaid who made her bed, the ladies who saw her every day, three doctors who had attended her for various minor ailments during the period in question – all these persons categorically rejected any suggestion that she had either been pregnant or been delivered of a living child.

On 7 June, Sophia Austin, wife of a former labourer in the naval dockyard at Deptford, appeared before the Downing Street committee and made a sworn statement to the effect that four years previously, that is on Sunday 11 July 1802, she had borne a son, baptized William, at the Brownlow Street Lying-In Hospital. Her husband having lost his job at the dockyard as a result of the peace treaty signed at Amiens in the spring of the year, Mrs Austin was obliged to seek charitable help and on Saturday 23 October had trudged the two miles to Deptford to Blackheath, carrying the three-month old William in her arms and clutching a petition from her husband asking the Princess of Wales to use her influence to get the dockyard to take him on again. She had apparently listened sympathetically to several such applications in the recent past and had acquired quite a reputation for benevolence in the neighbourhood. Lord Malmesbury would have been proud of her in this respect at least.

On her first visit Mrs Austin had seen Thomas Stikeman, who said that if her baby had been younger, 'about a fortnight old', he could probably have got it taken care of for her. However, she was told to come back and on 6 November she saw Caroline and was asked by one of the ladies present if she could make up her mind to part with the child, who would be treated like 'a young Prince'. The mother answered that she would rather part with it to a lady like the Princess than to 'keep it to want'. She was then given a pound note and told to start weaning the infant at once. Fanny Lloyd remembered being ordered to give her some arrowroot with instructions on how to make it up. A week later, William or Billy Austin, or Willikin as Caroline always called him, was duly delivered up at Montague House, and he had been there ever since. His mother continued to visit him at intervals – 'I saw the child last Whit Monday', her statement ended, 'and I swear that it is my child.'

Mrs Austin's evidence was corroborated by an entry in the Register of Births and Baptisms of children born at the Brownlow Street Hospital and seems to account pretty comprehensively for the origins and parentage of the 'Deptford child'. It certainly satisfied the Delicate Investigators, who reported their 'perfect conviction that there is no foundation whatever for believing that the child now with the Princess of Wales is the child of her Royal Highness, or that she was delivered of any child in the year 1802'. But although the Commission concluded that Willikin had, beyond all reasonable doubt, been born as advertised in the Brownlow Street Hospital 'of the body of Sophia Austin', the gossip-mongers naturally preferred to go on believing (and propagating) the more scandalous and/or romantic versions of the story, and they were encouraged in this by the fact that Willikin continued to occupy a uniquely privileged place in Caroline's affections.

The other pauper children she had taken under her capacious wing (there were about eight or nine of them) were all boarded out with respectable working-class families in the district to be brought up in a manner suited to their station in life. The boys were destined to become seamen, the girls well-trained, industrious housewives. According to her German admirer, Herr Campe, the Princess had told him that some people had criticized her for not doing more for her protégés in the way of expensive clothes and education, but she knew what she was about. She wanted them to become 'useful, virtuous and happy members of society' and had no intention of unfairly raising their expectations 'in despite of Providence and natural destination'. However, it appeared she had no such scruples in regard to Willikin, who was, in truth, always treated 'like a young Prince'.

Exactly why this particular child should have been so singled out has never really been explained. He was not, by all accounts, an especially attractive specimen. 'A nasty, vulgar-looking little brat' was the verdict of the outspokenly patrician Lady Hester Stanhope – an opinion widely shared by the other dinner guests at Montague House who were treated to the unappetizing spectacle of Willikin, bawling and kicking over their wine, as he was held up by a footman to snatch at anything he fancied from the dessert. The Princess Charlotte remembered him as a sickly-looking child, with fair hair and blue eyes; and as he grew up young Austin was said to bear a strong resemblance to his natural mother in features and complexion.

Knowing Caroline, there was pretty certainly an element of defiance in the attachment – yet another manifestation of that disastrous and seemingly irresistible urge to *épater les bourgeois* which, when somebody once referred to Willikin as her son, led her to cackle, 'Prove it and he shall be your King!' Apart from this, Willikin had, of course, become an essential ingredient in the elaborate half-fantasy, half-practical-joke she had begun to act out for Lady Douglas's benefit and which had gradually acquired its own reality, so that, for a time, the Princess may have more than half convinced herself that she *had* brought Willikin to bed. And so, in a sense, she had. He was at least all her own to love, as her daughter had never been. Everybody needed something to love, she once remarked to a friend, and as she frankly detested lap-dogs and parrots, that really only left babies. But to do her justice, she remained devoted to the egregious Willy long after he had ceased to be a baby, nor did she ever shirk her responsibility for his welfare.

The Downing Street committee finally submitted its report in mid-July, and their lordships were happy to be able to assure the King of their conclusion that all the allegations of pregnancy and childbirth as a result of illicit intercourse levied against the Princess of Wales had been satisfactorily disproved. Nevertheless, they felt in duty bound to add a rider to the effect that some of the evidence they had heard in the course of their enquiry contained 'other particulars respecting the conduct of her Royal Highness such as must, especially considering her exalted rank and station, necessarily give occasion to very unfavourable interpretations'. For example, the commissioners were of the opinion that 'the circumstances . . . stated to have passed between her Royal Highness and Captain Manby must be credited, until they shall receive some decisive contradiction; and, if true, are justly entitled to the most serious consideration'. In other words, while there might be no proof admissible in a court of law that Caroline had committed adultery, the presumption that she had been sleeping around was exceedingly strong; and when her footmen summed up the situation in flat Anglo-

Saxon terms, they were most probably and regrettably quite right – the Princess *was* very fond of fucking.

The report got a mixed reception from the two people most intimately concerned. The Prince of Wales, who had been hoping at the very least to be given grounds for divorce, was bitterly disappointed by its 'weakness, irresolution and pusillanimity'. He accused the commissioners of 'false delicacy' and of showing far too great a degree of leniency towards the Princess. Maybe there was not quite enough evidence to charge her with high treason, but the circumstances of her indiscretion, 'amounting nearly to positive proof', were such that they should have recommended the King immediately to bring in an Act of Parliament to dissolve the marriage.

Caroline, on the other hand, believed she had won a famous victory and wrote off to her father-in-law in confident anticipation of 'that happy moment when I may be allowed to appear again before your Majesty's eyes and receive once more the assurance from your Majesty's own mouth that I have your gracious protection, and that you will not discard me from your friendship . . . which must be my only support and my only consolation in this country'. She was soon to discover that it was going to be a lot more complicated than that.

FOUR

A Most Engaging Child

> *I quite tremble at the uncommon parts and cleverness of Charlotte, as
> I think she is likely to discover by that means the sad variance which
> reigns between her parents.*
>
> The Princess Royal to Lady Elgin, February, 1801

The panel of Royal Commissioners entrusted with the task of
conducting an investigation into the manners and morals
of the Princess of Wales had been too genteel to call on any
witnesses for the defence, but the Princess herself, who was not
at all genteel, had no intention of allowing her case to go by
default – especially as it began to dawn on her that her
'victory' was by no means so clear cut as she had at first
supposed. The report of the Lords Commissioners might have
cleared her of 'the enormous guilt of High Treason, committed
in the foul crime of Adultery'; but imputations remained,
'strangely sanctioned and countenanced' by that same report,
on which the Princess could not keep silent without incurring
fatal consequences to her honour and character.

Although the weight of the legal profession might appear
to have been heavily stacked against her, Caroline was not
without friends in high places – her husband's political
opponents were always grateful for an opportunity to
embarrass him by championing her – and on this occasion
she was able to command the services of Mr Spencer
Percival, who had lost his job as Attorney-General in the
government reshuffle following the death of Mr Pitt and was

consequently free to devote his energies to helping the Princess prepare a detailed rebuttal of all the allegations made by the Douglases. This 'artful' – and long-winded –, document, dated 2 October 1806, was drawn up in the form of a letter addressed to the King by his 'most affectionate and dutiful Daughter-in-law and subject', but was plainly intended for wider circulation and was, in fact, printed that winter under the somewhat ambiguous title of *The Book*.

In *The Book*, Caroline set out to contradict, as decisively as possible, those discreditable 'circumstances' left in doubt by the Royal Commissioners and to establish her innocence by exposing the injustice, the malice, the malevolence, and the glaring improbability of the story which had been put about by her enemies. The improbability, not to say absurdity, of Lady Douglas's statement was Caroline's strongest card. For why, she now demanded, if she had indeed been guilty as charged, should she have gratuitously and uselessly confessed so dangerous a secret and then, having put her life and character in the other woman's hands, gone on wantonly and without provocation to quarrel with her, insult her, and attempt to ruin her reputation? So blatant a farrago of nonsense must surely be enough to stagger the belief of any unprejudiced person – unless, of course, such a person also believed that Her Royal Highness was as insane as Lady Douglas insinuated.

To all those unprejudiced members of the great British public whose knowledge of the Princess of Wales was limited to generally favourable newspaper reports and perhaps an occasional distant glimpse of a graciously smiling figure waving from a carriage window or theatre box, Lady Douglas's narrative did seem incredible; but those privileged to have some first-hand knowledge of the Princess were not so easily convinced. Charlotte Douglas may very likely have indulged in a little judicious embroidery and had certainly omitted no scrap of damaging gossip, however irrelevant; nevertheless her story carried an unmistakably authentic echo of Caroline's voice, her reckless irresponsibility and mischievous compulsion to do and say the most outlandish things. Although not clinically insane – at least not by the standards accepted in her day – she was unquestionably unstable, and on this occasion at least the pressures of boredom, frustration, a corroding sense of grievance, and also perhaps simple envy of another woman's pregnancy, seem to have combined to push her temporarily across the never very well defined border between eccentricity and madness.

Whatever the truth about its underlying causes, the abberation was now over, and Caroline was back in the real world, facing the dismal necessity of regaining her place, such as it was, within the royal circle. But although it was easy enough to pour scorn on the pregnancy story – which, in any case, had already been rejected by the Delicate Investigators – it was not quite so easy to refute the more generalized charges of moral turpitude levelled against her. In all her various outpourings the Princess had never gone so far as actually to give a name to the father of her supposed child; she had retained just enough discretion for that. But significantly no one showed any particular surprise over the presumption that she could have been so caught out. Princess Charlotte apparently always took it for granted that Captain Manby had fathered Willikin, and Sidney Smith another of her mother's 'foundling' protégées known as Edwardina Kent.

In *The Book*, Caroline indignantly denied that anything improper had ever occurred with any of her gentlemen friends. Certainly Sidney Smith had been a frequent visitor to Montague House. Lodging as he did with the Douglases he had been a near neighbour and welcome to drop in whenever he was passing, but there had never been any question of his having his own key, as Robert Bidgood had alleged. The Princess hoped, with heavy sarcasm, that it would not be taken as a confession of guilt if she admitted having found Sir Sidney an amusing conversationalist – his accounts of the 'extraordinary events and heroic achievements' of his naval career were naturally most entertaining and informative. He

had also been kind enough to take an interest in her plans for
'fitting up' one of her rooms after the Turkish style, giving
her a drawing of the tent of Murat Bey which he had
brought home from Egypt, and showing her how to draw
Turkish arabesques. She did not deny that she had been
alone with him on frequent occasions, just as she had often
been alone with other men, with tradesmen calling for orders
or with visiting masters for painting, music, English, and so
on. It had all been perfectly innocent and above board, and,
in any case, she had always understood that it was quite
customary for ladies of the first rank to receive morning visits
from gentlemen unchaperoned. If she was wrong, then she
hoped fair-minded people would make allowances for her
ignorance and put it down to her foreign education and
habits. The footman, William Cole, might very likely have
seen her sitting on the same sofa with Sir Sidney Smith, but
the Princess of Wales felt certain the King would agree with
her that it was the hardest thing imaginable to be called
upon to account for what corner of a sofa she had been
sitting on four years earlier, or how close Sir Sidney had
been. 'I can only solemnly aver to your Majesty', she went
on, 'that my conscience supplies me with the fullest means of
assuring you that I never permitted Sir Sidney Smith to sit on
any sofa with me in any manner which, in my own
judgement, was in the slightest degree offensive to the
strictest propriety and decorum.'

As for the other men with whom she was alleged to have
had improper relations, namely Mr Lawrence the painter and
Captain Thomas Manby RN, it was true that Mr Lawrence
had slept two or three nights at Montague House while he
was painting her portrait back in the spring of 1801, and he
had spent some time in the evenings sitting with her and her
ladies. Sometimes there had been music, in which he joined;
sometimes he had read poetry aloud, or they played chess.
Nothing could have been more decorous, and William Cole's
stories of having heard them whispering together behind a

locked door late at night should be treated with the utmost suspicion. Cole had contradicted himself on several occasions in his evidence to the commissioners and he was, moreover, a prejudiced witness. Caroline had found him a most unsatisfactory servant – he had been educated above his station, which made him disagreeably forward and obtrusive in manner – and she had therefore sent him back to London to wait on her only when she came to Carlton House, a banishment which he had apparently greatly resented.

Turning to Captain Manby, she explained that she had made his acquaintance through her charitable work. A naval officer she believed to be of great merit, he had been introduced to her by mutual friends and had agreed to accept two of her 'charity boys' as members of his ship's crew. In token of her gratitude for his trouble, she had presented him with some trifling gifts of linen and plate for his cabin and had been pleased to receive him at Montague House while the *Africaine* was fitting out at Deptford. But neither there, nor at Southend nor Ramsgate had they ever been alone together – Robert Bidgood's evidence to the contrary was as foul, malicious, and wicked a falsehood as was ever invented by the malice of man.

Sir Sidney Smith was now back at sea in further pursuance of his adventurous career and did not trouble to enter a defence, but Thomas Lawrence and Captain Manby both swore affidavits fiercely rejecting the aspersions which had been cast on their virtue. Manby had never, upon any occasion or in any situation, had the presumption to salute the Princess in the manner alleged, or to take any such liberty or offer any such insult to her person; nor had he ever slept under her roof at Blackheath, Southend, Ramsgate, or anywhere else. Manby, it seems, was considered something of a rough diamond and not 'from his situation, birth, or manners' at all the sort of person one would normally expect to meet in the society of a Princess of Wales. Thomas Lawrence, on the other hand, might be encountered blending smoothly in the most exclusive company – a refined, soft-spoken fellow of whom it was said that he could not write an answer to a simple dinner invitation without its assuming 'the tone of a billet-doux'. He was, however, forthright in his denial that he had ever been alone with Caroline late at night behind a locked door. He had certainly spent a few nights at Montague House in 1801 but only for reasons of practical convenience while he was engaged in painting Her Royal Highness's portrait. The musical evenings to which she had graciously admitted him had always been chaperoned by the ladies-in-waiting, and nothing had ever passed between them which could not have been seen and heard by anybody.

An inscrutable silence followed the submission of Caroline's defence, and on 8 December she returned to the attack, drawing the King's attention to the torments of anxiety and suspense she had been subjected to while fondly indulging the hope that every day as it passed would bring the happy tidings that His Majesty was satisfied of her innocence. Nine long weeks had now passed and brought her nothing but disappointment. She remained in total ignorance of what had been done or what was intended about her future, and was becoming increasingly worried about the prejudicial effect this delay must be having on her reputation; for the outside world, not knowing the true facts of the case, would naturally begin to assume that she must be guilty. She knew she had no chance of clearing her name unless and until the King made some public demonstration of his belief in her, or until a full disclosure of the facts exposed the malice of her enemies and did away with every ground for 'unfavourable inference and conjecture'. She therefore once again took the liberty of throwing herself at the King's feet, entreating and imploring him for justice.

Despite the eloquence of her plea, the Princess had to wait another seven weeks before a rather grudging formal message from her father-in-law was relayed by the Lord Chancellor's office. After mature consideration it appeared that the Cabinet had agreed to take no further action in the matter – unless it was a prosecution of Lady Douglas for perjury – and had consequently advised the King that he need no longer refuse to admit the Princess of Wales to his royal presence. His Majesty felt bound to add, however, that certain aspects of Her Royal Highness's behaviour as revealed by the Douglas affair still caused him serious concern, and he hoped she would in future take care to conduct herself in such a way as to justify 'those marks of paternal regard and affection' which the King always wished to show every member of his family.

Taking this as a limited victory. Caroline at once wrote expressing 'unfeigned happiness' at her reinstatement and announcing her intention of hurrying down to Windsor to receive the royal blessing of which she had been so long and so unjustly deprived. The King was noticeably less enthused. He would prefer to see the Princess in London and would let her know a convenient date in due course. Ten days later she heard that since the Prince of Wales was now proposing to put 'certain documents' in the hands of his lawyers, the King considered it incumbent upon him to defer naming a day to the Princess of Wales 'until the further result of the Prince's intention shall have been made known to him'.

Caroline's old friend George Canning thought this 'very unfortunate' and likely to cause a public sensation. Everybody had expected to see the Princess at the Drawing-Room on 12 February, and the disappointment would inevitably give rise to a fresh burst of conjecture. Many people too, in Canning's opinion, would be shocked by the 'refined malice' displayed by the Prince in waiting until this last minute before bringing forward a mysterious new initiative – the more so as he had previously made such a point of telling everybody that he had nothing to do with 'exciting the proceedings' against his wife.

Caroline's response to the determined rearguard action being fought by the royal family was to despatch another letter complaining bitterly about the 'unparalleled injustice and cruelty of this interposition of the Prince of Wales' and once more rehearsing the long list of her grievances – as far back as April 1796 and her husband's original letter of dismissal when she had not been 'much above a year' in England. Caroline had never made any secret of her resentment over the way she had been snubbed and rejected in the past; on the contrary, she regularly bored her acquaintance to death on the subject. But what now emerged from the dense verbal thickets of complaint and self-justification was her refusal to accept continued social ostracism while her character was 'whispered away' by gossip and innuendo. If any further charges of immorality were to be brought against her, she claimed the right of reply in open court, together with the benefit of the presumption of innocence until proved guilty; if no such charges were contemplated, then she demanded full and prompt restoration of her former 'respect and station' as a member of the royal family, plus the use of apartments in one of the royal palaces, essential for convenient attendance at Court. Should these very reasonable requests be refused or ignored, the Princess would feel obliged, however reluctantly, to publish her own side of the case to the world, and on 5 March she issued an ultimatum: publication of the proceedings alluded to would not be withheld beyond the following Monday.

Not all her supporters were convinced of the wisdom of this course – publicity might, after all, prove a two-edged weapon – but Spencer Percival believed that 'the mere publication of the Princess's business, and our experience of the conspiracy against her and the injustice with which she has been treated, would give the government such a shock in point of popularity and public opinion that it would be very difficult for them to stand'. As it happened the unlucky Ministry of All the Talents was not destined to stand for much longer, though it was the long-running dispute over Catholic Emancipation which brought it down, not the publication of 'the Princess's business'. The change of government, however, brought the Princess's Tory friends back into office – George Canning to the Foreign Office, Lord Eldon as Lord Chancellor, and Spencer Percival as Chancellor of the Exchequer. There was no longer any question of stirring up public opinion. Ironically enough Spencer Percival found himself having to spend several thousand pounds of public money on retrieving a dozen or so prematurely leaked copies of *The Book*. And the whole rather undignified affair was finally settled by a Cabinet minute dated 21 April which declared that all the charges examined in the course of the Delicate Investigation were to be regarded as either satisfactorily disproved or else based on 'evidence underserving of credit'. The ministers, therefore, unanimously recommended that the Princess should be readmitted forthwith to the King's presence and received in a manner proper to her rank and station. On 18 May it was noted that there had been 'a prodigious exhibition of the Princess of Wales at the Opera and Drawing-Room'. At the former 'the tumult and applause was most unbounded', but at the Drawing-Room her public reception by her mother-in-law was marked by an all too obvious coldness. However, as Gilbert Elliot told his father, 'She is received at Court and they have been able to keep her quiet without insisting upon anything impossible or unreasonable, so that I hope that subject is at rest for ever.'

It was not, of course. The Delicate Investigation would remain on the record, to be picked over by the gossips and remembered against the Princess of Wales for ever. The Douglases, their credibility destroyed, disappeared from view – Sir John lost his job on the Duke of Sussex's staff and was even expelled from his Masonic Lodge. But Caroline had won a hollow victory, which was perhaps all she deserved. Nobody, in fact, had emerged with their personal credit much enhanced, though the principal loser – at least in his own estimation – was the Prince of Wales. Not merely had he been robbed of a heaven-sent opportunity of putting an end to his disastrous marriage by the weakness, irresolution, and pusillanimity of the Royal Commissioners, but Caroline infuriatingly had kept her winning lead in the popularity stakes. In spite of her disgraceful and, if the truth were known, almost certainly treasonous behaviour, the general consensus of opinion still held that she was the injured party, prevented from establishing her innocence on the flimsy pretext that a public inquiry would have been a violation of privacy – a prying into confidential royal family affairs. The unfairness of it all was almost too much, especially when the Prince recalled some of the more wounding insults so obligingly repeated by Lady Douglas: how Caroline had laughed at his complaisant cuckoldry, how she had declared that she should have been the man and he the woman, how he asked nothing better than to have his slippers under any old dowager's table and sit there all day scribbling notes. The lawyers having failed him it seemed he was powerless to retaliate, but he did refuse to allow his wife to go on using her old rooms at Carlton House – he was not going to risk running into her on the stairs. In fact, he was to go to considerable trouble to avoid the possibility of ever running into her again, although there was to be one last encounter at the King's Birthday Drawing-Room in June 1807 when, according to Lady Bessborough, they did not speak and 'coming out close together both looked contrary ways'.

While there was undeniably risible element in the spectacle of the overweight, overdressed playboy Prince and that over-rouged, over-generous lady his wife ostentatiously cutting one another dead for the benefit of a tittering Court, the situation had its serious side: for this comic-opera couple, now seemingly trapped for ever in their own peculiarly unholy estate of matrimony, were also the future King and Queen of England and parents of an heir presumptive who, to many thoughtful folk, represented the best, if not the only, hope for the future of the British monarchical system.

Princess Charlotte of Wales had remained in the care of

Lady Elgin until the autumn of 1804 – a circumstance for which her aunt Charlotte (George III's eldest daughter, now married to the Hereditary Prince of Württemberg) was devoutly grateful. 'Poor infant!' wrote the former Princess Royal, 'if, amongst so many dangerous, intriguing people, she had not the blessing to have a person about her capable from good principles, age and situation in life, to guard her from falling a victim to these examples, what would become of her?' Aunt Charlotte received regular bulletins on her dear little namesake's progress from Lady Elgin and reciprocated with a series of letters full of earnest advice on the proper management of this so precious child.

Charlotte was not an easy child to manage. Morning visitors were charmed by the bright, pretty little girl, bubbling with eager high spirits, who chattered away to them in the friendliest manner possible. 'The . . . most sensible and genteel little creature you would wish to see', commented that formidable educationist and social reformer Miss Hannah More after being shown round Carlton House by her four-year-old hostess; while Dr Porteous, Bishop of London, who spent a day down at Blackheath in the summer of 1801, found the young princess 'a most captivating and engaging child'. But the flaxen-haired moppet, entertaining Miss More with a rendition of 'How Doth the Little Busy Bee', or begging a blessing from the gratified Dr Porteous, could all too easily be transformed into a red-faced, screaming termagant. There was nothing in the least genteel or captivating about Charlotte in the throes of one of her uncontrollable temper tantrums.

Nevertheless, Aunt Charlotte remained resolutely opposed to the use of any harsh or violent methods of correction, which, she was convinced, only served to make a child obstinate and deceitful. Instead, from the safe distance of North Germany, she urged a policy of patient, gentle firmness in the campaign to moderate the effusions of young Charlotte's excessive sensibility. If nothing but mildness and steadiness were opposed to her 'little passions' she would soon grow to be ashamed of them, while, 'her being strongly impressed with the omnipresence of God' was the surest way of rooting out her disposition to tell stories.

In general, though, the older Charlotte was less concerned over these comparatively minor character faults than with the danger of her 'lovely little niece' becoming too hopelessly spoilt. 'I wish she had a child a little older than herself to play with, as that by degrees would teach her to prefer others to herself, and would prevent her thinking that everybody must attend to her.' But there was no move to revive that sensible practice of earlier times, when a royal child was always educated with a group of carefully chosen companions, and Aunt Charlotte continued to worry at the problem of how to combat the swollen-headedness encouraged by all those thoughtless grown-ups praising the little princess's beauty and cleverness. 'As she has once found out she is clever, nothing but being with older children will ever get the better of this unfortunate vanity.'

Apart from vanity, which was 'a little in the blood', there was Charlotte's tendency to stammer, another failing unfortunately 'very common to all sides of the Brunswick family' and attributable to a weakness of the nerves – Aunt Charlotte hoped that sea-bathing at Weymouth would prove strengthening. Other suggestions and recommendations – ranging from the best methods of inculcating a love of religion and checking an inclination towards the sin of covetousness, to correcting bad posture – continued to flow from the busy pen in Württemberg throughout the years 1798 to 1804. Presents arrived, too: silver toys from Stuttgart, dolls in national costume, and a dolls' tea-service specially bespoke in Louisbourg china; while in June 1801 the eldest aunt was made happy by a kind letter from the Prince of Wales enclosing 'a beautiful locket with Charlotte's hair'.

The Württemberg Princess had always been anxious that dear little Charlotte should be a comfort and blessing to the whole royal family and that the child should be kept in ignorance of the rift between her father and mother for as long as possible. Indeed, she shared with Lady Elgin a sentimental fancy that the little creature might one day be a means of reuniting them. But although Lady Elgin is to be congratulated on her efforts to ensure that her charge remained 'equally attached' to both parents, Charlotte was destined to become not an instrument of reconciliation but a weapon of war in the increasingly bitter family faction fights.

The old King had continued to take a deeply affectionate interest in his granddaughter, and Charlotte at five years old was weaving tasselled cape strings as a present for Grandpapa. The King also continued to champion the cause of the Princess of Wales – at least until the revelations of the Delicate Investigation finally destroyed his illusions. He dined with her regularly at Blackheath and was moved to bestow the office of Ranger of Greenwich Park upon her. These attentions naturally did nothing to improve his never very harmonious relations with his eldest son, which were particularly strained in the early years of the new century. The King stubbornly refused to allow the heir apparent any military rank or employment, at a time when England was under hourly threat of invasion by Napoleon's army camped at Boulogne, and as a result father and son were no longer on speaking terms.

However, in July 1804 it began to look as if young Charlotte might possibly become a means of reuniting her father and grandfather, if not her father and mother. It appeared that the King had expressed a wish to have the Princess Charlotte under his immediate care. The Prince, scenting an opportunity to exert pressure on the immovable royal object, responded by letting it be known that nothing could be more gratifying to him than to see his daughter taken under His Majesty's 'special direction', always providing this was His Majesty's 'sole and exclusive' direction. In order that there should be no misunderstanding about the significance of this proviso, HRH entrusted his special friend Lord Moira with a verbal message for the Lord Chancellor to the effect that 'exclusive' meant the continued exclusion of the child's mother from any say in her upbringing. The King, on the other hand, was making it equally clear that, if he were to undertake the guardianship of his granddaughter, he did not intend 'to destroy the rights of the mother', whose conduct he regarded as 'exemplary'.

Negotiations for a *rapproachement* between Windsor and Carlton House were still in a preliminary stage when Lady Elgin had 'a very extraordinary circumstance' to report to the Prince of Wales. She and Charlotte were spending their usual summer holidays at Shrewsbury Lodge, Shooters Hill, and on the morning of Sunday 19 August received an unscheduled visit from the Princess of Wales, who had driven over from Blackheath in great good spirits, bringing the exciting news that they were all invited to Kew on the following day. The King, Caroline told her daughter, had written to say he wanted them both to come and take leave of him before he went to Weymouth.

Lady Elgin was immediately struck with 'the uncommon style of the invitation', for she had never before been summoned to see their Majesties without a command from the Queen written by one of the princesses, and she was conscious of 'a sort of uneasiness'. But when she and Charlotte presented themselves at Kew to find the King was there alone, her ladyship became 'quite stupified' – especially when His Majesty told the little princess: 'I have got you all to myself', adding: 'The Prince has given up the child to me but it is not settled.' Caroline then arrived, and she and the King disappeared into an inner room for a long private conference, leaving Lady Elgin to walk her charge around the gardens.

The governess was by this time thoroughly scared, not only that she had been trapped into committing a dreadful breach of etiquette but that she might have become involved in something even more serious. She knew, of course, all about the King's history of mental illness, and fear that he and the notoriously irresponsible Caroline might now be concocting a scheme to snatch Charlotte out of her father's control could very well have been contributing to her ladyship's disquiet. But when the party presently sat down to dinner together she was slightly reassured to see that His Majesty ate his pudding and dumplings with his usual hearty appetite. The table talk was mostly about Weymouth, an innocuous enough topic of conversation, and the King, although appearing somewhat agitated, was a kind and attentive host, insisting on making the coffee himself.

The Prince of Wales's reaction to news of the unauthorized party at Kew was to issue top-secret instructions that Lady Elgin was not to let the Princess Charlotte out of her sight for a moment 'on any account or under any pretence whatsoever', while the radical politician Charles Fox injected a further element of drama into the situation by warning the Prince of 'the desperate attempt that is making to take the Princess from your Royal Highness'. Fox had heard on good authority that it was highly probable that the King would attempt to gain possession of his granddaughter 'by violence or stratagem' and take her to Windsor, and he urged the Prince to send for the child to Carlton House immediately and 'maintain the possession of her person by all legal means . . . For God's sake, Sir, let no one persuade you that this is not a matter of the highest importance to you.'

The Prince's factotum, Colonel McMahon, was also busy spreading reports of the King's erratic behaviour: he was abusing the Queen, talking openly of parting from her and setting up house with a mistress, while at the same time loading the Princess of Wales with favours and caresses, promising her apartments at Windsor where she could be 'comfortable and independent', and swearing he would never forgive his eldest son for various past injuries. His Majesty had 'fasten'd his mind to getting the little Princess Charlotte entire to himself' and would do 'almost anything on earth to bring it about'. The Lord Chancellor, however, did not believe the King would take any further steps in the matter until his return from Weymouth and begged the Prince of Wales not to do anything which might be construed as provocative in the mean time. The King did, after all, have certain rights over the care and education of the younger member of the royal family, and Lord Eldon, anxious to avoid more damaging domestic dissension, urged that this important business should be conducted with 'the delicacy and caution' which alone could lead to an arrangement satisfactory to the 'just and natural feelings' of all concerned.

Much to the relief of His Majesty's ministers, the furore over the King's intentions towards his granddaughter quickly subsided. The King and Queen went down to Weymouth. The Prince of Wales went off to Brighton, and Charlotte and Lady Elgin seem to have stayed on at Shrewsbury Lodge. But when the Court returned to town at the end of October the King, apparently under the impression that Charlotte would soon be coming to occupy the house at Windsor which he had ordered to be got ready for her, set about drawing up an ambitious scheme for her future education. The training of 'the presumptive heir of the Crown' must obviously be of a more extended nature than the smattering of elegant accomplishments considered sufficient for the average young English gentlewoman. Charlotte's schoolroom was to be under the overall direction of a bishop, who would recommend a clergyman to instruct her in religious principles and Latin and read daily prayers. There were to be instructors for history, geography, English literature, and French, as well as writing, drawing, and music masters. The day-to-day care of the Princess would be entrusted to a governess, and the King felt that the excellent Lady Elgin should now be replaced by someone 'whose age and activity may be more suited to the age of the Princess'. This lady must be supported by a sub-governess and an assistant sub-governess, so that Charlotte would, both day and night, be constantly under the supervision of responsible persons.

The face-to-face encounter between the King and the Prince of Wales which would, it was hoped, witness the burying of several years' accumulation of hatchets finally took place at Windsor in November with outwardly encouraging results. But the battle over the custody of Princess Charlotte continued to be conducted through intermediaries and consequently dragged on inconclusively and long-windedly for the best part of eighteen months.

The chief stumbling-block to a settlement remained the Prince's deep-rooted fear that Caroline would be bound to gain in influence and prestige from any concordat which ceded control to the King. His Majesty was, after all, still paying his daughter-in-law a very marked degree of attention and showering her with expensive presents. 'His mind is ever employed for her comfort and pleasure,' commented her lady-in-waiting Mrs Lisle, and the frequency of his visits to Blackheath had begun to attract ill-natured comment in the outside world.

In the circumstances a conscientious papa might legitimately hesitate. A conscientious papa might legitimately regard a woman of Caroline's temperament and reputation as an unsuitable mentor for an impressionable little girl. Then, again, there was the doubtful propriety of trusting the child to the hands of her grandfather, an elderly man who had already exhibited symptoms of mental disorder and who was, moreover, 'averse to her father, and siding with her mother against him'. But quite apart from these considerations, it seems probable that the Prince of Wales had never had any real intention of parting with Charlotte, who was potentially his most valuable bargaining counter in dealing with the King and his ministers. In January 1805 he announced that, while he had no objection to Charlotte's spending some part of the year with her grandparents at Windsor, her 'nominal headquarters and town residence must be Carlton House'. He also reserved to himself the right to appoint the members of her household, while remaining 'ever desirous to consult His Majesty's inclinations in the formation of it'.

Eventually a compromise of sorts was reached. Apart from therapeutic seaside holidays at such newly fashionable resorts as Worthing, Bognor, or Weymouth, Charlotte would in future divide her time between her father and grandfather, spending roughly half the year at Lower Lodge, Windsor, but remaining at Carlton House during those months when the Prince of Wales was normally to be found in London. In fact, however, her 'nominal headquarters and town residence' were soon transferred to Warwick House, a gloomy down-at-heel building which adjoined the Carlton House complex.

By the time this arrangement was agreed on, the princess's household had been radically reorganized and enlarged. Lady Elgin had resigned and been replaced as governess in January 1805 by the Dowager Baroness de Clifford. Mrs Alicia Campbell, widow of a former Governor of Bermuda, became sub-governess, and a Mrs Udney, nicknamed Mrs Nibs by Charlotte, was also added to the strength. John Fisher, Bishop of Exeter, was appointed superintendent or inspector of education and recommended the Reverend George Nott for the post of chaplain and sub-preceptor with special responsibility for religious knowledge, English, Latin, and Ancient History. There were two additional sub-preceptors for English literature, modern history, French, and German, and visiting masters for writing, music, dancing, and drawing.

Every effort, so her grandfather hoped, was being made to surround the princess with persons who would cultivate her mind and furnish it with the sort of principles likely to prove a blessing to the dominions over which she might later be called to preside, and the Bishop of Exeter set to work to draw up the outlines of a plan regulating the education of this promising child. This plan or timetable as submitted for the King's approval certainly regulated every moment of her day. At 8.00 a.m. she was to enter the schoolroom, where she would find Mr Nott ready to read morning prayers and give her religious instruction until nine. This would be followed by breakfast and a walk. Then lessons with Mr Nott until 11.30.

Half an hour's break and another lesson period occupied the rest of the morning. Dressing and dinner, the main meal of the day, lasted from 1.30 to 3.00 p.m., and then came a carriage airing or some other form of amusement. The hours from five to seven were to be allocated to writing practice, music, or dancing, and the day rounded off with a final recreation period before bed at eight.

It was certainly high time something was done about Charlotte's education. Lady Elgin had declared with an air of pious self-congratulation that she was handing over a pure and innocent child 'free from all fault whatever, both in character and disposition', whose progress in learning had been 'uncommonly great'. But the Reverend Mr Nott found the princess to be practically illiterate. Her handwriting was simply shocking and she made spelling mistakes which 'a common servant would blush to have committed'. Greatly scandalized Mr Nott tried hard to remedy the situation, but it was uphill work. 'Where, may I ask your Royal Highness, is this to end,' he wrote in May 1805 after his pupil had presented him with a particularly careless and ill-spelt piece of composition, 'or when are we to have the satisfaction of seeing your mind animated with a becoming pride and a generous resolution to improve? More than three months have passed, during which the most unremitting exertions have been employed by those about you, and what is the progress you have made?' Ignorance, he went on sternly, was disgraceful in proportion to the rank of the person in whom it was found, and negligence, when the means of improvement were readily available, was nothing short of criminal in the eyes of the Almighty.

But if Mr Nott lacked the ability to stimulate the interest of a lively ten-year-old in academic matters, his integrity and patient kindliness quickly earned him her affection and respect. She genuinely wanted his approval – 'never shall another lie come out of me!' – and when he was ill in the summer of 1806 Charlotte agonized over her past misdeeds, which, she had obviously been told, were the cause of his breakdown. 'What should I have had to answer for, if you had been taken out of the world? . . . Oh, what a dreadful recollection that would have been! But now I shall labour to recover your health by my industry, and wish to please and make you happy.'

She felt no desire to promote the well-being of the principal director of her studies. The Bishop of Exeter – soon to be translated to the see of Salisbury – enjoyed a long-standing connection with the royal family, having once been tutor to the Duke of Kent, chaplain to the King, and Canon of Windsor, and had been chosen by King George for his present appointment on the strength of his mild disposition and engaging manner, which, His Majesty believed, would be 'likely to gain the esteem of any young person'. John Fisher did not, however, succeed in gaining the esteem of the Princess Charlotte. A dull, solemn-looking man with a projecting under-lip, he was a pedantic, self-important, humourless bore, and Charlotte could not stand him. She christened him 'the Great U.P.', from his irritating trick of referring to himself as the BishUP, and whenever his back was turned would shoot out her lower lip and imitate his voice and mannerisms with wicked accuracy. A classical scholar and fastidious connoisseur of the fine arts, the Great U.P. for his part found the Princess bad-mannered and uncouth – he was particularly revolted by her vulgar habit of wiping her nose on her sleeve.

It cannot be said that Charlotte's new governess was having any very noticeable success in polishing her charge's social graces. Described by an acquaintance as 'a good commonplace person' and by her grandson 'as a most agreeable companion', the Dowager Lady de Clifford (who was not, in fact, very much younger than the departed Lady Elgin) does not seem to have possessed the force of character necessary to make a strong-willed, rebellious little girl do as she was told. Charlotte was apparently in the habit of bursting into her governess's room at all hours, usually leaving the door open.

'My dear Princess,' expostulated her ladyship on one such

occasion, 'that is not civil. You should always shut the door after you when you come into a room.'

'Not I, indeed,' was the rudely shouted reply: 'if you want the door shut, ring the bell.'

The Princess and Lady de Clifford both had hot tempers and were often at loggerheads during their eight-year-long association; but although she used to grumble about her strictness and her stinginess, Charlotte grew to feel a certain rather grudging affection for the Dowager. 'After all,' she would remark to young George Keppel, 'there are many worse persons in the world than your snuffy old grandmother.' She was very fond of her other governess, Mrs Campbell, and disliked Mrs Udney with equal fervour.

Like many such establishments, the menage at Warwick House proved a fertile breeding ground for petty intrigue and jealousies. These, of course, were encouraged by Charlotte's outspoken preferences and prejudices and presently erupted in the great row over the Affair of the Princess Charlotte's Will. This remarkable documents was firstly drafted in the spring of 1806. 'I make my Will,' announced the ten-year-old testatrix. 'First, I leave all my best books, and all my books, to the Revd Mr Nott. Secondly, to Mrs Campbell my three watches and half of my jewels. Thirdly, I beg Mr Nott, whatever money he finds me in possession of, to distribute to the poor. . . . I leave with Mr Nott all my papers which he knows of, and I beg him to burn those he sealed up.' The BishUP was to have a Bible and Prayer Book and his daughters 'all my playthings'. To Lady de Clifford, 'the rest of my jewels, except those that are most valuable and those I beg my father and mother, the Prince and Princess of Wales to take'. Charlotte hoped the King would make Mr Nott a bishop and begged that her two devoted maids, Mrs Gagarin and Mrs Louis, should be very handsomely paid and given a house. But, darkly, 'nothing to Mrs Udney, for reasons'.

The first casualty of the ensuing rumpus was Mrs Campbell, who found herself most unfairly accused of having put the idea of making a Will into Charlotte's head with a view to her own personal gain. The sub-governess was forced to resign her post on a plea of ill-health, and the sub-preceptor also became a target of in-house back-biting and spite, although Mr Nott seems originally to have incurred the Prince of Wales's displeasure by writing Charlotte a note reproving her for unpunctuality in terms which HRH considered insufficiently deferential. Mr Nott appeared to have altogether misunderstood his situation. He was paid to wait for the Princess, 'instead of being entitled to expect that she should wait for him'. Nor was he entitled to subscribe himself as her 'most faithful friend', thus attempting to put their relationship on a quite unacceptable footing of intimacy.

In April 1809, the tutor faced further accusations of having 'laboured by artful and improper means' to gain the young princess's confidence, to have used his influence to put her against her father and Lady de Clifford, to have allowed her to develop 'the idle habit of gossiping conversation' and encouraged her to speak disrespectfully of Mrs Udney. Mr Nott indignantly denied all the charges against him, and John Fisher, who believed Mrs Udney to be the principal trouble-maker, brought counter-charges, accusing the governess of letting Charlotte spend far too much time with the servants. Mrs Udney, moreover, had shown the child an indecent drawing and *explained its meaning* to her. But the ladies won the battle. Nott was suspended from duty and, despite Fisher's spirited defence, not reinstated.

Charlotte felt his loss very keenly. 'If we never meet again,' she wrote to him a few days before they were parted, 'keep for me your regard and affection. If I go into other people's hands, rely on me, I shall ever remember your kindness and your good advice . . . but I shall be more miserable than I can tell you if you leave me.' Charlotte had always been in the habit of openly referring to Mrs Campbell and Mr Nott as her adopted parents and undoubtedly cared far more for both of them than she did for her real father and mother.

Not that this was in any way surprising. Back in July

1804, when the plan to barter custody of the child in exchange for political and financial favours had first been under discussion, Lord Moira, was advising the Prince of Wales quite cold-bloodedly to let himself be seen 'testifying some ostensible kindnesses to Princess Charlotte' in order to show the public what a sacrifice he was making to please the King. But although he took very little notice of his daughter in the ordinary way – as she got bigger her uninhibited behaviour probably reminded him painfully of her mother – the Prince was not unmindful of the need to attach her to his interest in the all too likely event of future domestic rows, and told Lady de Clifford shortly after her appointment that he wanted Charlotte to be aware of his readiness to indulge 'every reasonable wish she may entertain'.

To Charlotte, of course, at this time Papa remained a remote and god-like being to be propitiated at intervals by prim little notes which bore every sign of having been drafted by other hands and laboriously copied at the schoolroom table. 'Forgive me, my dearest papa', in November 1806, 'for writing to you when you have so much business, but I saw you so unwell last night that I could not help writing to enquire how you are.' And on New Year's Day: 'Accept from me, my dearest papa, my congratulations of the season, and that you may live to see many happy returns of it is my sincerest wish.' In August 1807 the young Princess was staying at Worthing with Lady de Clifford and Mrs Udney in attendance, and wrote from there to wish dearest Papa many happy returns of his birthday on the 12th: 'may I become every year more worthy of so kind a father and be a comfort to him when I am grown up'. There had evidently been some sort of recent unpleasantness, perhaps connected with the matter of the will, for she went on to beg forgiveness for having shown lack of proper filial feeling. 'I was ungrateful to a father who, tho' he had a great deal of business, I am sure never had me out of his mind, but I was sufficiently punished, for you could not bear your daughter ungrateful and therefore you would not see her. I assure you, my dear papa, I will struggle to get the better of my lessons and of all my learning and to do everything I can to please you.' Happily Papa was in a benevolent mood and rewarded the penitent with an invitation to Brighton to see a review of his own regiment of hussars and have dinner at the Pavilion afterwards, but treats of this nature were very few and far between.

Charlotte's relations with her mother were rather more complicated. Although never given an opportunity of seeing her child unchaperoned by the governesses appointed by her estranged husband, and rigidly excluded by him from any say whatever in the manner of her upbringing, Caroline supported by the King's determination to uphold her maternal rights, had nevertheless been able to have the little girl with her at Blackheath pretty well as often as she liked – until, that is, the Douglas scandal broke. All intercourse was broken off during the progress of the Delicate Investigation, and when it was resumed, after Caroline's eventual vindication in the spring of 1807, the Prince stipulated, not altogether unreasonably in the circumstances, that Willikin should no longer be allowed to play with his daughter and that the continuity of Charlotte's education must not be unduly interrupted. Her visits to her mother therefore became effectively restricted to Saturday afternoons, when she would be taken either to Montague House or to Kensington Palace, where the Princess of Wales now had a set of apartments, the Prince remaining adamant in his refusal to allow her back into Carlton House. Warwick House, too, was out of bounds, and when Caroline had the gall to show her face there in April 1808 when Charlotte was getting over the measles, Lady de Clifford received a warning that on no account should this be regarded as the thin edge of the wedge.

It is hard to say with any degree of certainty what Caroline really felt about her daughter. She certainly appeared to resent the royal family's efforts to keep them apart and was always quick to register a public protest whenever her maternal rights came under attack, either from her husband or from her mother-in-law; but whether this proceeded from mother love or – more likely – from self-interest must be a matter of conjecture. According to Mrs Louis, 'a very respectable woman', who was Charlotte's dresser and personal maid throughout her life and loved her dearly, Caroline never showed the least affection for the child. On the other hand, the King declared in February 1805 that it was quite charming to see the Princess and her child together, and three years later the Princess herself told Miss Hayman: 'I must entertain you with the wit and amiableness of my daughter. She has been for two months at Bognor, and she wrote to me twice a week without the assistance of bishop, tutor or governess: and she wrote just as she felt and thought, from first impulses; and if she remains so natural in her thoughts and feelings she will be very delightful for the private as well as the public.'

Charlotte's own first recorded thoughts and feelings towards her mother were nothing if not natural and arose out of an episode in 1805 when she and Lady de Clifford were cut dead by the Princess of Wales while out driving. This was presumably unintentional, but nine-year-old Charlotte was comically furious at the apparent slight – her mother was a monster, seized by pride and the Devil! Plainly Mama inspired none of the deferential respect with which Papa was to be approached, but by the time she was nine years old Charlotte would have picked up enough information from servants' gossip and her own sharp-eyed observation to have realized that Mama's lifestyle was not such as to command any kind of respect.

It is to her credit that she would always remain loyal to a mother who, as time went by, was to show less and less concern for her young daughter's welfare, but she grew up with few illusions about either of her parents. 'My mother was bad', she is reputed to have told a friend years later, 'but she would not have become as bad as she was if my father had not been infinitely worse.'

FIVE

A Pretty Queen You'll Make!

. . . buckish about horses and full of exclamations very like swearing.
                                    Lady Glenbervie, October 1812

The Princess Charlotte was a person of great abilities, tolerably well cultivated . . . Her temper was somewhat violent and irascible, and her preceptors had failed in taming it.
                                    Lord Brougham, Autobiography

What will be her fate? It is impossible not to feel an interest in any human being, upon whom such a weight of responsibility is placed.
                                    Lady Charlotte Bury, Diary of a lady-in-waiting.

In January 1810 Charlotte was fourteen years old, and Lady Charlotte Bury, the Princess of Wales's new lady-in-waiting who met her at Kensington Palace towards the end of the year, pronounced her to be 'a fine piece of flesh and blood'. Her manners were still those of a hoyden schoolgirl, but she could 'put on dignity when she chooses, though it seems to sit uneasily upon her.' Certainly young Charlotte very rarely chose to 'put on dignity', and Charlotte Bury soon found there was something very captivating about her unselfconscious openness and candour. 'I pity her that she is born to be a queen. She would be a much happier being if she were a private individual,' commented her ladyship, who went on to describe an incident at one of those Kensington visits which seemed to illustrate her point. Dinner was over and the ladies settled in the drawing room when Princess Charlotte ran down to the other end of the room to fetch herself a chair – a simple little act of the kind which princesses of the blood were not expected to perform for themselves.

'I rose and said how shocked I was that Her Royal Highness had not commanded me to do her bidding,' wrote Charlotte Bury in her journal of Court life.

'Oh,' said the Princess of Wales, with one of her sudden disconcerting flashes of casual malice, 'I assure you she likes it; it is an amusement for her; she is kept so very strict, it is like feeling herself at liberty to fly about – is it not, Lady de Clifford?'

The Dowager, not surprisingly, took offence – 'I assure your Royal Highness the Princess Charlotte has liberty enough with me' – and the visit ended in a distinct atmosphere of huffiness.

Actually Lady de Clifford had every reason to be annoyed, for at this period of her life Charlotte was anything but downtrodden, and seems to have enjoyed a remarkable degree of liberty for one in her rarefied social position. There are some cheerful glimpses of her on holiday at Bognor, collecting seashells or trotting down to Richardson's the baker about the time she knew his buns would be ready, and sitting in the shop munching and chatting away to the worthy baker in the friendliest manner, 'as if she took an active interest in his concerns'. It was also at Bognor that, in a spirit of 'youthful mischief', she once drove her pony carriage at speed over a bumpy field, ignoring the protesting shrieks of her unfortunate governess, who expected to be overturned at any moment, and shouting, 'Nothing like exercise, my lady! Nothing like exercise!'

An affectionate and graphic portrait of the adolescent Charlotte can be found in the memoirs of Lady de Clifford's grandson. Young George Keppel (whose great-great-grandfather had come to England in the train of William the Dutchman in 1688 and been rewarded with the earldom of Albermarle) first made the Princess's acquaintance in 1808, when he was rising nine years old and a new boy at Westminster School, and she had just passed her twelfth birthday 'She had blue eyes', he remembered,

> and that peculiarly blonde hair which was characteristic rather of her German than of her English descent. Her features were regular, her face, which was oval, had not that fulness which later took off somewhat from her good looks. Her form was slender . . . her hands and feet were beautifully shaped. When excited she stuttered painfully. . . . She was an excellent actress whenever there was anything to call forth her imitative power. One of her fancies was to ape the manners of a man. On these occasions she would double her fists, and assume an attitude of defence that would have done credit to a professed pugilist.

When in this mood Charlotte would pummel her younger playmate unmercifully, but although 'excessively violent in her disposition', she was also 'easily appeased, very warm-hearted, and never so happy as when doing a kindness'. Indeed, to her friends she was 'generous to excess'. 'From Princess Charlotte I received my first watch,' wrote George Keppel; 'from her, too, my first pony, an ugly but thoroughly good little animal.' George also received sundry 'tips' and was not above applying for financial assistance. 'My dear Keppel,' Charlotte wrote to him on one of the occasions,

> You know me well enough to suppose that I never will refuse you a thing when there is no harm in it. But tho' I send you the money, still I must give you a little reprimand. . . . You will, if you go on asking for money and spending it in so quick a manner, get such a habit of it that when you grow up you will be a very extravagant man, and get into dept [sic], etc. etc. Your grandmamma de Clifford allows me £10 a month. But although I

spend it I take care never to go further than my sum will allow. Now dear, George, if you do the same you never will want for money; say you have a guinea, well then, never go beyond it, and in time you will save up. That is the way everybody does, and so never get into dept. [Charlotte never did learn to spell].

Having delivered her 'little reprimand', which had a special piquancy coming from her father's daughter, the Princess relaxed her high moral tone sufficiently to inform George that, if he called at Warwick House, the porter would have a guinea for him.

George was, in fact, already a frequent visitor to the porter's lodge, Warwick House being close enough to Westminster to make 'a skip out of bounds' a risk worth the taking, especially on summer evenings. There was, as he freely admitted, a strong element of cupboard love about this assiduous attendance. Like most schoolboys of the period, he was permanently hungry, and Charlotte used to make him sandwiches to supplement the starvation rations at Mother Grant's boarding-house. On one occasion, however, he took it into his head that so much good fare ought to be shared and decided to extend the hospitality of Warwick House to include his chief crony, one Bob Tyrwhit – a vicariously generous impulse which nearly ended in a nasty accident. 'As I was a privileged person at Warwick House', George remembered, 'I passed with my companion unquestioned by the porter's lodge, and through a small door which opened from the court-yard into the garden. The Princess greeted us with a hearty welcome. In the garden was a swing, into which Charlotte stepped, and I set it in motion. Unfortunately, it came in contact with Bob Tyrwhit's mouth and knocked him over.' It must have been exceedingly painful, and the victim 'set up a hideous howl', as his friend unsympathetically described it, causing an agitated throng of sub-governesses, pages, dressers, and footmen to come surging out of the house. But before these personages could reach the scene, the Princess had descended from her swing, assumed an air of offended dignity and was discovered lecturing Master Keppel on the extreme impropriety of his conduct in bringing a strange boy into her garden without her privity or consent. 'The marvel is how she or I kept our countenance,' he wrote.

There was never any standing on ceremony with Charlotte. Indeed, the extreme informality of her approach sometimes made it difficult for her contemporaries to remember, 'to preserve the decorum due to her station'. Her new tutor, the Reverend William Short, lived in Dean's Yard, next door to the headmaster of Westminster, and one day young George Keppel, scurrying through the archway connecting Little with Great Dean's Yard on an errand for his fagmaster, suddenly caught sight of the Princess's carriage bowling into the school precincts. Uncomfortably aware of his scruffy appearance, he tried to sneak past unobserved – but too late. Peremptorily hailed by 'a loud and well-known voice', he found himself swept up in the royal visit just as he was, 'in the ordinary garb and dirt of a Westminster fag'.

Charlotte was being entertained to lunch by Dr Short, a rotund and jovial individual who looked as if 'he were not indifferent to the good things of this world'. The Princess insinuated as much over the luncheon table, and master and pupil engaged in some light-hearted banter on the subject – she preaching rigid abstinence, he solemnly protesting that he took no more than nature craved. After lunch the party adjourned to the College Garden, the first and only time that George or, so he believed, any other Westminster boy had ever been privileged to tread 'that sacred sod'. Years later George could still recall his sense of the awesomeness of the occasion, but Charlotte would have been quite unimpressed. Another time when she had driven down with Lady de Clifford to fetch George from school, a fist-fight between two notable combatants happened to be in progress in the Great Cloisters. While the Dowager wandered about examining the various 'quaint monumental inscriptions' on the ancient walls, her grandson vividly remembered her royal charge gripping the cloister railings and eagerly following the fortunes of the two pugilists slogging it out on 'the fighting-green'.

When she was in town Charlotte's Sundays were spent either at Lady de Clifford's suburban villa at Paddington or as the guest of George Keppel's parents, who had a house at Earl's Court in the village of Brompton, another pleasantly rural suburb of orchards and gardens on the western fringes of the capital. Once outside the gloomy confines of Warwick House, the princess was like 'a bird escaped from a cage'. She would tear up and down the stairs of any house she was taken into, 'one moment in the garret and almost in the same moment in the kitchen'. George Keppel recalled various merry pranks perpetrated by Charlotte in holiday mood, including a mutton chop sent into Lady de Clifford's dining parlour 'so ill-dressed and so well-peppered as to be uneatable'; the Dowager's bell rang indignantly, and further enquiry revealed that 'the good old lady's royal charge had acted as cook and her favourite grandson as scullery maid' – an incident which prompted the scullery maid to say to the cook: 'A pretty Queen you'll make!'

The princess usually came to Earls Court in Lady de Clifford's carriage, but on one Sunday afternoon she arrived in her own, and the distinctive royal scarlet liveries quickly attracted a crowd of sightseers anxious for a glimpse of the presumptive heiress to the throne. When she heard 'how desirous the people were to have a sight of her', Charlotte's immediate reaction was to exclaim: 'They shall soon have that pleasure!' And slipping out of the garden gate into the road, she ran among the crowd from the rear, appearing more eager than anyone to have a peep at the princess. She was in especially boisterous spirits that day and urged George to mount one of his father's hacks, which she had saddled and bridled herself. But before he was properly on board she gave the animal a 'tremendous cut' on the hindquarters with the groom's heavy whip, sending it off at full gallop with George hanging on to its mane for dear life 'roaring lustily'. Their destructive progress continued through Lord Albermarle's pleasure-gardens until the horse, irritated past endurance, finally threw up its heels and deposited its unhappy burden on the lawn in full view of the drawing-room windows just as Charlotte, red-faced and panting, emerged from the bushes too late to make her planned interception. The commotion had brought the whole family out, and the Princess got 'a tremendous scolding' from her much mortified governess, which she took coolly enough; but was not prepared for Lord Albermarle's disapproval – the more quelling for being expressed by looks rather than words – and as soon as they were alone again she vented her chagrin on poor George. 'The heavy riding-whip was once more put into requisition,' he remembered, 'and she treated my father's son exactly as she had just treated my father's horse.' In spite of this, the friendship survived, Charlotte more than once attempting to shield her partner in crime from the consequences of truancy or neglected homework, but, since her Latin was even worse than his, her well-meant efforts in this respect were apt to do more harm than good.

George's three little sisters had also from time to time to suffer the dubious advantages of Charlotte's patronage. Her taste for rough games apparently used to lead her to entice them to climb to the top of a mound in the orchard at Earls Court in order to roll them down into a bed of nettles below. To do her justice, if the girls 'refrained from crying and from complaining to their governess' they would be rewarded for their reticence by a doll. 'Indeed the Princess, never so happy as when making presents, kept their nursery well supplied with dolls.'

The Keppel children seem to have been her only regular playmates, but Charlotte was growing up fast and physically at least she developed early. When she was fifteen Charlotte Bury remarked that she had the figure of a women of five and twenty, 'her bosom full, but finely shaped; her shoulders large, and her whole person voluptuous'. But Lady Charlotte could see that unless she was very careful HRH would soon have a weight problem. Her skin was white but curiously opaque – 'there is little or no shade in her face'. Her features were good, though, and her hands and arms 'finely moulded'. She still had her slight stammer – 'an additional proof, if any were wanting, of her being her father's own child', commented Charlotte Bury slyly, but it seemed that in every detail she was 'his very image'. In the circumstances perhaps that was just as well.

Charlotte appeared to want to be admired as 'a lovely woman', but beneath that formidably well-developed bust there still lurked the Madcap of the Upper Fifth, the untamed Terror of St Trinian's 'in awe of no one', who slouched or swaggered about 'twanging hands' with all the men, 'forward and dogmatical on all subjects, buckish about horses, and full of expressions very like swearing'. At fifteen Charlotte was horse mad, an accomplished and fearless rider galloping and leaping over every ditch like a schoolboy. 'Very quick and very lively, and very ill-brought up' was the verdict of one censorious lady, and Charlotte Bury wrote: 'I fear that she is capricious, self-willed and obstinate. I think she is kind-hearted, clever and enthusiastic. Her faults have evidently never been checked nor her virtues fostered.' It had long since been remarked that the Princess Charlotte was 'her own governess', and certainly Lady de Clifford had precious little control or influence over her.

'My dear Princess Charlotte, you show your drawers,' exclaimed the Dowager at Kensington one day as Charlotte sat with her legs stretched out in front of her – a favourite but ungainly attitude.

'I never do, but where I can put myself at my ease.' was the reply.

'Yes, my dear, when you get in or out of a carriage.'

'I don't care if I do.'

'Your drawers are too long.' Long drawers or pantalettes

were a rather daring new fashion, meant to be seen only in occasional titillating glimpses.

But Charlotte was unrepentant. 'I don't think so – the Duchess of Bedford's are much longer, and they are bordered with Brussels lace.'

Lady de Clifford had learned over the years when to admit defeat, and Her Grace of Bedford's drawers offered an easy way out of this latest in a long line of losing arguments. 'Oh, if she is to wear them she does right to make them handsome.'

Charlotte might be argumentative, 'dogmatical', and brash. She might lack grace and elegance and social poise, but in spite of these obvious shortcomings, in spite of her casual manners, her rattling tongue, and over-loud laugh, she still had 'a peculiar air' about her, that mysterious but unmistakable glamour which is conferred by the possession of royal blood and royal self-confidence, and which, as Charlotte Bury reflected in her Journal, in defiance of the higher powers of reason and justice, cast a dazzling lustre through which it was difficult to see individuals as they really were. 'Never was a truer word spoken by man,' concluded her ladyship, 'than that Princes are a race apart.'

Charlotte's membership of the princely race was highlighted with dramatic poignancy just a month after her fifteenth birthday when the lengthening shadows of illness and dementia finally closed around her grandfather. The old King was seventy-two now, blind, and shattered by the death of his youngest and favourite daughter, Amelia. 'He is quite lost', wrote Charlotte sadly, 'and takes no notice of anything that goes on in his room and knows *no one.*' In January 1811 the government decided to bring in a Regency Bill. The King was handed over to the doubtful mercies of the 'mad-doctors', and on 6 February 1811, at a meeting of the Privy Council convened at Carlton House, the Prince of Wales was formally sworn in as Regent. Princess Charlotte of Wales had not been invited to witness any part of this historic ceremony, though she could be seen riding up and down in the gardens trying to catch a glimpse of the proceedings through the ground-floor windows.

Later in the year Carlton House was to be the setting for a grand fête, ostensibly held in honour of the exiled remnants of the French royal family, but in reality to celebrate the inauguration of the new regime with an entertainment as brilliant and as sumptuous as its host could contrive. Charlotte wanted very much to be present and wrote wistfully to her old friend Miss Hayman: 'The Prince Regent gives a magnificent ball on the 5th of June. I have not been invited, nor do I know if I shall be or not. If I should not it will make a great noise in the world, as the friends I have seen have repeated over and over again it is my duty to go there; it is proper that I should. Really I do think it will be hard if I am not asked.' She was not. Her father, only too well aware that she would be an object of intense curiosity, did not intend to risk being upstaged at an occasion specially devised to give him the starring role; and, so far from being asked to the party, Charlotte was packed off down to her grandmother and aunts at Windsor – 'Heavens how dull!' – to be out of the way of all these 'violent doings' as her mother put it.

The Carlton House ball was, of course, the social event of the season. But, as the Regent, sporting the long-coveted (and individually inspired) uniform of a field marshal, moved regally among his guests, those present did not fail to remark on the absence of both his wives. Maria Fitzherbert, insultingly refused a place at the Prince's table, had chosen to stay away, and the beginning of the Regency marked the final ending of a more than twenty-year-long special relationship. The Princess of Wales – who liked to annoy her in-laws by saying that her only real sin had been to commit adultery with Mrs Fitzherbert's husband – had not expected an invitation and spent the evening of the ball in her rooms at Kensington Palace with only Horace Walpole's friends the Misses Berry to keep her company.

In the years which had passed since the Delicate Investigation, Caroline's social prestige had been steadily eroded, largely, it must be admitted, as a result of her own behaviour – 'How true it is that vulgar familiarity breeds contempt!' – and it was no longer smart to be seen at Blackheath or Kensington. Bored, lonely, and resentful, the Princess would drive her ladies to the point of mutiny with interminable recitals of her many grievances – 'all day and all night long, complaints poured forth from which there is no remedy or relief' – and embarrassed them horribly with diatribes against the royal family. 'All the day long her Royal Highness continues to talk of wishing people dead.' sighed Charlotte Bury, who had joined the household in 1810. 'I have been an accomplice in murder many a time if silence gives consent.'

Her Royal Highness would also often do 'the most extraordinary things, apparently for no other purpose than to make her attendants stare'. Strolling in Kensington Gardens and dressed quite unsuitably for the public highway, she would suddenly take it into her head to bolt out of one of the smaller gates and go rambling round Bayswater and along the Paddington Canal at the risk of being insulted, or, if recognized, mobbed, all the while mischievously enjoying the terror of the unfortunate lady-in-waiting fated to accompany her. On one occasion she got into conversation with an elderly couple on a bench in Kensington Gardens. They had no idea who she was, and Caroline began to ask them 'all manner of questions about herself, to which they replied favourably', expressing a flattering desire to see the Princess of Wales. This particular Haroun al-Raschid escapade passed off happily, but Charlotte Bury confessed she dreaded its possible repetition, for it was said that listeners seldom heard good of themselves.

Antics of this sort, although certainly ill-judged and calculated to give her attendants nervous spasms, were harmless enough, but 'about this time her Royal Highness the Princess of Wales was introduced, by a very injudicious friend of hers, to a set of low persons, totally unfitting her private society'. These were a family of Italian musicians named Sapio 'whom her Royal Highness encouraged to treat her very disrespectfully' and whom a deeply disapproving Charlotte Bury christened the Squallinis. The Squallinis – father, mother, and son – became constant visitors, very much at home in the Princess's drawing room. Caroline sang, or squalled, endless duets in her loud and distressingly untuneful voice, showered her new friends with expensive presents, paid their bills, and even rented a cottage in Bayswater where they could foregather free from the restraints of etiquette and the remonstrations of her household. Lady Charlotte Bury believed the pleasure she took in the Sapios' company originated in 'her love of ease and indolence, which is indulged by living with persons of inferior rank; but', she went on, 'in after times I much fear there were other reasons for submitting to such an unworthy set of persons'. The sight of Sapio junior's horse waiting in the stables at Kensington at all hours made it pretty plain what those reasons were.

Faced with the prospect of having to hob-nob with the Squallinis and Willikin, it is perhaps not very surprising that more and more people should have chosen to send their excuse when invited to Kensington or the 'tinsel and trumpery' of Blackheath. All the same, Charlotte Bury noted that the wives of the nobility had continued to call on the Princess of Wales 'till the King was declared too ill to reign, and the Prince became in fact Regent'. From that moment, it seems, these high-born ladies vanished from Kensington and were never seen there more. 'It was', according to Lady Charlotte, 'the besom of expediency which swept them all away.' Society, in short, did not mean to risk getting off on the wrong foot with its new supremo by being found keeping the wrong company; for although the doctors had at first expressed some hope that the old King might recover (as indeed he had done once before), this time it was soon obvious that he would not again emerge from the world of shadows he now inhabited, and in February 1812 the restrictions on the powers of the Regent for a precautionary twelvemonth period were removed. The Prince of Wales was thus confirmed as both Head of State and head of the royal family, which boded little good to his estranged wife, and rumours were soon circulating that he was planning to turn her out of Kensington Palace, to send her out of England, to divorce her, marry again, and perhaps beget a son, who would replace her daughter as heir to the throne.

Although Charlotte, advised by her strong-minded new friend, Margaret Mercer Elphinstone, was doing her best to stay out of her parents' quarrels, her relationship with her father was becoming increasingly stressful. This was a pity, for normally the Prince of Wales got on well with young people. He took an affectionate, interest in Mrs Fitzherbert's foster-child little Mary Seymour, and his own younger sisters, Amelia especially, doted on him. But then 'Minny' Seymour and the princesses were sweetly pretty, perfectly mannered young ladies, studied in the arts of pleasing. Charlotte, big, boisterous, and uncouth, often grated horribly on her papa's exquisite sensibilities and reminded him of her mother, for whom his loathing continued unabated. Charlotte, for her part, was nervous and ill-at-ease in his presence, and the fact that while he remained intensely unpopular her public appearances were greeted with enthusiastic cries of 'God bless you!' and 'Never forsake your mother!' did nothing to improve the situation.

However, despite the stories of rabid jealousy industriously spread by his political enemies, it does not seem that the Regent actually disliked his daughter. He could be 'very kind and attentive' to her, even sometimes 'VERY KIND INDEED'. But there were other times when his mood was not so sunny, and, for no obvious reason, he would either cut her dead or, if he did condescend to notice her, his manner would be so chilly that 'it was very distressing'. This blowing hot and cold naturally made poor Charlotte even more nervous and edgy – her stammer, which irritated her father, becoming more than usually pronounced – while his determination to keep her in the schoolroom, clashing with her longing for escape into the world of balls, parties, and young men, led inevitably to conflict. Already she was straining at the leash. 'Have you had many pleasant parties?' she asked Mercer Elphinstone in one of her letters from Windsor in June 1811. 'I assure you a little London news to such a country lady as I am is quite a charity.' For the time being she had to resign herself. That summer, flanked by governesses, she went as usual to Bognor, her 'quizzical figure' (Charlotte Bury had been quite right, she was already putting on weight) puffing over packing her trunk in a spell of hot weather, and in October she was ordered back to Windsor, lamenting that 'it will be dreadfully dul to be shut up for 5 hours in the evening in the royal menagerie'.

Charlotte frankly hated the gloomy, claustrophobic atmosphere of the Castle, where no one could forget the unseen and unmentionable presence of the poor old mad King, and the four remaining spinster princesses, sitting silently over their needlework, lived on in resentful subjugation to their mother's tyranny. Advancing age, ill health, and adversity had not mellowed the Queen's temper. But although she regarded her grandmother without affection, Charlotte was not afraid of her and could even sometimes make the grim old lady laugh, standing over her chair, talking and joking away as naturally as she did with her aunts. Not that she cared much for her aunts either. With the possible exception of the youngest, Sophia, she suspected 'the old girls' of spying and carrying tales to her father. As for the uncles, and surely 'no family was ever composed of *such odd people*', she thought little of Clarence, with his quarter-deck manners and pointed head, or Cambridge, who in any case, spent most of his time in Hanover. In common with nearly everyone both inside and outside the royal family, the princess feared and detested Cumberland, 'Prince Wiskerandos', whose sinister scarred countenance, unsavoury reputation, and rabidly reactionary Toryism made him, not entirely fairly, the bogeyman of popular imagination. Kent and Sussex were more sympathetic, both in their politics and in their attitude towards their niece. Sussex in particular was to be her champion, while Kent, for all his pomposity and obsessive preoccupation with the trivia of daily life, was always uniformly kind and good natured as far as she was concerned. But it was left to the Duke and Duchess of York to show her real constructive kindness. The Duchess's passion for whist, her insomnia, and her preference for the society of an unmanageable number of pet dogs, monkeys, and parrots earned her a reputation for eccentricity; but Charlotte, who was also an animal-lover, always enjoyed her visits to the Yorks at Oatlands, and 'the little Duchess', as she was known in the family, seems to have been the only person to make any effort to provide the princess with entertainment and congenial company of her own age.

In November 1811 there was a particularly gay and successful house-party at Oatlands. Anne and Georgina Fitzroy, the Duke of Wellington's nieces and 'remarkable, pleasing, amiable girls' who sang charmingly, were among the guests with their mother, Lady Anne Smith, née Wellesley, and their stepfather. Also present were Lord Erskine, Richard Sheridan the dramatist and Whig politician, who disgusted the Princess by getting 'beastly drunk', and another Whig MP, William Adam, Chancellor of the Duchy of Cornwall and a great favourite – 'Mr Adam and I *flirted* amazingly and we had a great many jokes and good stories.' The royal family was represented by the Prince Regent and the Dukes of Cambridge and Cumberland, but not even her father's distant manner towards her (which was noticed with surprise, she thought, by the other gentlemen) or the unwelcome presence of ogreish Uncle Ernest could spoil Charlotte's pleasure. She drove about with her hostess, to nearby Hampton Court, which she was glad to have seen in spite of its frightful air of gloom and coldness, and to Claremont, that house of ill omen, where they inspected the gardens laid out for Lord Clive by Capability Brown. At Oatlands there was music every evening and on two nights a dance which the Princess enjoyed most of all things, enthusiastically practising the waltz, that daring new import from Germany which she hoped would continue in fashion through the winter. She had been 'amazingly happy', and, when the time came for going home, the parting was softened by her father saying she might return whenever the Yorks would have her and the Duchess promising that it should be soon. In fact, she returned for a brief visit early in December to see the Regent, who was laid up with an injured foot. The little Duchess was, as always, 'as kind as possible', and everyone else seemed flatteringly pleased to see her again. Even her father was 'more easy in his manner than I have seen yet', although he could not be persuaded to give permission for Charlotte to go to the theatre.

Back at Warwick House life seemed horribly flat. The weather turned very cold, and the Princess, who felt the cold acutely, was like a '*shriveled lemon*'. She was bored and depressed as well as cold. 'I have not been out for these four days', she told Mercer Elphinstone on 20 December. She was worried about her weight and knew she ought to take more exercise, but riding was impossible with snow on the ground, and she really could not bring herself to go walking for walking's sake, especially as 'there is no lady in town that I like well enough as an agreeable companion to walk with. Alas!' she went on, 'I have no one to waltz with or to play at billiards, or any of the gymnastic games which I should much delight in. I feel the cold most amazingly and begin to think that a warm pelisse would not be a disagreeable thing.'

But, as she surveyed the political scene, Charlotte had other, weightier matters on her mind that winter. She herself was an enthusiastic Whig, just as her father had been in his salad days, but now that he was at last in a position of power, it had begun to look ominously as if he meant to renege on his former friends, 'party, promises, professions and everything'. This would be a betrayal of all those progressive, radical causes such as Catholic Emancipation, electoral reform, or the ending of the war in Spain with which the Prince of Wales had previously been associated and it shocked and saddened his daughter. 'What will become of us all?' she wrote. 'I begin quite to despair! When this is known in the world . . . how very unpopular it will make the P[rince]. . . . All these things must make *all good wigs* [sic] *tremble – but not give up, as the motto must undoubtedly be perseverance.*' Charlotte was inclined to blame her grandmother's influence for the Regent's threatened apostasy – 'the Queen has got quite *master* of the Prince . . . and *whatever* he *dislikes most* she makes him *agree to*'. So when Her Majesty made one of her rare excursions from Windsor to preside at a family dinner at Carlton House celebrating Charlotte's sixteenth birthday, the Princess noted the 'good understanding' currently existing between her father and his mother with misgiving. It was not, in her opinion, 'a good sign with regard to his measures in Government and politics'.

All was sweetness and light at the Carlton House dinner – everyone present from the Queen and Regent downwards quite going out of their way to be civil. There was much joking and good humour over the meal, served by the footmen in their State liveries, and afterwards the Prince rose to drink to his mother's health and that of his brothers and sisters, declaring he was never so happy as when in the bosom of his family. His daughter, remembering the sibling jealousies, the grievances, the petty feuds and squabbles which normally rent the family bosom, was not surprisingly '*thunderstruck*' by this sudden and unnerving display of fraternal solidarity, which she couldn't help but suspect, must have some underlying and probably sinister purpose.

Although everyone had exerted themselves to be gracious and 'very *very* kind' Charlotte's enjoyment of her birthday party was somewhat marred by the fact that she had to go straight on to visit her mother. 'I was upon thorns, being obliged to eat, tho' I was to dine at Blackheath afterwards.' At Blackheath more relations were assembled – her cousin Princess Sophia of Gloucester, the Duke of Brunswick, his two young children, and the old Duchess. Back in October 1806 disaster had struck the family in Brunswick. The old Duke, fighting with the Prussians against Napoleon, had been defeated and mortally wounded at Auerstadt; his duchy, like many another small German state, was overwhelmed by the apparently irresistible advance of French imperialism, and his widow and the new Duke his son were driven to seek sanctuary in England.

The Princess of Wales had shown no particular pleasure over the reunion with her mother and brother; in fact, Charlotte Bury commented on 'a hardness of manner in the Princess towards her mother . . . which sometimes revolts me'. After spending several months at Kensington and Montague House, reluctantly lent by Caroline, the old Duchess moved into lodgings in Hanover Square, where she lived lonely and neglected, 'a melancholy spectacle of decayed royalty'. Princess Charlotte saw her maternal grandmother on her regular weekly visits to her mother – following the report of the Delicate Investigators it had been decreed from on high that the old lady should always be present on these occasions – but there is no evidence of the growth of any bond of affection between them. Charlotte was, however, enthralled by Duke Frederick, a glamorous figure with his deep-sunk eyes, bushy brows, bristling moustaches (an unusual sight in clean-shaven England), and general air of romantic gloom. 'The uncle and niece, in their demeanour, were the very opposites,' remembered George Keppel:

> His, sedate and silent; hers, impulsive and voluble. He seemed well satisfied to be a listener, and much interested in the Princess's lively and careless prattle. On her part, she almost worshipped him. Once after a visit from the Duke, she improvised a mustache, swaggered up and

down the room, then making a sudden stop, with arms akimbo, she uttered some German expletives which would probably have hardly borne a translation, and thus sought to give you her conception of a 'Black Brunswicker'.

Charlotte had been eleven years old when she first encountered her fascinating uncle. At fifteen she was beginning to take an altogether more advanced interest in the opposite sex, dreaming optimistically of 'baux' to waltz with. In the autumn of 1811 she made the acquaintance of her cousin George, eldest of the numerous brood of natural children fathered by the Duke of Clarence on his long-suffering partner, the actress Dorothea Jordan. Despite the disapproval of their aunts, Charlotte and George Fitz-Clarence, a captain in the Prince of Wales's Regiment, enjoyed some delightful rides in the Great Park at Windsor, and when George's leave came to an end, another young officer, Lieutenant Charles Hesse of the Eighteenth Light Dragoons and reputed to be a by-blow of the Duke of York, took his place. The lieutenant was rather too short to be regarded as truly handsome, but his lack of inches did not show on a horse. He had charm and social address and made an agreeable companion riding by the side of Charlotte's open carriage. Hesse was only too willing to engage in a little dalliance, and it all seems to have been innocent enough – a matter of pretty compliments, sighs, and languishing glances, the touch of a hand, the exchange of trinkets and billets-doux – but it was nevertheless unwise for anyone in Charlotte's constitutional position, as well as being potentially dangerous, especially considering her parentage and her warmly emotional temperament.

Either from indolence or misplaced indulgence, Lady de Clifford very foolishly allowed the affair to flourish for some six weeks. When she did at last try to put a stop to it, Charlotte defied her, flatly refusing to part with her 'little Lieutenant'. Then the Princess of Wales decided to take a hand and with irresponsibility bordering on the criminal deliberately set out to assist her daughter on a course which could very well have ruined her for life, encouraging the young couple to meet unchaperoned at Kensington and even, apparently, on one occasion ushering them into her own bedroom and turning the key on them. Fortunately for all concerned these typically unsubtle tactics seem to have acted as an effective antidote to passion, and Charles Hesse may well have been rather relieved when he had to rejoin his regiment down at Portsmouth, although he and Charlotte continued to correspond – something which the Princess was later to regret.

Eighteen twelve was turning into a wretched year for Charlotte. Her relations with her father worsened when he did finally turn his back on the Whigs that spring; indeed, she showed her disapproval so openly that he retaliated by forbidding any further intercourse with her bosom friend and confidante Mercer Elphinstone, who was, he believed, an undesirable – and Whig – influence. Charlotte had first got to know Margaret Mercer Elphinstone (known as Mercer to her intimates) some time in 1809. Eight years older than the princess, Mercer – daughter of Admiral Lord Keith and heiress through her mother to a handsome fortune and a couple of Scottish baronies – was a beautiful girl, intelligent, forceful, common sensible, and a loyal and supportive friend. Charlotte was devoted to her and bitterly resented their enforced separation – 'an unjust and cruel requisition'. Unsurprisingly in the circumstances she was not impressed by a homily from the Queen urging the necessity of regarding her father as 'the only source of her happiness' and the person who 'not only by right but by experience' must know best what was good for her. Old Charlotte went on to warn young Charlotte of the danger of forming particular friendships – especially political friendships – adding that any member of the family who took sides against the Crown would be lowering it 'most essentially'.

Charlotte had been dispatched to hated Windsor – the *grand convent* – early in June that year and left to languish there, so that when an opportunity of reopening her correspondence with Mercer presented itself, she seized it without compunction. 'I detest everything that bears the name *clandestine'* she wrote on 24 August, 'but I call this not so. I hold myself *absolved* from the promise that was *extorted* from me, not to hold any communication *whatever* with you·. . . it is too great a sacrifice to be demanded.' The princess was thoroughly miserable isolated at Lower Lodge, a house she had always detested. 'My residence is deplorable and irksome, deprived *now* of *all possibility* of seeing *any of my friends, surrounded by spies* that detail everything; and by people that can neither be *trusted* or *liked* – a *perfect prison.*'

Poor Charlotte was so bored that she was obliged to occupy her thoughts with 'studdy', once disliked but now her greatest resource for passing away hours of ennui. Even so no one could accuse her of bookishness or, despite her own artless conviction that she had changed and 'grown very serious and thoughtful at times', of showing any signs of taking on the slightest tinge of the dreaded 'blueness' which denoted the learned woman. On the contrary, Charlotte had remained resolutely resistant to education as purveyed by Bishop Fisher and his cohorts, not one of whom appears to have had the least notion of how to interest her naturally lively and enquiring mind in matters academic. In fairness, though, it does have to be remembered that this was a time of widespread intellectual stagnation, with the educational establishment still sunk in its eighteenth-century torpor and the era of New Woman, of Miss Buss and Miss Beale, Girton College *et al.* as yet undreamt of. In 1812 higher education for girls was largely a matter of acquiring elegant accomplishments in spite of the fluently expressed disapproval of evangelical moralists like Hannah More, who would have preferred to see greater stress being laid on character building and the cultivation of virtue and piety. 'The bishop', wrote Charlotte from Windsor, 'is here, and reads with me for an hour or two every day from Mrs Hannah More's *Hints for Forming the Education of a Princess*: this is I believe what makes me find the hours so long.'

The austere Miss More regarded music as coming under the heading of time-wasting and trivial accomplishments, but fortunately for the princess, who had a genuine love and feeling for 'musick', her preceptors did not agree. She had lessons on the piano and harp and even learned to play the guitar. She also read widely, though not always the sort of literature which would have been approved of by Miss More. A Gothic novel with the promising title of *The Sicilian Mysteries* was pronounced 'most interesting. . . . It is in 5 vol. *full of mistery* and remarkably well worked up.' Charlotte shared her father's admiration for Jane Austen, enjoying *Sense and Sencibility* (sic), which was also 'interesting, and you feel quite one of the company'. She could see points of similarity between herself and Miss Austen's heroine: 'I think Maryanne and me are very like in *disposition*, that certainly I am not so good, the same imprudence, etc., however remain very like.' The Princess in company with all other young ladies of a romantic turn of mind, swooned over the mad, bad, and dangerous Lord Byron and devoured his poetry. 'I have got Lord Byron's Bride of Abydos', she wrote the following year, 'and have already read it *through twice*. I am *quite captivated* by it and think it quite equal to his *Giaour*.'

Apart from 'studdy', music and drawing lessons, and novel reading, Charlotte filled in the dragging hours at Windsor with daily rides, but these were not agreeable because they always had to be taken in company with her aunts. On the whole, though, she saw little of the family at the Castle. I '*never dine there* except upon birthdays, or *if* the Prince *comes down*, which is but seldom . . . The Queen nor none of them come down here.' In spite of this, she felt '*persecuted sometimes* (I cannot say often) by their officious civilities, by their *uncertain temper*, directions and advice (none of wh. I attend to)'.

As well as the general wretchedness and depression always brought on by Windsor and 'this infernal dwelling', Charlotte was unwell, sleeping badly and suffering from colds and bad headaches. Lower Lodge was undoubtedly damp, and the drains were probably bad. She was also oppressed by the knowledge that another major row was brewing between her parents. Mercer would, of course, have seen newspaper reports of 'the unpleasant circumstances relating to the Princess coming here'.

One of the consequences, and pretty certainly one of the reasons for her prolonged banishment to Lower Lodge, had been the cutting down of her regular visits to her mother from once a week to once a fortnight. When, on one convincing pretext or another, these too began to be cancelled, Caroline embarked on a campaign to draw public attention to this latest attempt to deprive her of her maternal rights. 'My daughter is now at Windsor', she wrote to Miss Hayman that August; 'she came to pay a visit to my mother on her birthday, for which reason I do not expect her this week, but next week and week following, if she does not come I shall certainly go to Windsor, and have the honour to be turned out by Her Gracious Majesty.' This apparently referred to the Queen's reported remark that if the Princess of Wales had the impertinence to show her face at Windsor, Lady de Clifford ought to have the power to turn her out. The Prince of Wales had already made it clear that his wife would not be permitted to see their daughter at Windsor as Charlotte was 'residing in a house appropriated for the use of the Prince Regent' and he was presumably afraid that they might run into one another. Caroline, however, was not to be put off. She still had a house of her own, bestowed on her by George III, within the precincts of the Castle and she now demanded that Lady de Clifford bring Charlotte to visit her there. This was refused. Her next move, a request for an audience with the Queen, was also turned down, but her daughter did not believe this would be the end of the matter: 'All I can say is that *feeling* her *claim* is *just*, she will *pursue* it till the *gains* her *point.*' Caroline did indeed return to the attack in September, only to be confronted by the Prime

Minister, Lord Liverpool, who again refused her demands to be allowed to see her child. 'Though I begged hard,' she wrote mournfully, 'the Regent and the stony-hearted old Queen would not let me see her.' The stony-hearted old Queen was, of course, reporting everything back to the Regent, who, for his part, solemnly thanked his mother for the prudent manner in which she had baffled the impudent attempt of 'this most mischievous and intriguing infernale' to create discord and confusion in the family by pretending to a maternal fondness she was incapable of feeling.

The battle rumbled on through the autumn. Caroline continued to bombard the unresponsive Queen with letters alternately insisting that Charlotte should come to London or threatening that she would again go down to Windsor. When Lady de Clifford developed an inflammation of the eyes which prevented her from escorting her charge to Kensington, Caroline demanded that someone else be appointed to act as chaperone. Miss Cornelia Knight, Lady Companion to Queen Charlotte, was chosen and given strict instructions not to let the princess out of her sight for an instant. A week later came another letter from Caroline again demanding to see her daughter, 'or else she would come down', and asking the Queen again to name a substitute for Lady de Clifford, who was still on sick-leave.

Caroline sent a copy of this letter to Charlotte, which gave rise to more commotion. The Regent appeared at Windsor in a furious temper, Lord Liverpool was summoned, and there was much conferring behind closed doors between the Prince, the Prime Minister, the Queen, and the Princess Mary, who was presently dispatched to order Charlotte to surrender the letter. 'My answer was that I had *burnt* it and had it not. Something of a threat was thrown out. Finding they could not succeed [they] gave it up quietly . . . Lord Liverpool saying that upon consideration it was not of importance enough to take up. Here it ended. Could I do otherwise, do you think', Charlotte asked her friend Mercer plaintively, '*being all alone*, and the first time I ever had anything of the kind to do with?'

The next time she saw her mother she 'told the Pss. every word that had passed, *as she asked me*'. Caroline was putting everything down on paper and was building up quite a dossier. She told Charlotte 'to be easy, that she did nothing without good advice, and that she might fight this battle thro' as she could'.

Charlotte might perhaps have guessed that battle as conducted by her mama was not likely to conform to any of the recognized rules of war but when, a week later, a full and accurate account of their conversation appeared in the press she was taken entirely by surprise. 'It came like a thunder clap,' she told Mercer. She realized, however, the importance of getting her story in first and managed to send a letter containing her version of events to the Regent a few hours before anyone else in the family. As it turned out, the consequences of Caroline's betrayal were not too dire, though Charlotte reported that her father had reverted to his old habit of ignoring her in public. 'The Prince did not say 5 words to me or take any notice whatever.'

By this time, the end of October, she was at least back at Warwick House for three days a week with the promise of some social life during the winter and at the beginning of December attended her first public function – the State Opening of Parliament – where, however, it was noticed that she often turned her back on Papa, who, for his part, was said to be 'much displeased at her manner'. Charlotte had been deeply offended by the fact that, on Papa's orders, her aunts were given precedence over her in the procession into the House of Lords; but she noted with some satisfaction that, while Papa's appearance had been greeted with perfect silence by the crowds lining the streets, they had been 'very civil and good-humoured' towards her, cheering and shouting her name as she passed.

In the circumstances it was hardly surprising that the day

should have ended badly, with the Prince in a thoroughly bad temper after dinner at Carlton House abusing Caroline to their daughter 'in the grossest terms possible' and accusing her of having put Charlotte against him. When Charlotte, who had remained silent until this point, 'respectfully disavowed it', he told her brutally that it was time she saw all the evidence about her mother's murky past and made up her own mind, adding, 'a great many shocking insinuations, to all which, of course, he thought I was ignorant'. Charlotte was, in fact, already pretty well informed on the subject and cherished few, if any, illusions regarding her mother's character, past or present. She also knew that Caroline's current activities were motivated less by genuine maternal concern than by a malicious, if understandable, urge to 'teaze and worry' the royal family.

Caroline's erstwhile champion, Spencer Percival, had had the misfortune to be assassinated in the spring of 1812, and she was now being advised by her Whiggish brothers-in-law, the Dukes of Kent and Sussex, and a group of Whig politicians with an eye to the future and a score to settle with the Regent. Foremost among these were the brewer MP Samuel Whitbread, an eager and eloquent advocate of root-and-branch reform, and the able and ambitious but unscrupulous lawyer Henry Brougham, who saw the Princess of Wales and her daughter as essential tools in the Whigs' campaign both to secure their position and establish a power base for the next reign, and to embarrass the present Tory government.

No one in politics could forget that only the poor mad old King at Windsor and the Prince Regent stood between Princess Charlotte and the throne. The old King was, of course, as good as dead already, while the Regent, who was no longer a young man (he would soon be fifty and had had a very serious illness the previous autumn), could not be regarded as a good life in actuarial terms. Charlotte had never made any secret of her Whig sympathies, and now that she was approaching her majority it was obviously good tactics to seek to cultivate her acquaintance and offer her any guidance and support she might require. As for her mama, Caroline's new friends were frank in their private appraisal of her as a light, vulgar, and thoroughly dislikeable woman, but her grievances – both real and imagined – represented an exploitable asset no party out of office could be expected to ignore. 'True patriotism, true knight-errantry, where is it?' sighed Lady Charlotte Bury, who considered Henry Brougham to be 'a man of inordinate ambition and . . . of little heart'. Not that Caroline harboured any false notions about the sincerity of Brougham's knight errantry. On the contrary, she rather disliked him. 'His manner does not please her,' recorded Lady Charlotte; 'they look at each other in a way that is very amusing to a bystander. The one thinks, "She *may* be useful to me"; and the other, "*He* is useful to me at present." It does not require to be a conjurer to read their thoughts; but they are both too cunning for each other.' Brougham did, though, usually offer sound advice and was the only person currently within her orbit who seemed to exercise any control over Caroline, who was a little in awe of him. The Princess of Wales was in high spirits at the end of 1812. More than anything the poor woman dreaded boredom and 'dulness' – the awful, stultifying pointlessness of her existence – and was therefore elated at the prospect of a little excitement, of being once more a centre of attention, and most of all of having an opportunity to make the Prince's life a misery. Of the possible consequences, both for herself and her daughter, she never thought. Nothing could be worse than her present circumstances, she told Charlotte Bury defiantly, but that lady was not so sure and feared her employer was goading the sleeping lion.

SIX

The Plan of Protracted Infancy

'If she had been my daughter, I would have locked her up.'
                                        Lord Eldon, January 1813

*Mr Brougham . . . said positively that till the Princess Charlotte was
one and twenty, the Prince might even lock her up if he chose, and had
absolute power over her.*
                    Lady Charlotte Bury, Diary of a Lady-in-Waiting

*I ought not to give way to lowness, I believe, but I nearly despair and
see things very black.*
                    Princess Charlotte to Mercer Elphinstone, August 1813

Eighteen twelve had been a miserable year for Princess
Charlotte, and 1813 too, got off to a bad start with an
especially upsetting piece of unpleasantness over the
resignation of Lady de Clifford. There had been a marked
deterioration in relations between governess and pupil since
the affair of Captain Hesse. 'I am far from being comfortable
with the *old dow*,' Charlotte had written to Mercer in
December 1812. 'She is so dreadfully *critique, jalouse, curieuse.*
She says little, but I see *evidently* at times does not think the
less. Sometimes she throws out ill-natured hints, wh. if I chose
I might take up, but wh. I appear never to understand.'
Charlotte did *not wish* to quarrel with the old lady, she might
get something worse, but it seemed that the Dowager, who
disliked the damp discomfort of Lower Lodge Windsor every
bit as much as Charlotte did, had had enough of the strains

and stresses of her situation. She told the Queen that she felt she had lost the Princess's confidence, and after that, of course, it was impossible to ask her to stay on.

The question of Lady de Clifford's replacement was the subject of much anxious discussion in the royal family, especially among the female members. It had been decided to ask the Duchess of Leeds to succeed Lady de Clifford as governess, but the Queen felt the Duchess would undoubtedly want an assistant before agreeing to undertake such an onerous charge; and since Charlotte was now rather too old for sub-governesses, a responsible and trustworthy younger woman, suitable for admission into royal society, should be designated her official companion. Her Majesty was also strongly of the opinion that this would be an excellent opportunity to change all the maids and other household servants with whom the Princess had been far too friendly in the past.

The Princess herself quite agreed that she was too old for sub-governesses. Indeed, she considered she was now too old for governesses of any degree and had been cherishing the hope that with her seventeenth birthday coming up on 6 January she might qualify for an establishment with proper grown-up ladies of the bedchamber. She was therefore deeply chagrined to hear from Lady de Clifford not only that her ladyship had resigned but that the Duchess of Leeds had already been appointed to replace her. Her immediate reaction was to announce that she would never submit to obey anybody in the capacity of governess – a defiance of Papa's authority which was greeted with rapture by Mama down at Blackheath. Lady de Clifford, too, was urging the Princess not to allow another governess to come near her, which piece of advice Charlotte Bury thought must proceed from the vanity of wishing to say that 'Princess Charlotte never had any governess after me.'

Lady Charlotte disapproved. After all, what right had the Princess to disobey her father? 'Those persons who are never governed', she moralized in the pages of her journal, 'are not, surely, fit to govern others. . . . I am sincerely attached to the Princess Charlotte', wrote Charlotte Bury, 'but I shrink from being obliged to say, "very firm, and very fine", when I think, "very obstinate, and very wrong-headed".'

Queen Charlotte, who was under no obligation to be tactful, told her granddaughter bluntly that she was too young to be her own mistress and had no right to expect her father to consult her over the arrangements being made for her welfare. Indeed, 'she was greatly mistaken if she thought any father *was bound* to tell a child of what he might think *proper* to do *by her* as *he* must know best *what was most best* for her good'. In the course of a comprehensive telling off, delivered in the presence of Lady de Clifford and the Bishop of Salisbury as well as the Princess Mary, the Queen, according to Princess Mary's report to the Regent, said everything she could to make Charlotte 'sensable [*sic*]' of her filial duty and 'of the consequences that might arise if she did not submit to the commands of a father'. But Charlotte had already written to her father refusing, 'in a very respectful manner', to have any more governesses. She had been very much hurt that he had not seen fit to take her into his confidence over Lady de Clifford's resignation – 'more particularly as the once kind and grateful promise you gave me of there never being a third person between us gave me hopes'. But she had been the last to know of it 'and not till every one talked of it and it reached my ears by hearsay'. She trusted her dear father would pardon 'the freedom and candor [*sic*]' with which she addressed him but could not help judging 'from the view of other young people of my own age who cease to have governesses at 17'. She had no personal objection to the Duchess of Leeds but remained fixed in her determination not to accept or submit to the Duchess or anyone else under the name of Governess.

This ultimatum was dispatched on 10 January with a copy to the Prime Minister and provoked an immediate reaction. Scenting the dreaded influence of the 'mischievous and intriguing infernale' of Blackheath as well as that of political opposition behind this piece of teenage rebellion, the Regent came storming down to Windsor in a furious temper. Charlotte was summoned to the castle to face a kangaroo court consisting of her father and grandmother and Lord Eldon, Lord High Chancellor of England, who had been brought along for the express purpose of explaining the law which gave the Prince virtually untrammelled power over her both as parent and as sovereign. Eldon, a reactionary right-wing Tory familiarly known as Old Bags, was something of a rough diamond – his grandfather having been a trader and owner of keels or barges on the coal wharves of Newcastle-upon-Tyne – and he performed his task with hectoring relish. The Queen and Regent then took up the attack, the Regent demanding to know what Charlotte meant by refusing to have a governess, calling her a fool, an obstinate, perverse, headstrong chit of a girl not fit to have any establishment of her own.

'Depend upon it,' he roared, 'as long as I live you shall never have an establishment unless you marry.' He knew all about those clandestine meetings with young FitzClarence and Captain Hesse, he went on, and if it were not for his clemency he would have had her shut up for life. He then appealed to Lord Eldon – what would *he* have done as a father?

The Chancellor hastened to take his cue. 'If she had been my daughter, I would have locked her up.'

'Rather violent language', commented Lady de Clifford, 'for a coal-heaver's son to the future Queen of England.'

It was this aspect of the affair which seems to have rankled most. Charlotte contrived to maintain her composure in front of her father but afterwards with one of her more sympathetic aunts, she had broken down in tears, sobbing, 'What would the King say if he could know that his granddaughter had been compared to the granddaughter of a collier?' She told Mercer in one of her smuggled letters that she was 'not beat' in spite of all the tyranny, threats, and abuse she had suffered. Though her health and spirits were affected – she had a heavy cold and cough and had lost sleep and appetite – she could still rise above the meanness, jealousies, and 'tracasseries' of family life at Windsor, the full story of which would scarcely be credited outside the pages of a Gothic romance. But while Charlotte assured her friends that she had not submitted without a struggle, she had nevertheless been forced to face the fact that Papa's word was indeed law, and no more was heard about her refusing to have another governess.

The Duchess of Leeds arrived at Lower Lodge in mid-January and proved to be an amiable non-entity, possessing few if any qualifications for her onerous position. The Duke's second wife, she had been born a Miss Anguish, daughter of a mere professional man, but displayed an unfortunate tendency to put on airs when in company. 'What can be expected of a *low woman*, who has been *pushed up* and *never* found her *level?*' commented her charge contemptuously. The 'pinchbeck Duchess' as she was quickly dubbed in Whig circles, belonged with her husband to the right wing of the Tory faction, which did nothing to endear her to the Princess. She was also, according to Charlotte, a bore whose irritating characteristics included 'no conversation, but stories of an hour's length; very *fidgety temper*, almost always ill, and keeping close to me whenever I am out in publick, of wh. I have cured her I believe'.

Charlotte had the sense to be polite to her unwanted duenna – 'For God's sake be civil to her,' she hissed at Mama the first time the Duchess chaperoned her to Kensington – but at the same time contrived to see as little as possible of her, their intercourse generally being limited to half an hour or so in the afternoon.

This arrangement suited both ladies. An easy-going soul, the Duchess of Leeds, unlike her predecessor, had no inclination to quarrel with anybody, and the household no longer rang with sounds of the warfare which had formerly been waged between the Dowager de Clifford and the Bishop of Salisbury, who 'seemed now to bless himself that things went on so well and quietly'. In fact, as long as she was left in peace to enjoy her bad health, which did not appear to interfere with her social life, to go for ambling rides on a quiet horse, dose herself with calomel, and spend her salary, the new governess was more than willing to allow her pupil to continue untrammelled by any restrictive supervision. When busybodying persons passed remarks about the extreme shortness of Princess Charlotte's petticoats (Princess Charlotte had pretty feet and ankles and liked to show them off), her careless habit of nodding instead of making a formal bow to her acquaintance, or the way she would chatter to the maids-of-honour in chapel during Divine Service, the Duchess became quite bilious with agitation, cried in her sleep, and begged her deputy to undertake the task of 'speaking' to HRH, 'for she did not like to venture on anything herself unless driven to the last extremity'.

The Duchess's deputy, who replaced the unloved Mrs Udney at the end of January, was the only bright spot on Charlotte's horizon just then. Cornelia Knight, she told Mercer, was 'an excellent, valuable person . . . straightforward, open and honourable'. A spinster in her mid-fifties, Miss Knight was the daughter of an admiral, widely travelled, cultivated, intelligent and used to moving in the highest circles. Charlotte regarded her arrival as a blessing, and her appointment as Lady Companion to the Princess had been intended as a conciliatory gesture which Sir Henry Halford – the royal family's general practitioner, confidant, and trouble-shooter – hoped would soothe the feelings of irritation stirred up by the manner of Lady de Clifford's departure. Unfortunately it also stirred up another major 'tracasserie', owing to the fact that the Queen regarded the valuable Miss Knight as *her* property and took great offence when asked to release her. Charlotte Bury heard there had been a tremendous battle between the Regent and his mother but that 'the old Begum' was forced to submit, which she did with a very bad grace.

Although worried sick in case she was being disloyal to the Queen, Cornelia Knight did not long resist the Prince's tempting offer. She told her friend Lord Moira that her sole motive in accepting was her desire 'to assist in rescuing a noble young person from surrounding persecution' and help her to realize her potential as one 'certainly capable of becoming a blessing to her country'. Miss Knight gave it as her opinion that the next year or two would be crucial for the development of Charlotte's character and that the repressive measures recently pursued with her might well drive her to despair and spoil her disposition 'if not counteracted by affection and tenderness'.

So, full of crusading zeal and romantic notions that she could be of use, Miss Knight had shaken the depressing dust of Windsor Castle and on 23 January came up to meet the princess on her return to London. She found Warwick House 'miserably out of repair' and the accommodation, though far from being uncomfortable for a private family, 'anything but royal'. But even shabby old Warwick House, tucked away at the end of a narrow court in the shadow of Papa, was to Charlotte 'a seat of happiness' compared to Lower Lodge at Windsor, and she was 'anxiously desirous' to remain in town as much as possible. It had been decreed that she should spend alternate weeks at Windsor, but she was promised visits to the theatre, balls and parties at Carlton House, and various other treats. Nevertheless when Miss Knight attended her to a dinner party at Carlton House on the 25th, the company consisted largely of uncles, and the only other lady present was old Miss Goldsworthy, one-time governess to the princesses, now very deaf and in the habit of falling asleep over the dinner table. Miss Knight could not help noticing how well Papa did himself in the overheated salons of Carlton House all fitted up 'with great splendour and elegance' and much ornamental decoration and bronze and china. It was a marked contrast to the modest accommodation provided for Charlotte. The Prince, too, hardly spoke to his daughter and showed her neither 'the manner or voice of affection'. His greatest attentions were reserved for Miss Goldsworthy, and this, Cornelia Knight believed, was all part of the plan to keep Charlotte, 'as long as possible a child'. All her attendants, it seemed, were to be regarded as nurses or governesses, and as such inferior to the former nurses and governesses of her aunts. Miss Knight was to be very much annoyed a few days later by seeing her own appointment described in the *Morning Chronicle* as 'sub-governess' – a misapprehension which she lost no time in correcting.

Dr Short was still coming to read English with Charlotte for an hour every morning; Dr Sterkey, a minister of the Swiss Church, came for French; and the Great U.P. put in an appearance three or four times a week to 'do the important' as her Royal Highness's preceptor. The schoolroom atmosphere was further heightened by the arrival of the Duchess of Leeds' fifteen-year old daughter, Lady Catherine Osborne, and her governess – 'an elegant little girl', according to Cornelia Knight, 'who danced well, could play a little on the pianoforte, and speak a little French'. She was to be a companion to Princess Charlotte, 'and it was proposed she should have, when in Town, parties of young ladies not presented – that is to say, children's balls'.

Charlotte was scornful of the idea of Lady Catherine's companionship and later came to detest her for her habit of listening at keyholes and hanging about in places where she had no business to be. 'That odious Lady Catherine is a convenient spie upon everybody in the house, with her *long nose* of bad omen, and her *flippant* way of walking so lightly that one never hears her.' Eventually Charlotte became so exasperated after encountering 'her little ladyship' loitering yet again in the passage outside her room that, she told Mercer, 'I *took courage* . . . walked on with her to the water closet, where I stopped, and finding the window open and very cold, contrived *before* she was aware to push her in and lock it, keeping her very agreeably for a quarter of an hour consoling her with the assurance that it *could* only be there she wanted to go to every evening . . . the young ladies dismay was not small, and her assurances thro' the door *very amusing*.' This rather ridiculous episode provided Charlotte and Miss Knight with a good laugh, but Lady Catherine's 'impertinent curiosity' continued to be a source of irritation, and Charlotte was always having to remember to guard her tongue when the 'elegant little girl' might be within earshot.

At the beginning of February the Queen came up to St James's and held a Drawing-Room on the 4th. The Duchess of Leeds and Miss Knight both went in to make their curtsies, but Charlotte was left to wait outside in the Duke of Cumberland's rooms. She was, says the sympathetic Miss Knight, 'greatly hurt by being thus treated as a child, but made no complaints, and was good natured with her family'. Miss Knight was of the opinion that the Regent's determination to keep his daughter in the background, if not in the nursery, was all to do with the switch in his politics. Charlotte, 'in understanding, penetration, and stature', was now a woman, eager to learn about public affairs and perfectly capable of forming judgements for herself – something which did not suit Papa's book at all.

However, on 5 February the Princess was to be allowed to attend a proper grown-up function, a ball at Carlton House ostensibly given in her honour and to which some members of the Opposition party were invited. Dressed in white and silver and for the first time wearing in her hair the ostrich-feather plumes of full Court dress, Charlotte appeared handsome and self-possessed and, rather to her own surprise, really enjoyed herself, although she was disappointed not to see the young Duke of Devonshire, whom she had expected as her partner, and nettled by the way her Aunt Mary pushed in to claim the privilege of opening the dance – 'always the cupple above me, as jealous and ill natured the whole night as she could be'.

The Queen and the aunts, 'the whole pack of devils' in fact, trundled back to Windsor by the end of the week, while Charlotte, who was still suffering from a nasty cough, managed to wheedle Papa into letting her stay in town – 'I have *got off going* at all.' But although thankful to be rid her most disliked relations at least for the time being, she was depressed, 'horribly and detestably out of spirits'. She had heard some disquieting rumours that her visits to Kensington were to be further curtailed and dreaded the prospect of yet another round in the ugly, unforgiving war between her parents. She told Mercer 'FOR YOUR OWN PRIVATE EAR' that a letter had been sent from her mother to her father and had been rejected and returned unread on three occasions at least. It had then been directed to the Prime Minister, who had finally been allowed to read it to the Prince, 'who gave no answer'.

This letter, although copied and signed by Caroline, had of course been composed by Henry Brougham. Caroline had been furiously disappointed by the collapse of Charlotte's attempted rebellion, and Brougham, aware that 'the young one' too was still simmering with resentment at the way she was being treated, deemed the moment – the young one's seventeenth birthday – to be ripe for a gesture, for addressing a formal remonstrance to the Regent as from a wronged wife and grieving mother cruelly deprived of the society of her beloved child. Caroline pointed out that although she had been cleared of all blame by the Delicate Investigators she was still, after seven years, being treated as a social pariah by her husband and his family and as unfit to have free access to her daughter. 'Let me implore you to reflect on the situation in which I am placed; without the shadow of a charge against me – without even an accuser – after an Inquiry that led to my ample vindication – yet treated as if I were still more culpable than the perjuries of my suborned traducers represented me, and held up to the world as a Mother who may not enjoy the society of her only Child.'

This affecting plea naturally ignored the matter of Caroline's questionable conduct in the years since the Commission of Inquiry had published its report – for example, her encouragement of the deplorable Sapio family, who were still very much in evidence at Kensington and

Blackheath. She was on somewhat firmer ground when she went on to protest over the eccentric manner of Charlotte's bringing up. 'The plan of excluding my Daughter from all intercourse with the world, appears to my humble judgement peculiarly unfortunate. She who is destined to be the Sovereign of this great country, enjoys none of those advantages of society which are deemed necessary for imparting a knowledge of mankind to persons who have infinitely less occasion to learn that important lesson.' Charlotte, in short, might find herself 'called upon to exercise the powers of the Crown, with an experience of the world more confined than that of the most private individual'. And there was another circumstance in every way distressing to Caroline's maternal and religious feelings – her daughter had not yet enjoyed the benefit of Confirmation, 'although above a year older than the age at which all the other branches of the Royal Family have partaken of that solemnity'.

No one with any inside knowledge of public affairs was at all surprised when the full text of the Princess of Wales's letter appeared in the columns of the leading Whig party newspaper, the *Morning Chronicle*. The Regent reacted to this blatant piece of coat-trailing by reopening the Delicate Investigation. The Privy Council, in its judicial role, was ordered to re-evaluate all the evidence taken in 1806, together with certain other, more recent disclosures regarding the manners and morals of the Princess of Wales, and then to pronounce on whether or not the intercourse between Princess Charlotte and her mama should continue to be subject to 'restriction and regulation'. In the mean time, Charlotte was 'deprived by a positive order' from seeing her mother at all.

This edict was conveyed by the Prince Regent '*himself* in person and *alone*'. He arrived at Warwick House accompanied by an embarrassed Lord Liverpool, who was left to make small talk with Cornelia Knight, while HRH saw his daughter in private. The interview, according to Charlotte's report to Mercer Elphinstone, was 'most painful', as it was 'constant *strong language* against her [Caroline] and all the expressions of the most violent affections towards me possible'. Miss Knight and Lord Liverpool were then summoned, since the Prince wished the Prime Minister, whom he described as 'his confidential servant', and Cornelia, as Charlotte's friend, to hear him repeat what he had been saying to her, 'namely that an investigation was being made with respect to the conduct of her mother, on the result of which depended her ever being allowed to visit her again'. The Prince added that 'it was a very serious investigation, and most probably would end in a manner most painful; but that whatever way it ended, his treatment of Princess Charlotte would be equally kind and considerate, as he should not consider her accountable for the faults of her mother'.

The sympathetic Miss Knight thought Charlotte looked 'penetrated with grief' and attributed her obvious misery to the pain of being obliged to hear 'family dissensions of so delicate a nature' discussed in front of outsiders. Certainly Charlotte was in a perfectly horrible position and she naturally felt the emotional stress and strain more acutely as she grew older and more aware. She bitterly resented the way in which both the warring factions sought to manipulate her for their own advantage and was, she told Mercer, 'disgusted and distressed to a degree with all the falseness'. Her father's current efforts to curry favour were beyond everything. 'Conceive only his saying to me that I need not be agitated as I should not lose my Balls or gaities [*sic*] at all.' She knew the Prince's friends were putting it about that they had quite won her over and persuaded her to abandon her mother's cause by promising 'gaities'. She also knew that it was '*these reports* that *reach* the *ears* of the *people* and which they believe'.

Charlotte had disapproved of the publication in the *Morning Chronicle*, for which she blamed Brougham, and retained no illusions as to the nature of her mama's indiscretions. All the same, she had no intention of abandoning her and, in any case, was determined to nail the gossip that she could be won over by the promise of treats. She therefore resolutely refused all invitations to the play or 'little parties at Carlton House', saying that it would ill become her to appear in public while her mother was under a cloud of 'so tremendous a nature'. This self-imposed seclusion was, however, brought to an abrupt end on 22 February by a morning visit from the Miss Herveys, two ladies 'very intimate at Windsor', who informed the Princess that if she did not show herself in public 'her character would be lost', for the most injurious stories were being circulated about her and Captain FitzClarence. It was, apparently, being whispered that she had had an affair with her cousin and was pregnant by him. So Charlotte ordered her carriage and went for an airing in the Park.

After this she and Miss Knight 'went almost every day for an hour or two up and down the road where only royal carriages are allowed to go', but even here she was not safe, as a hurried note to Papa makes clear:

> I am this moment returned from my drive in the park, and do not delay an instant informing you that I met the Princess, who stopped her carriage and spoke to me for five minutes as she came to town to see the Duchess of Brunswick. I trust this circumstance will not happen again, but as it was entirely unexpected by me I wished to give you the earliest intelligence, as I make it a point never to have any concealments from you.'

Charlotte was still anxiously awaiting the result of the Privy Council's deliberations. 'Many days passed,' wrote Miss Knight, 'and no visit from the Prince. He sent one or two messages to excuse himself, and we heard that everyone talked of this unhappy affair.' They also heard that those two birds of ill omen, Sir John and Lady Douglas, had been rehabilitated and were 'constantly with the inhabitants of Carlton House' – a piece of information scarcely calculated to reassure the inhabitants of Warwick House. At last, on 1 March, the Duchess of Leeds returned from a summons to Carlton House with the news that 'the Princess's affair had finished dreadfully'. A copy of the Council's report was delivered that evening, addressed to the Duchess, but Her Grace, with unexpected delicacy, handed the document over to Charlotte unopened. 'Her Royal Highness', says Miss Knight, 'ran over the paper, and then said, "I have no objection to anyone hearing this".' To her great surprise and relief Charlotte had found the dreaded report to be nothing more than 'a sort of answer' to Caroline's letter in the *Morning Chronicle*, 'but so vague and incomprehensible and undefined . . . as hardly to be called an answer'. The Privy Councillors, in short, had merely confirmed the verdict of the 1806 inquiry and consequently agreed with the Regent that Charlotte should only be permitted to see her mother under supervision and subject to the restrictions he imposed. 'After all this farce it leaves you just where you were before,' was Charlotte's exasperated comment.

In the world outside the walls of the Carlton House complex the news of the Princess of Wales's second vindication was greeted with uninhibited delight. Loyal addresses and letters of congratulations on 'having escaped a conspiracy against her life and honour' poured into Kensington Palace from all sides, and Caroline pressed home her advantage by writing a letter to the Speaker of the Commons which she requested should be read to the House without delay. The Princess of Wales had, she said, seen a report made to the Prince Regent by the Privy Council on certain aspects of her character and conduct. This report was of such a nature that her Royal Highness felt persuaded no one could read it without considering it as 'conveying aspersions' upon her; but it was so vaguely worded as to make it impossible to discover precisely what it meant 'or even what she had been charged with'. She had not been permitted to know what evidence the Privy Council had proceeded upon, still less to be heard in her own defence.

Until the result of the inquiry had been communicated to her, her only source of information had been 'common rumour'. She thefore felt compelled to throw herself upon 'the wisdom and justice of Parliament' and make it known that she feared no scrutiny however strict, provided only that it was carried out by impartial judges. Indeed, she would positively welcome a full, fair, and open investigation of her whole conduct during the period of her residence in England. Her one desire was 'that she may either be treated as innocent, or proved to be guilty'.

This sort of appeal always went down well. Samuel Whitbread, who had appointed himself Caroline's champion in the Commons, made several impassioned speeches on her behalf, while a number of honourable members wanted to know whether Sir John and Lady Douglas were to be prosecuted for perjury or treason or both, and if not, why not. Unsurprisingly, no satisfactory answer was forthcoming, the government sticking to its line that no good could result from parliamentary interference in the private concerns of the royal family. The popular press were less fastidious, and some ladies began to burn their newspapers so that the servants might not read such improprieties.

Caroline continued to be mobbed by enthusiastic crowds whenever she appeared in public, and Charlotte Bury considered that this was perhaps 'the proudest moment of the Princess's troubled life'. Afterwards, she wrote, there was 'more pomp and greater public demonstration of feeling for her, but then it was a storm of passion and of party, not the sober current of honest feelings, which moved justice to stand forth and defend her'. Within the royal family, however, no one was moved to stand forth and defend the Princess of Wales, and in Court and government circles it seemed her social ostracism was to continue unabated.

At the end of March the old Duchess of Brunswick died in her lodgings in Hanover Square. This was a circumstance which could not be ignored, and the Duchess was interred in the family vault at Windsor in recognition of her status as the King's sister. Queen Charlotte did not hesitate to express the view that 'the poor Dutchess's [*sic*]' demise had been hastened by anxiety and by suppressing her feelings over her daughter's behaviour, but there had never been much love lost in that quarter, and the old lady had long since washed her hands of Caroline, remarking that the poor creature's only excuse was that she was not quite right in the head. Nevertheless, the Regent was obliged to allow Charlotte to pay a visit of condolence at Blackheath. This took place on 26 March with the Duchess of Leeds and Cornelia Knight in attendance, the latter recording that 'we passed a very quiet and comfortable day' and adding: 'the Princess of Wales looked better than I ever saw her. She appeared to be affected and subdued and was particularly so when we came away, saying how uncertain it was when she should be allowed to see her daughter again.'

In spite of the Privy Council's ruling, Charlotte's fortnightly visits were not resumed, and she had to apply for special permission to go down to Blackheath on Caroline's birthday, 17 May. Permission was reluctantly granted, but for a brief morning visit only. Charlotte was not to stay for dinner, when she would run the risk of being exposed to the sort of society of which Papa could not approve. Caroline, as usual, felt herself slighted, and the occasion was not a success – 'as dry and as formal as possible'. Charlotte, in convoy with the inevitable governesses, went away soon after two o'clock, and Caroline was left to a tête-à-tête with the Duke of Kent, her only other birthday visitor.

Charlotte was changing. Although evidently determined to go on observing all the proprieties, her manner towards her mother was becoming noticeably cooler, and Charlotte Bury and Cornelia Knight both attributed this to the influence of Mercer Elphinstone. After a gap of more than a year, the two girls were being allowed to see one another again – a concession which, Cornelia Knight was convinced, had only been granted on condition that Mercer used her very considerable influence with the Princess to 'open her eyes to her mother's imprudence and break the confidential intimacy between them'. Charlotte Bury, too, heard that 'Miss E. was not friendly to the Princess of Wales' and commented that 'since her return to Princess Charlotte, the latter is not half so kind to her mother'.

Certainly the hard-hearted Mercer had always urged Charlotte to remember the importance of keeping on civil terms with her father, and may very well have warned her against the dangers of appearing too much at home at Blackheath. But Charlotte was nobody's fool and would hardly have needed to have her eyes opened to her mother's imprudence, especially not in the spring of 1813. Although she had always known a good deal and guessed a good deal more about Caroline's indiscretions, she had been deeply shocked and upset by the disclosures which followed the Privy Council's report – 'the publication of things I was wholly ignorant of before, really came upon me with *such a blow and it stagger'd me* so terribly, that I . . . shall *not ever recover* from it'. Gossip and surmise were one thing; actually being able to read reports of the evidence given by Caroline's servants to the 1806 Commission, now printed in the Tory press, and Spencer Percival's *Book* in her defence, reissued by her political friends, was something else again and sank her so very low in her daughter's estimation that their relationship had suffered an irreversible change. 'The horror of the knowledge of the whole can never make those feelings ever return again that might have allowed influence.' Nevertheless, Charlotte remained stubbornly loyal to her mama and wished to show her all affection and respect due to her position, perhaps even more than before, for '*she had her aggravations . . . she was ill-used*, and is *still* more *now* than before, after this double clamor [*sic*]'.

One thing about Caroline – it was impossible to have anything much to do with her and remain indifferent, and

Princess Charlotte's feelings of revulsion and disapproval mixed with pity and a reluctant, exasperated affection were not unlike those of Charlotte Bury, Caroline's lady-in-waiting. 'This Princess is a most peculiar person – she alternately makes me *dislike* and *like* her – her conduct and sentiments vary so in quality every time I see her.' Lady Charlotte had been shocked and repelled by Caroline's callousness when one of her postilions was thrown from his horse as her carriage drove – much too fast – out of the gates of Kensington Palace: 'the Princess ought not to have allowed the boy to ride on, but should have ordered him to go home and be taken care of'. But a few days later, down at Blackheath, she found Her Royal Highness 'in a low, gentle humour' and was once more moved to genuine pity. The two women walked together in the grounds of Montague House, and Caroline cried as she said that the garden and shrubbery were all her own creation but that she would soon have to leave them for ever, for she could no longer afford to keep a house at Blackheath and one in London. In any case, the last winter she had spent there had been so very dreary, she could not face the prospect of another. She spoke, remembered Lady Charlotte, 'with a desolation of heart that really made me sorry for her'. Then, with one of her sudden changes of mood, she smiled; 'an expression of resignation, even of content, irradiated her countenance', and she exclaimed:

'I will go on hoping for happier days. Do you think I *may?*'

'I trust your Royal Highness will yet see many happy days,' responded Lady Charlotte 'with heartfelt warmth' – what else could she say to the 'poor soul' for whom, in spite of everything, it was impossible not to feel great compassion.

Meanwhile, Princess Charlotte, still in a sort of limbo at Warwick House and leading, thought the indignant Miss Knight a life of quiet monstrous dullness, might also legitimately be hoping for happier days. But there seemed no immediate prospect of any relief from the boredom, frustration, and nervous tension which oppressed her spirits and, not surprisingly, gave her headaches, insomnia, and indigestion. 'I feel so *constantly in a fever* about things', she told Mercer early in March, 'and I have had so many unpleasant and painful things to go through, and to bear also secretly, that I am always prepared from one day to another for something else disagreeable, and if one day passes without, and in peace, I feel almost *uneasy* with the apprehention [*sic*] of what another day may bring.'

The first thing that summer brought was the sorrow of bereavement with the death of her much loved former nurse, personal maid, and dresser, Mrs Gagarin. According to Cornelia Knight, who was told her romantic story in confidence by Charlotte, the excellent Mrs Gagarin was an Englishwoman who had made an unfortunate marriage to a Russian prince 'whom she afterwards discovered to be the husband of another, and whom she therefore left without even claiming a provision'. Mrs Gagarin had been with the Princess from her infancy and had taught her her first lessons. Charlotte was devoted to her and, when her health began to fail, bestowed on her, 'every care, every attention, which the kindest and most considerate affection could suggest'. While the sick woman was still capable of taking airings, 'her Royal Highness constantly sent her out in a carriage, and when she grew so weak as to be confined to her room, visited her two or three times a day, carried her in her arms to the window, and exerted every faculty to soothe and comfort her.' Sadly all these loving exertions were in vain. Mrs Gagarin died on 1 July, and Charlotte, 'who might be said to have known no other mother', was deeply affected. 'She was very low for a long time afterwards,' records Miss Knight, 'though she endeavoured to suppress and conceal her feelings.'

Like all children whose natural affections are denied or suppressed, Charlotte had sought other outlets and lavished love on her servants and pets. She had several dogs – including a beautiful white Italian greyhound with cropped ears, taken from aboard a captured French ship and given to her by her father. Later there is mention of another 'little French dog . . . a small *white poudel*' which had been taught to perform tricks by the prisoners of war at '*Dartmore* French prison'.

During the early summer of 1813 the Princess's difficult relationship with her father was temporarily a little cosier. He gave her what had once been the central sapphire of the Stuart Crown and was generally unusually kind and attentive. The iron hand was, however, only thinly disguised by the velvet glove. On 4 June at Frogmore, where the royal family had assembled to celebrate the King's birthday, the Regent was again 'all courtesy' and apparently in high good humour, but before the party broke up he tapped Miss Knight on the shoulder and, using one of Charlotte's pet names for her, remarked: 'Remember, my dear Chevalier, that Charlotte must lay aside the idle nonsense of thinking that she has a will of her own; while I live she must be subject to me as she is at present.'

The Chevalier knew better than to repeat this to Charlotte, but what Brougham called 'the little flirting' between father and daughter was already over. There were complaints about Charlotte's visits – heavily chaperoned of course – to the studio of the artist George Sander, who was painting her portrait as a present for the Regent's birthday. It was felt more suitable that the sittings should take place at Warwick House, and explanations that Warwick House was too dark for the purpose were not considered sufficient. The real objection was that Charlotte might meet unsuitable people, and it's true that various ladies took the opportunity to come and look at the portrait and afterwards to 'talk over the balls and parties of the night before'. Poor Charlotte, starved as she was of the gaiety enjoyed by her contemporaries 'doing' the Season, listened eagerly to their accounts of the assemblies, balls, and routs from which she was excluded; and they would sometimes call in at Warwick House for a little while in the evening, before going on to dance the night away in the glittering social whirl she longed to join.

Virtually the only social occasions Charlotte was allowed to attend were family dinner parties and even these were often spoilt by some 'tracasserie'. For example, there was trouble one evening in June at the Duke of York's, when the Regent saw the princess sitting on a sofa and chatting with his cousin the Duke of Gloucester. The Regent detested Gloucester, an amiable if vacuous individual variously known as The Cheese, The Slice, or Silly Billy, and sent Lady Liverpool to break up the tête-à-tête. Charlotte, angry and humiliated, stalked off into another room and later, when her father had gone, apologized to the offended Cheese and his sister, Princess Sophia of Gloucester, for what had happened. This, according to Cornelia Knight, gave occasion to the Duke to say that 'he meant to take no liberty, but that she might consider him as devoted to her and ready to come forward whenever she would cast her eyes on him'.

There was still more trouble over the young Duke of Devonshire, a highly eligible bachelor who was 'followed by all the mothers and all the misses in London'. Charlotte liked William Cavendish, who was one of her regular partners at Carlton House balls, but now rumours of a romance began to circulate, and Brougham told his friend Thomas Creevey that 'Young P and her father have had frequent rows of late, but one pretty serious one. He was angry at her for flirting with the Duke of Devonshire, and suspected she was talking politics' (the Cavendishes were a leading Whig family). The Regent continued to harbour dark suspicions about the Devonshire connection, and reports that Charlotte had twice been seen in the vicinity on a day when the Duke was entertaining at Chiswick House provoked thunderbolts from Carlton House. Miss Knight hastened to explain that she had proposed the excursions to give Charlotte the amusement of seeing the ducal guests and their carriages. The Princess's life had so little variety in it, and her health and spirits were at that time so indifferent (it was just after Mrs Gagarin's death), that her Lady Companion had been anxious to do anything that could cheer her up.

This excuse was coldly received. Charlotte's own plea to be

allowed a seaside holiday was refused, and she and her entourage were ordered back to hated Windsor. Everyone was in disgrace in this 'sudden fit of ill-humour'. Cornelia Knight especially should have known better after her years of service with the Queen; the Duchess of Leeds was accused of using her supposed ill-health as an excuse for neglecting her duty; and even Lady de Clifford came in for retrospective blame for not having informed the princess 'of things that were proper'. No wonder there was an atmosphere of gloom and simmering revolt at Lower Lodge. Cornelia Knight felt the injustice of it all so deeply that she became quite ill, and even the placid Duchess was roused to complain how very hard it was that the Regent 'should so easily give in to such wrong accounts of things, and that it would never answer to go on so'. As for Charlotte, who had been told that her rides and drives were to be confined to the Great Park and Forest of Windsor and that morning visitors only would be allowed, she was deeply depressed. 'I ought not to give way to lowness, I believe', she told Mercer on 14 August, 'but I nearly despair and see things very black.'

There was, of course, one obvious escape route from all this. Marriage would at least buy her freedom from Papa's heavy handed regime, from Lower Lodge, from boredom and governesses, family quarrels and intrigues. Charlotte knew this as well as anyone, and it is surely some measure of her desperation that while resolutely denying rumours of the *tendre* for the Duke of Devonshire, she was apparently seriously considering the Duke of Gloucester as a bridegroom. When a startled Miss Knight said she was convinced neither the Regent nor the rest of the royal family would ever agree to the match – poor pop-eyed Cheese was nearly forty and a violent Whig and suffered from the additional handicap of having had a non-royal mother (she was the bastard daughter of Sir Edward Walpole) – and went on to murmur that she had never seen anything to make her believe that the Princess had any particular partiality for Gloucester, Charlotte replied calmly that all that was quite true. However, she knew she could never expect to marry from inclination, and 'the Duke's character and temper were so good that she might reasonably look forward to being 'treated with kindness'. It is a little hard to credit that, even with her background, Charlotte's expectations could have been quite so limited, and few people at the time believed she was serious, a suspicion that she was using Gloucester deliberately to distract attention from Devonshire persisting in some quarters. In fact, neither duke was ever a serious proposition, but marriage was now definitely in the air, and that summer the name of the Hereditary Prince of Orange, Charlotte's first fully accredited suitor, was being mentioned with elaborate casualness in the corridors of Windsor Castle.

SEVEN

The Orange Match

The Prince's great object is to get the Princess Charlotte out of the way, to Holland.

Brougham to Lord Grey, March 1814

Plagues you must expect, but on the one hand if you are firm they are for a limited time, while on the other, should you yield, the decisive event may last as long as you live.

The Duke of Sussex to Princess Charlotte, July, 1814

God Almighty grant me patience!

Princess Charlotte

By the summer of 1813 the possibility of an Orange match for Princess Charlotte had been under active discussion for several months. It was a proposition with much to recommend it in official circles. The connection between the English and Dutch royal families, dating back to early Stuart times and culminating in the joint reigns of William and Mary, had proved beneficial to both countries and its renewal would no doubt be warmly welcomed by public opinion at home; but the marriage brokers in London and The Hague were thinking more in terms of the wider context of international diplomacy.

For almost as long as anyone could remember, the international scene had been dominated by the empire and wars of Napoleon Bonaparte, but now, following Napoleon's Russian débâcle of 1812 and the duke of Wellington's recent run of success in Spain, the French were at last being driven back behind their own borders. In Berlin and Vienna, London and St Petersburg, the map of Europe was being unrolled again as the peacemakers began to bend their minds to the exhilarating task of drafting treaties and redrawing frontiers.

Twenty years earlier – three years before Princess Charlotte was born, in fact – Britain had gone to war to prevent the domination of the Netherlands by revolutionary France. Now the Foreign Office was proposing the setting up of a new state of the United Netherlands, incorporating the southern, French-speaking provinces of Belgium and ruled by the Dutch house of Orange Nassau, which it was hoped would be 'a strong bulwark' against any future French expansionism. The United Netherlands and the United Kingdom would, of course, be closely bound by treaty, but a marriage between the Orange heir and the British heiress would obviously be of immense value in strengthening an alliance so vital to Britain's security.

Charlotte had known of the existence of this project for some time – Mercer had warned her in February that the government wished to hasten the progress of its 'favourite plan' – but her reaction was negative, and she remained deeply suspicious of the whole scheme. With the awful warning of her parents' example constantly before her, and knowing her father as she did, she was understandably nervous of finding herself being manipulated into a potentially 'worse than death' situation. Her present circumstances might leave a great deal to be desired, but that was no reason to rush into making a possible change for the *worse*. Never, she told Mercer, never would she be tempted 'to purchase temporary ease by *gratifying* the *Windsor and Ministerial* cabals'. She was prepared for battle: 'we may have a scene, but only one I think, as a positive declaration of refusal must, I should think, *amply satisfy*. *Force* will never do anything with me, nor intrigue.'

These were brave words, but that August back at Lower Lodge, 'that abominable and infamous place' where she was always depressed and out of sorts, Charlotte began to dread the prospect of having to meet the 'P. of O.'. 'I am sure my miseries will be much added to by the *plagues about him*,' she wrote gloomily. She had by this time made the acquaintance of the P. of O.'s father in circumstances hardly calculated to make a favourable impression. The king elect of the United Netherlands had been among the guests at a dinner held at the new Military Academy at Sandhurst to celebrate the Regent's birthday, where most of the men got leglessly drunk. The Regent himself had to be retrieved from under the table, glassy-eyed and speechless, to escort his mother to her carriage. The Duke of York fell and cut his head open on a wine cooler, while William of Orange senior was to be seen wandering about in his shirt sleeves, having shed both coat and waistcoat somewhere in the course of the general Bacchanalia. It was, admittedly, a very hot night, but such uncouth behaviour did nothing to improve Charlotte's opinion of a family she was already inclined to dismiss as 'intriguant and violent', and news that young William was actually on his way to England threw her into a flutter of nervous anticipation.

The Hereditary Prince was currently employed on Wellington's staff and had been chosen to carry the dispatches giving details of the Duke's latest triumph over Marshal Soult in the Pyrenees. But Charlotte, rightly or wrongly, felt convinced that his real purpose was courtship and was determined not to allow herself to be tricked into any unrehearsed encounter with 'the little hero', as she had begun sarcastically to describe him. She therefore refused a dinner invitation from Lord and Lady Liverpool, on the excuse of illness, suspecting that both Oranges might be present. She was not well – she had a chronic pain in her side for which Sir Henry Halford had prescribed a blister – but she did nevertheless put in an appearance at the Egham races, sitting in her carriage.

There was to be another family party at Frogmore on 16 August for the Duke of York's birthday, and again Charlotte dreaded the possibility of being brought face to face with the Prince. As it turned out, she need not have worried. To the disappointment of the other Windsor princesses – 'a set of ill-natured spinsters, who only regret not being young enough to seize upon him themselves', observed their niece in a burst of spite – the hero was not present at the Frogmore fête, and Charlotte heard that he would be returning to the army 'almost *immediately*' at his own request. She was, however, cornered at Frogmore by Lord Yarmouth, one of the Regent's cronies, who reproached her for not getting on better with her father.

'It is all your own fault,' he said. 'You might so easily get ascendancy over him if you took pains about it.' In any case, he went on, in a few months' time she would be her own mistress, able to carry all before her.

Lord Yarmouth was not the only person to be thinking of the approach of Charlotte's eighteenth birthday, when she would become of age to succeed to the throne without a regency. She herself was looking forward keenly to the moment when she must surely be granted an establishment and some measure of emancipation. The Regent, on the other hand, was palpably unenthused by the prospect. Never noted for his consideration for the feelings of others, he had shown a consistent lack of sensitivity in his dealings with his daughter, but it is understandable that he should have recoiled from the thought of Charlotte – 'twanging hands' and showing her drawers – at large in London society. Not merely would she be an easy prey for unscrupulous Whig politicians, but the risk of her forming unsuitable romantic attachments, with their attendant horrid scandals, or worse besmirching her good name, seemed all too real. It was all very well for the Prince to warn Miss Knight that Charlotte would remain subject to him for as long as he lived, but with the best will in the world it would not be possible to keep a determined, hot-blooded young woman, who was moreover heir apparent in all but name, in a state of permanent tutelage.

The obvious solution to the problem was marriage. The princess would then become her husband's responsibility and, with any luck, would soon be too busy child-bearing to get into mischief. Charlotte's aunt Mary told her that her father very much wanted her to be married by the following year, and, as autumn approached, she found herself on the receiving end of a remorseless propaganda campaign designed to wear down her resistance to the idea of the Orange match.

Henry Halford, in his dual capacity of family doctor and old and trusted family friend, was employed as the Regent's principal intermediary in this delicate affair and was continually in and out of Lower Lodge charged with messages from the Castle. Although Charlotte was well aware that everything she said was being noted down and might be used in evidence, Sir Henry occupied a uniquely privileged position – 'there are none that have the P.'s belief and confidence like him' – and there was no avoiding his visitations.

'The little Dr was a full hour and a half with me yesterday,' the princess wrote to Mercer on 15 October. He had evidently been instructed to sound her opinion on the subject of marriage and to hint how much more desirable it would be to have this settled before any establishment took place. He went on to speak strongly in favour of the Prince of Orange, 'saying that there were very few choices to be made that would at once please the family and satisfy the nation'. Another possible candidate, Prince Charles of Mecklenberg-Strelitz, the Queen's nephew, was rejected because *she* was so unpopular. Asked about her own preferences, Charlotte replied that, 'situated as she unfortunately was', she could make no objection to marriage in principle, but reiterated her determination not to accept the Prince of Orange and again suggested the Duke of Gloucester, an Englishman well known and esteemed in the country – an important consideration for one who considered herself *'the publick property'* and responsible to the country for her choice. Nothing would look worse than a future Queen of England marrying a foreigner, she announced, brushing aside Halford's reminder that young Orange had had an English education and had made many English friends in the course of his army service.

Next day Sir Henry was back again with the news that the Regent himself would soon be coming down to Windsor. It seemed that matters were being pushed towards some sort of crisis, and Charlotte was 'in a dreadful fuss' at the prospect of another painful scene with her papa. But when the Prince appeared at Lower Lodge on 18 October the worst of his spleen was reserved for the Duke of Gloucester, whom he proceeded to abuse in language which neither Charlotte nor Cornelia Knight (who was present at the interview) could bring themselves to repeat. By contrast he spoke very highly of the Prince of Orange, but utterly disclaimed any thought of proposing him as bridegroom. However, since Charlotte apparently wanted to be married, he would do his best to find her a suitable husband. There were plenty of fine young men on the Continent whom he would invite over to England, to see if any of them would please her. He would never attempt to 'force her inclinations', he went on virtuously, or even try to persuade her into a distasteful marriage. He would simply say who there was for her to choose from and leave the rest to her.

Unfortunately all this display of sweet reason had been spoilt by his venomous attack on Gloucester. The Regent had even had the gall to accuse his daughter of having had too much to drink on that evening at the Duke of York's, which offended her very much and she was also deeply wounded by his implied suggestion that she was hungry for a man. 'He spoke as if he had the *most improper ideas of my inclinations*,' she told Mercer, adding sadly: 'I see that he is *completely poisoned against me*, and that he will *never* come round.' At the family dinner party at the Castle which followed their encounter, the Prince was at his most charming, chatting away to his daughter and treating her to a public display of affection which only served to impress her with his fluency as a liar and the conviction that 'there does not live one who is a greater coward or a greater hypocrite'.

Feeling in need of allies, Charlotte, in consultation with Mercer Elphinstone, had already written to Lord Grey, the leader of the Opposition peers, asking for his advice in her present predicament: how far could she safely go in 'maintaining her own resolution, to refuse the Prince of Orange and, by implication, how much support could she expect from the Whig party in Parliament? Grey's reply, which reached Lower Lodge on 23 October, was an elegantly composed study in tact and diplomacy. He began by reminding the princess of the duty she owed to the Regent, as both a sovereign and a father, and urged her to avoid 'by all proper means the appearance of a public opposition to his pleasure'. She was now standing on the threshold of a public career which Grey hoped might be long and glorious, and it was thus 'indispensably necessary', both for her own sake and for that of the crown she would one day inherit, that she should do nothing to risk alienating the confidence and affection of the nation. They were, after all, living in a society which believed with King Lear that sharper it was than a serpent's tooth to have a thankless – or a disobedient – child.

That said, there were limits to the demands of filial piety, and Lord Grey went on to acknowledge that the Regent's authority was by no means absolute. It was his parental duty to advise, his right to recommend in the matter of his daughter's choice of husband, and he had a legal right of veto, at least until she was twenty-one; but no law, human or divine, gave him the power to force her into a distasteful marriage. Grey was careful not to become involved in personalities – he was sure Her Royal Highness would not expect him to give an opinion between the various illustrious candidates whose names had been mentioned – and his considered advice was that she should, if pressed, ask for delay: 'the suspension, for a time at least, of the further consideration of a subject much too important to be hastily determined upon'. Charlotte was still very young and had hitherto lived in 'almost total seclusion'. The hardship of being hustled straight from the schoolroom and against her wishes into the 'sacred and irrevocable engagement of marriage' would be obvious to everyone, and nobody could reasonably take exception to her asking for a breathing space to look round, enjoy such intercourse with society as her exalted station would allow, and acquire some knowledge and experience of the world on which to base a proper judgement.

This was all sensible, expectable agony-aunt/uncle advice, and Charlotte was delighted with it, since it was very much what she had wanted to hear. 'Believe me,' she told Mercer, 'I have not the smallest inclination at present to marry, as I have seen so little, and, I may add, *nothing* of the world as yet.' What she really wanted, of course, was a year or two of independence, of fun and freedom, before settling down with someone other than the Prince of Orange. She was not over-optimistic about her chances of independence. Her father was saying she already had more liberty than most girls of her age, and she felt certain that all kinds of difficulties would be made over giving her an establishment. She did, however, believe that she had gained two points. The Prince had *positively* (and in front of a witness) given her his word that she would '*never be persuaded or forced*' into an alliance she did not like; and 'the Orange business' was now quite out of the question, and quite given up.

But if Charlotte really believed the Orange business was given up she was soon to be disillusioned. She came back to London in November and on the 29th was writing to Mercer: 'My *torments* and *plagues* are again beginning *again spite of all* promises made at Windsor. I have had a *violent orange* attack this morning; it is *too true* he is *coming* over here directly on his way to Holland, that the P. is to give him a *great diner by way* of introduction.'

This latest onslaught was again being spearheaded by the 'little *Baronetted doctor*', who, wrote Charlotte, 'began *every argument of seduction* you can possibly conceive to *shake my firmness* and turn *my head*. By power, by riches, by liberty, by splendor, by pleasure, by society and lastly by the *general* wish of the nation it would give universal delight, as the grand object now was to keep Holland affixed to this island as much as possible, and that nothing would promote it so well as by an alliance with the young P.' Everyone who made vows was sure to break them, declared Sir Henry, and he was convinced that Charlotte would change her mind as soon as she saw the young man. As regards appearance, he was not at all of 'the Dutch make', and as to his being fair and 'delicate looking', that had nothing to do with his 'manlyness of character'. Halford seems to have got the idea that the princess was harbouring doubts about her suitor's masculinity, for he went on to speak in terms of such frankness as she 'never had herd before from *anyone* and certainly never expected to have done'. She herself had heard from various sources that the Prince was nothing to look at – 'thin as a needle', light blond hair with white eyebrows, a complexion burnt brown by the Spanish sun, and protruding teeth. On the credit side he was said to be very gentlemanlike with excellent manners, agreeable, sensible, lively, fond of fun and amusement, and a good dancer, especially of the waltz. Lady Georgina Fitzroy pronounced him to be the best waltzer she had ever met.

Although Charlotte was certainly not going to commit herself to Henry Halford – she had treated him to a display of 'excessive pride and haughtiness' and had refused to see him the next time he called – the general pro-Orange pressure was becoming well-nigh irresistible, and there were signs that her curiosity was beginning to overcome her misgivings. 'I have agreed without any demur or hesitation to see the young P. when he comes', she told Mercer on 8 December. She meant to do all that was fair and give the young man a chance. The immediate consequence of this apparent change of heart was a dramatic improvement in her relations with her father. The Regent became uncommonly kind and affectionate all of a sudden and, when Charlotte asked if she might go to Kensington to see her mother, replied almost carelessly that she could do as she liked. He would leave it entirely to her discretion and what she knew to be right.

Events now began to move with bewildering speed. The Prince of Orange landed in England late on the evening of 10 December, and Mercer Elphinstone, who got a quick look at him as he passed through Plymouth, was able to send a favourable report to Warwick House. 'I really admire the victory a single glimpse of his form has had upon you', Charlotte wrote back on the 13th , 'and give my permission to your being in love with him for my sake.' Mercer's approval eased Charlotte's mind considerably, since by this time she not only had seen the Prince for herself but had accepted him.

Their meeting had taken place the previous day under cover of a select dinner part at Carlton House, and Cornelia Knight (who had not been invited and was therefore inclined to be huffy) recorded that Charlotte had gone next door wearing an unbecoming gown of violet satin trimmed with black lace and looking 'pale and agitated'. The agitation was understandable, for her father had made her promise that she would make up her mind about the Orange match on the strength of this one encounter. The young Prince (he was actually twenty-three years old) was seated on Charlotte's right at the dinner table and made a genuinely favourable impression. He was shy, 'but presented himself gracefully and perfectly, and tho' he talked little, was master of the subjects he talked of'. He was certainly very plain, but was so lively and animated that the effect of his unprepossessing appearance soon wore off.

After dinner more guests arrived, and according to custom the company walked up and down the ornate, overheated salons of Carlton House making polite conversation. Then came the moment of decision. The Regent appeared and bore Charlotte away into another room to ask her what she had to say. She hesitated for a moment, and he cried out in alarm, 'Then it will not do?' No, replied Charlotte, he was mistaken, she approved what she had seen so far. It does not sound much on which to base a lifetime's commitment to matrimony, but it was more than enough for the Regent, and before she knew where she was Charlotte was being congratulated, embraced, and wept over by her greatly relieved papa, who declared himself to be 'happiest person in the world'. The Prince or Orange was then summoned, and a highly emotional scene ensued which left Charlotte feeling 'quite unstrung', for her father's 'whole heart and soul seemed moved with real parental affection'. Young Prince William behaved uncommonly well, appearing awestruck by the solemnity of the occasion. The Regent joined the betrothed couple's hands and gave them his blessing, but went on to warn them that the engagement must be kept very quiet until the political future of the Netherlands had been settled, and also until the news had been broken to the Queen, who would undoubtedly make things very unpleasant if she were not the first to be informed. Charlotte and the Prince of Orange were left alone to talk and walk about together, and she found it 'really singular' how much they agreed about almost everything. They sat next to one another at supper, and finally parted with a promise from the Regent that he might call at Warwick House on the following day. It was one o'clock before Charlotte herself returned to Warwick House to tell the faithful Chevalier, who had been sitting up for her, that she was engaged to the Prince of Orange. Miss Knight could only remark that the Princess had evidently gained a great victory over herself.

'No,' said Charlotte, 'you would not say so if you were to see him; he is by no means as disagreeable as I expected.'

Next day the Prince came to make his visit, escorted by Lord Bathurst, the Secretary for War, and Miss Knight was able to form her own judgement. On the whole it was favourable. The Chevalier thought him plain and sickly looking (his nickname in the army was Slender Billy), but he shook hands 'very good-humouredly'; and if his manner was a trifle over-hearty and boyish, this was not altogether unpleasing in a young soldier. For her part, Charlotte continued to find her fiancé so amiable and kind that she was encouraged to hope that any lingering shyness in his presence would soon disappear. Sadly, though, her unexpected pleasure in her own status as an engaged girl was to be short-lived.

On the following day, Tuesday 14 December, the Prince of Orange called at Warwick House again, this time escorted by the Prince Regent, who left the young people together while he sat by the fire with Miss Knight in an adjoining room. He told her, in confidence, about the engagement but said the marriage would not take place until the spring, since Dutch affairs had to be settled first. No alterations would be made to Charlotte's household before then and he hoped Miss Knight, as the princess's friend, would give her good advice, 'particularly against flirtation'. As they were talking, the sound of loud sobbing was suddenly heard from across the corridor. The Regent started to his feet and, followed by Miss Knight, hurried to the door of the other room, where they found Charlotte in floods of tears and the Prince of Orange looking 'half frightened' and wholly embarrassed. 'What!' cried the Regent. 'Is he taking his leave?' and without waiting to hear any more declared that they must go, as it was time to leave for the banquet being given by the City in the Prince's honour.

As soon as they had gone, Charlotte sobbed her troubles into Cornelia Knight's sympathetic ear. It seemed the Prince had told her that she would be expected to spend two or three months of every year in Holland when they were married. It was important, he explained, to conciliate the Dutch, who were a stiff-necked lot and would take offence if they got the idea that the wife of their Hereditary Prince thought herself too grand to come and live among them – or that their Hereditary Prince preferred another country to his own. The thing would be for them to try and divide their favours as evenly as possible. Charlotte must never forget she was an English princess but should be prepared to think herself more a Dutchwoman when she was in Holland. Of course, he had added hastily, they would go backwards and forwards constantly and have a house in England as well as Holland. He felt quite an Englishman himself and hoped Charlotte would invite what friends she liked to The Hague to keep her company.

Miss Knight was obviously puzzled by the princess's violent reaction to what, in the circumstance, appeared a not unreasonable demand, but Charlotte had unfortunately convinced herself that, as heiress presumptive, she could not be asked to leave the country. What had really upset her, though, was the fact that no one had seen fit to tell her in advance that she would have to spend some time abroad after her marriage, and she was conscious of a growing sense of having been deliberately deceived. Not by the Prince of Orange – *he* had been all openness and honesty – but by her father, whose recent display of kindness and graciousness it now appeared had been nothing but a trick to catch her.

Charlotte's feelings were in turmoil, her soul, she told Mercer excitedly, 'wrung out to the bottom'. It was true that she had been most agreeably surprised by William. Indeed, the little she had seen of him had delighted her. 'Our tempers and minds I think will perfectly suit,' she wrote on 16 December. 'He is both open, frank, generous minded, warm and affectionately hearted, very lively and sencible and cheerful.' They were fully agreed in their dislike of politics and their desire to keep clear of family quarrels and disputes. They had both promised 'to use no disguise or concealments from one another, and to have perfect and mutual confidence', which, Charlotte believed, was the only way 'to go on well and have a comfortable marriage'. The Prince had shown every sign of wanting to consult her wishes and do all he could to make her happy, and although she was not in love – to say anything of the kind would be absurd – she was persuaded that she would come to have a very great regard for him, which was perhaps 'better to begin with and more likely to last than love'.

Given the circumstances which surrounded so many royal marriages of the period, this all sounded promising, unusually so in fact, but it did not alter Charlotte's resentment at the way in which she had been hustled and outmanoeuvred over the matter of her engagement. She found it especially hard to forgive her father's duplicity. He had never said a single word with regard to her going abroad, and if young William had not the honesty to warn her, she would still have been ignorant. 'I shall ever say to the last moment of my life that the P. *used me ill and deceived* me throughout the whole affair.' But whatever underhand methods had been used to promote it, the Orange match would at least offer an escape route from her present bondage and from the necessity of 'having to submit to every caprice of the P. or his family', and Charlotte did not now wish to undo what had been done.

Meanwhile, William had had to go home to assist at the settlement of his country's constitutional affairs, and Charlotte had to face the prospect of Christmas at Windsor. Visits to the Castle were always an ordeal, but this time there would be the added trials of family reaction to the news of her engagement and her Confirmation, which was to take place in St George's Chapel on Christmas Eve. 'What with *congratulations*,' she wrote to her friend Priscilla Burghersh, 'ill-concealed joy, as ill-concealed *sorrow*, *good* humour and *bad peeping out*, my Confirmation and the Sacrament, and little jokes and witty sayings that were circulating, I was both excessively put out and overcome.' All the same, it might have been worse. The aunts, poor souls, were doing their best to be kind; the Duchess of York, as always, was 'very friendly and affectionate', and the Regent, naturally enough, remained in high good humour, giving his daughter an early birthday present of a diamond bracelet. Even the old Queen was making an effort to be gracious, although she obviously disapproved of the Orange connection, and Charlotte remarked that this was the first time she had ever been treated with any distinguishing civility by her relations.

Eighteen fourteen came in with fog and frost. Charlotte saw the New Year in at Windsor but was back in London in time for her birthday on 7 January. This much-looked-forward-to event was, however, allowed to pass without official notice, and the coming of age of the King's only legitimate grandchild went unmarked by public rejoicing of any kind, 'the war and the great expenses of the nation' being put forward as not very convincing excuses. The Regent himself was out of town, and, apart from a late evening visit by the Dukes of Kent and Sussex, the occasion appears to have been ignored within the royal family as well. Charlotte was understandably hurt. 'My birthday', she wrote, 'was kept quietly at home, and, except for a few cadeaux, totally neglected.' She had gone to see her mother, now installed at Connaught House in Bayswater, but this had done little to cheer her up.

Caroline had declared herself delighted with her new home but she seemed in bad spirits, frequently dissolving into tears of self-pity which would then be 'smothered in *indignant* feelings'. The Princess of Wales, her daughter found,

feels *extremely* her situation, that is to say the *very few* who will visit, who will come near her, and the numbers who now refuse, decline and keep out of her way. She has a great deal of pride and high spirit and feels *mortified*, and fears she may be lower'd in people's eyes. She likes society, hates being shut out of it, and yet if she were to give parties people would then see *who she* is *reduced* to.

Charlotte hated to see her mother unhappy – 'too well do I know the smarts and cuttings of a wounded heart not to feel for her' – and believed her to be 'a very unfortunate woman', who, for all her great faults and errors was 'really oppressed and cruelly used, not even to be treated with the common attentions fitted for her situation'. Not even, indeed, with the common attention of being told of her daughter's engagement before the news was publicly announced.

Charlotte Bury, too, continued to pity her 'poor Princess', despite her unmatched talent for always showing herself in the worst possible light. Caroline, it seemed, had learned nothing during her years in England – learned nothing and forgotten nothing. The regrettable Sapios, father and son – the old Orang Utang [*sic*] and Chanticleer, as Lady Charlotte had privately christened them – were still very much in evidence, and so was Willikin. To the great regret of his benefactress, poor dear Willikin was growing up; and, to Charlotte Bury's horror, Caroline had begun to talk about getting '*another* little boy'. She could not do without a little child in the house, and although she loved Willikin dearly, he was growing too big, too much of a man. Lady Charlotte said nothing – 'What could I say?' she inquired rhetorically in her Journal – but her thoughts were full of foreboding. If the Princess were to adopt another very young child, no matter how innocent the transaction, the worst construction would inevitably be put upon it. Poor foolish woman! sighed Lady Charlotte. Could she not see that, by taking another child under her protection, she would lay herself open to fresh accusations of immorality? But although Caroline kept up the tease for several days, returning to her strange obsession for babies and child-bearing and giving the household heart failure by mischievously hinting that she was pregnant, she changed her mind about staging a re-run of the William Austin scandal and, to everyone's intense relief, went back to her regular after-dinner occupation of sticking pins into a wax effigy of the Regent, which she would then put to 'roast and melt in the fire'. 'Her Royal Highness really has a superstitious belief that destroying this effigy of her husband will bring to pass the destruction of his royal person,' wrote Charlotte Bury, torn between compassion, exasperation, and a strong desire to laugh. Her long-suffering ladies did their best to fill the long dull evening hours, but nothing really entertained the Princess of Wales except the old, stale, and unprofitable recital of her grievances.

Princess Charlotte dined at Connaught House a couple of times during January and February but she, too, seemed 'low spirited'. There were a number of reasons for this. Charlotte was worried about the letters she had been unwise enough to write to Lieutenant, now Captain, Hesse at the time of their brief 'romance' back in 1812. She had authorized Mercer to try and get them back, but Hesse, now abroad on active service with his regiment in Wellington's army, was proving disturbingly difficult to pin down. It would be embarrassing, especially just now, if any of these records of her weakness, as she described them, were to fall into the wrong hands. Other vexations included the freezing weather, which left Charlotte congealed in a state of 'complete stupidity and listlessness', suffering from a persistent cold and cough, and the remonstrances of the Duchess of Leeds, who was 'more odious and severe about bills and money than anything ever was'. Charlotte was finding it impossible to manage on her £15 a month pocket-money and £800-a-year dress allowance. In fact, she does not seem to have tried, and was already in debt to the tune of some £15,000. Matters were not improved by the Prince Regent's return to London after a hectic round of country-house visits. He brought with him a royal hangover, a bad attack of gout, and a querulous temper which he proceeded to take out on the unlucky Cornelia Knight, who was summoned to Carlton House to listen to his complaints that Charlotte had ordered a carriage from a firm recommended by the Duke of Kent instead of his own coach builders, and that the offending vehicle was to be painted green instead of yellow like his own. The Regent went on to grumble that his daughter was spending far too much on jewellery. It was no good her trying to keep such things hidden from him, because tradesmen always talked, and he thought it shameful that young ladies of immense fortune should accept valuable gifts from Princess Charlotte. (This was a dig at Mercer Elphinstone, who had received an expensive Christmas present from the princess.) Charlotte, her father continued disagreeably, must be content to do without amusements that spring, as he was quite unable to entertain for her 'under present circumstances'. In any case, she should not now be thinking of frivolity; she was about to be married and must think of the duties of a wife.

Unfortunately, the more Charlotte thought about her duties as the wife of the Hereditary Prince of Orange, the less she liked them. Shut up in Warwick House with nothing to do but yawn over her piano and sketchbook, act little French 'proverbs' or charades written by Miss Knight, and watch the skaters disporting themselves in the white Siberian landscape of St James's Park, she had ample leisure to think – and to listen to the voices of those warning her to beware. Prominent among the Cassandras was her Uncle Augustus. From his stance on the far left of the Whig party, the Duke of Sussex approved of the Orange match in principle. He knew and 'delighted in' the Prince's character, and Charlotte would find it much easier to assert her own opinions as a married woman. But she must never forget her position or allow her husband to forget it. As for her going abroad, it was all a trick on the part of the government, possibly even a plot to get her out of the way. There could be absolutely no question of the heir presumptive leaving England, it would be quite improper, and if necessary Sussex would raise the matter in the House of Lords.

Charlotte was, perversely, almost sorry. Now that she had got used to the idea, she had quite begun to look forward to the prospect of a little foreign travel – just a *short tour* of course, perhaps three summer months, which should be enough to become acquainted with the *most desirable portions* of the European Continent. But having made up her mind to be guided by the Opposition, she wrote again to Lord Grey, who replied on 7 February, agreeing that it was 'unquestionably of the utmost moment' that she should not be pressed to go abroad against her inclinations and equally important that her habits should be formed among the people she was to govern. However, Grey did not believe there was anything intrinsically impossible or improper about her going 'at any time' out of England – always providing the time of going and length of residence abroad were left entirely to her discretion. He was against the idea of having the matter discussed in Parliament, except as a last resort, and suggested that Charlotte should try to settle it privately and amicably with her future husband.

The Prince was still in Holland, and apart from 'a very kind and really a manly feeling' letter written to her on her birthday, Charlotte and her betrothed do not appear to have had much communication during January and February, though she was told he constantly wore a gold ring she had sent him.

At last, on 2 March, things began to happen. Charlotte was sent for to Carlton House, where the Regent still had his gouty foot propped up on a chair, to be shown the letters brought over by Baron Van der Duyn Van Maasdam, Grand Master of the Dutch royal household, in which the newly enthroned King of the Netherlands and his son formally asked for her hand in marriage. On the following day the Baron paid a visit of ceremony at Warwick House. 'A sulky boy in petticoats' was his verdict on the future Hereditary Princess of Orange. Van Maasdam had also brought a portrait of the Hereditary Prince and a sum of money to be spent by Charlotte on jewellery.

The marriage was now being openly talked about. It had already been announced to the States of Holland and would, it was expected, be officially communicated to Parliament at Westminster before Easter. Charlotte, however, was growing steadily more uneasy – especially over the matter of her future domicile. She had written very frankly on this subject to her fiancé, and his response had not been reassuring. After the freedom and excitement of his army service, Slender Billy was already bored with the slow pace of life in his native land and the stiff, old-fashioned manners of his parents' Court. (To Charlotte, stories of the Dutch royal ladies spending their evenings virtuously sewing comforts for the troops must have sounded horribly reminiscent of Windsor, with its grim circle of aunts sitting silently over their needlework.) But while young William would have been only too pleased to spend his time enjoying the amenities of English society, he was not his own master, and it now appeared that he and his bride would be expected to live in Holland for at least six months of the year. Indeed, arrangements were already in hand to provide them with houses in town and country. What was worrying Charlotte was that nothing had yet been said about a house in England.

She was by this time taking the advice of that shrewd legal and political operator Henry Brougham. Brougham had no doubt that the Regent's 'great object' was to get his daughter out of the way and living with her in-laws. Knowing Charlotte and the prevailing climate of British public opinion, he felt equally confident that any attempt to keep her in Holland against her will could quickly be frustrated by 'a few lines of remonstrance' or, if necessary, an appeal to Parliament. All the same, he wrote to Lord Grey on 17 March,

> upon constitutional grounds, and wholly independent of her personal convenience or feelings upon the matter, it should seem that Parliamentary notice ought to be taken of the singular situation in which this marriage will place her – viz., under control of a person *not amenable to our laws*, and who may carry her out of the realm. Then if she is carried abroad, and the crown devolves on her, as it may any day, can any situation be conceived more absurd than for the Queen of this country to be abroad as a subject of a foreign state? and a subject, by the laws of that state, incapable of leaving its territory without the consent of her husband?

Such a situation would clearly be undesirable as well as absurd; but while the Opposition lawyers continued to consult and seek for precedents, external events temporarily at least pushed

Charlotte's problems into the ground. 'Affairs began to take the most favourable turn on the Continent,' commented Cornelia Knight in her Autobiography. News arrived of the defeat of the French army by Lord Wellington and of Bordeaux opening its gates and declaring for the Bourbons. On 31 March the Allied armies entered Paris, and shortly afterwards 'this delightful intelligence' was followed by the news of Napoleon's abdication and the restoration of Louis XVIII to the throne of his ancestors. London was illuminated, and 'joy and good order reigned throughout the metropolis'.

Yet there was little joy for Princess Charlotte. Her marriage contract was now being drawn up, but she had not been consulted on any of its provisions, and it looked as if she would not see it at all until it was presented for her signature. Lord Grey was still against raising the matter in Parliament – he feared it would do Charlotte's cause no good if she were to become too closely identified with the Opposition at a time when the Tory administration was riding high on the tide of victory. Instead he suggested she should write to her father 'upon the subject of her proposed residence in Holland, and stating what she feels with respect to it'. But his lordship cautioned that the Princess must not shut her eyes to the dangers of embarking on a personal contest with the Regent, and should 'consider her own ability to support the attacks to which she will be exposed . . . both to cajole and to intimidate her'. Grey confessed that he dreaded the sort of struggle in which she might find herself engaged, and felt the responsibility of advising her in what was 'altogether a most trying and a most cruel situation'.

Charlotte can have harboured few illusions about the sort of reaction her letter would be likely to provoke, but on 15 April she wrote to her 'dearest father, her natural friend and protector', asking to be allowed to see the draft of the marriage contract, on which, after all, the whole happiness of her future life must depend. As she reminded her dearest father, not a word had been said on the subject of domicile when the Orange match was first proposed to her, and if she had then had the slightest suspicion that her home was not to be in England she would never have accepted. She therefore hoped it would be 'stated as a condition in the treaty that I shall never be obliged to leave England contrary to my inclination'. She also wished it to be clearly understood in advance that her residence should 'permanently be fixed in this country', and expressed her sense of unease at hearing of 'no house being provided, nor establishment named'.

The Regent was predictably enraged by this evidence of insubordination and summoned Cornelia Knight to his presence to receive the first intimations of his displeasure. There was absolutely no question of anybody planning to banish Charlotte, but it was a wife's duty to follow her husband, and to include the sort of stipulation she was demanding in the marriage contract would be tantamount to providing for a divorce. As far as a house was concerned, he had been considering various possibilities in the neighbourhood, but it was not easy to find anything suitable, and he might have to build. Meanwhile, she and the Prince of Orange could perfectly well stay at Carlton House when they were in England. Charlotte, he repeated, had nothing to fear. Neither she nor her fiancé had any business to see the marriage contract, that was something to be settled by fathers, but a generous provision of £50,000 a year plus the clause that her eldest son, as a future King of England, was to be brought up and educated in the country, should be proof enough that nothing prejudicial to her interests was intended. If she persisted in her unreasonable demands, then the matter would have to be discussed in Cabinet; the engagement would be broken off, and he, the Prince Regent, would certainly not consent to a marriage with anyone else. If, on the other hand, she withdrew her letter and renounced her demands, then he was prepared to forgive and forget 'what had so deeply offended him'. Miss Knight was then dismissed, with instructions to repeat all this to Charlotte and return next day with her answer.

The answer was not, however, such a one as to procure the Chevalier a favourable reception, for, she recorded, 'Princess Charlotte adhered firmly, though respectfully and very affectionately, to the purport of her first letter.' She was grieved at having caused Papa displeasure but could not retract one word of her determinations. She also refuted the Regent's quite outrageous assertion that the Orange marriage had been first proposed by her and was being arranged to gratify her wish. If her father really believed this to be the case, then he had been deceived and it could only have been by Sir Henry Halford.

The battle of wills continued through April and May. The Duke of York and Charlotte's old friend William Adam, Chancellor of the Duchy of Cornwall, were brought in to 'try and talk her over but failed to make any noticeable impression. When her uncle Frederick cited the case of Princess (later Queen) Mary, daughter of James II, who had married a previous Prince of Orange and gone to live in Holland, Charlotte retorted with Queen Mary Tudor, who had married Philip of Spain but had never left England. When the Duke remarked that she appeared to regard herself as the heir apparent, whereas she could 'hardly be considered as presumptive heiress', Charlotte replied coldly that she was perfectly aware that *legally* she was only heir presumptive, but in the circumstances she thought the difference was rather nominal than actual. When William Adam observed that it was supposed Princess Charlotte must have access to legal advice, as her letters 'were not those of a woman', Cornelia Knight reminded him that the Princess had gone through a course of study on the laws of England. Adam only smiled, but the well-founded suspicion that his daughter was being guided by his political opponents was certainly contributing to the Regent's displeasure.

Early one morning towards the end of April, Miss Knight was called downstairs to see a Captain St George, just arrived from Holland and sent by Lord Bathurst. The visitor, she found, was the Hereditary Prince of Orange himself, summoned by a harassed Lord Liverpool in the hope that he might prove to have superior powers of persuasion. Charlotte was still in bed. She was unwell and was irritated by this unheralded arrival. At first she refused to see her fiance but presently relented, and they had an amicable conversation. Charlotte had nothing against the Prince personally, she told him, and promised he should see copies of all the correspondence that had passed on the subject of residence. William then went next door to see the Regent. An hour or two later, says Miss Knight, 'he flew back' with the news that the Regent wanted them both to go over, and 'all would be forgiven'. Charlotte at once scented another trap. She was not about to be tricked a second time and 'most earnestly entreated to be left quiet for the rest of the day'. Much letter writing and anxious toing and froing between Warwick House, Carlton House, Downing Street, and The Hague went on during the next few weeks. But as it became clear that Charlotte could neither be threatened nor be cajoled out of her determination to retain full powers of discretion over whether, when, and for how long she went overseas, the Cabinet grudgingly agreed that an article to this effect should be drafted for inclusion in the marriage treaty, and the matter was referred to the Dutch government for its approval.

Meanwhile London had been filling up with foreign royalty in anticipation of the forthcoming peace celebrations. So much so, in fact, that the Prince of Orange was obliged to make do with lodgings over his tailor's shop in Clifford Street. The Queen was to hold two Drawing-Rooms in honour of the distinguished visitors, but what should have been a joyful reunion of 'illustrious personages' – most of whom were connected by blood or marriage or both – only provided an opportunity for yet another demonstration of the royal family's implacable hostility towards the Princess of Wales. She would not be welcome at Buckingham House, she was informed, since the Regent intended to be present and remained fixed in his unalterable resolution never to meet his estranged wife 'upon any occasion either in public or private'.

Caroline's advisers had differed over her response to this latest outrage. At Samuel Whitbread's dictation, she wrote to the Queen, submitting, more in sorrow than in anger and from 'motives of personal consideration towards her Majesty', to the harsh proceedings of the Prince Regent. Brougham thought this 'mealy mouthed' and that Caroline should have stood on her rights and gone to Court 'in spite of the Regent and his whiskers'. However, care was taken to publicize the reason why the Princess of Wales was absent from her appointed place in the Queen's Drawing-Room, and Caroline wrote to her husband protesting bitterly at the injustice of his decree excluding her from the society of so many of her own kinsfolk, and reminding him that the time was coming when he would have to meet her in public – as for example at their daughter's marriage. (When Charlotte was presently sent a list of the guests to be invited to her wedding from which her mother's name was missing, she promptly returned it with her own name crossed out.)

Caroline was not the only person to be conspicuously absent from the festivities of the victory summer of 1814. Charlotte did attend one of the Drawing-Rooms – the first time she had done so – but she was still in deep disgrace with her papa and was not invited to any of the parties at Carlton House or to any of the other entertainments provided for the visiting royals.

The Prince Regent was not enjoying the banquets and balls, the parades and receptions of the brilliant social season now in full swing. He and his mother were hissed and hooted at in the streets, but when his hateful, horrible wife appeared at the Opera the whole house rose to applaud her, and her carriage was mobbed by a sympathetic multitude who enquired hopefully if she would like them to burn down Carlton House. His tiresome daughter, too, was surrounded by cheering throngs whenever she appeared in public, although, said Cornelia Knight, she did nothing to encourage them.

The Regent's temper was not improved by the attitude adopted by some of his guests, notably the Grand Duchess Catherine, widow of Prince George of Oldenburg and favourite sister of the Tsar of Russia. The Grand Duchess and the Prince Regent disliked one another on sight. She thought he looked 'used up by dissipation' and was unimpressed by his famous charm. Seated next to him at dinner she brought up the subject of Charlotte. Why did the Princess never appear with her father?

'My daughter is too young, Madam, to go into the world,' came the reply.

'But not too young for you to have fixed on a husband for her.'

'When she is married, Madam, she will do as her husband pleases; for the present she does as I wish,' came the reply.

'Ah, yes,' murmured the Grand Duchess, poisonously sweet, 'your Highness is right. Between husband and wife there can only be one will.' After that, of course, it was war.

The Grand Duchess took a close interest in Charlotte, whom she described as being white, fresh-looking, and 'as appetizing as possible'. Rather too well covered, though, especially over the hips. Charlotte Bury had also remarked recently that the young princess was losing her figure and would soon be as stout as her mother. Both ladies were in agreement about Charlotte's pretty hands and feet, and the Grand Duchess also praised her handsome nose, delicious mouth, and lively, pale blue eyes, although they did sometimes display that fixed stare so characteristic of the House of Brunswick. The Russian thought it a crime that so delicate a creature should have been allowed to fall into such tomboyish ways. The English princess's vigorous handshake, bouncing walk, and general lack of royal dignity and reserve were really quite breathtaking. For her part Charlotte took a great fancy to Duchess Catherine, and the two became very friendly – to the added annoyance of the Regent, who suspected the Russians of intriguing against the Anglo-Dutch alliance. Nor did Anglo-

Russian relations improve with the arrival of the Tsar at the head of the other Allied sovereigns. His Imperial Majesty upset all the arrangements by refusing to stay in the accommodation prepared for him at St James's Palace and going instead to join his sister at Pulteney's Hotel. He snubbed the Regent's current mistress, hobnobbed with the Opposition, and threatened to visit the Princess of Wales. Worst of all from his host's point of view was the rapturous excitement with which he was greeted by the Londoners – especially the ladies, who were all wild for the handsome Alexander. The welcome accorded to the Tsar, and indeed to the other visiting grandees in their picturesque uniforms mounted on the very steeds they had ridden in battle against the Corsican ogre, served cruelly to emphasize the plight of England's fat, stay-at-home Prince, who dared not venture on to the streets of his own capital for fear of insult. Small wonder poor Prinny was reported to be 'worn out with fuss, fatigue and *rage*'.

Certainly he was in no very good temper when he arrived at Warwick House on 6 June to inform his daughter that she had won her battle over the terms of her marriage contract. Seeing the Dutch were prepared to concede all her demands, he had withdrawn his objections, and a clause guaranteeing that she could not be taken or kept out of the country without her consent would now be written into the treaty. Assuming 'a half-threatening, half-cajoling tone', the Regent then suggested that having gained her point Charlotte might now retract as a gesture of goodwill to the Orange family, who had done so much for her – more than he would have done – and who might be offended at her persistence. Charlotte, naturally enough, refused. She was sure the Dutch royal family would continue to give her their 'cordial support'.

On the face of it everything should now have been plain sailing, but Charlotte seems to have remained in a state of painful indecision about her future. She told her mother that she was determined *not* to marry the Prince of Orange. Apart from the fact that his being approved by the family was quite enough to make him disapproved of by her, he was so ugly that she was sometimes really obliged to turn away in disgust when he spoke to her. A couple of weeks later, according to Lady Charlotte Bury, she was saying that everything was fixed for her marriage, that she did not love the Prince of Orange, but that she must be married. 'It only shows what faith is to be placed in her words', commented Lady Charlotte, who thought Princess Charlotte's inclination would continue to vary 'with every wind that blows'.

It was undoubtedly true that a number of contrary winds were blowing round the unfortunate Princess Charlotte at this time. Her mother was against the marriage. She naturally opposed anything the Regent favoured and in any case had always disliked the Orange family. The Whigs, too, had raised another bogy. If Charlotte got married and went to live in Holland, there would be nothing to keep Caroline in England – she was already talking of going abroad. The Regent would then be able to divorce her, marry again, and perhaps have a son. And where would Charlotte be then? It seems likely that the Opposition, or at least its more irresponsible fringe, was more concerned with keeping mother and daughter at home, where they could be more easily manipulated for party advantage, than with the credibility of this interesting scenario. It was, however, being canvassed with every appearance of seriousness, and its effect on Charlotte was said to be magical.

Even more magical, it appears, was the effect of the charms of one of the Prussian princes whom she had encountered at the one Carlton House dinner party she had been allowed to attend. There is some doubt as to the identity of this individual, but the most convincing candidate was Frederick William Henry Augustus, usually known as Augustus and referred to by Charlotte as 'F', a 35 year-old notorious womanizer and the black sheep of the Prussian royal family. Charlotte fell heavily for 'F' and, with the assistance of Cornelia Knight, contrived to have several secret assignations with him at Warwick House. It was a foolish and potentially damaging episode with no future in it, but it did nothing to increase the Princess's enthusiasm for her approaching nuptials. Despite her father's efforts to keep her out of harm's – and temptation's – way, Charlotte was becoming increasingly aware of her own sexuality and of the fact that there were many more and more seductive fish in the sea than the Hereditary Prince of Orange. Apart from the enigmatic 'F', there was a selection of Russian grand dukes, described in glowing terms by Grand Duchess Catherine, and there was the good-looking, soft-spoken Leopold of Saxe-Coburg, who had come to London in the Tsar's train.

Slender Billy was not helping matters by accepting invitations to all the Carlton House parties from which Charlotte had been excluded, getting tipsy, and neglecting his betrothed, who was growing steadily more disenchanted with her situation. Her grandmother was now ordering her trousseau – telling her she would only need one Court dress, as hoops were not worn in Holland – and her Aunt Mary wrote to say that, as soon as the Tsar and the King of Prussia had gone home, 'it was the intention of the Prince [Regent] to send for the Orange family and to have the wedding immediately'. This, according to Miss Knight, threw Charlotte 'into great alarm'. She was still deeply suspicious that a plot was hatching to get her married and out of the country before she could open her mouth to protest, and she made up her mind to have 'an explanation' with the Prince of Orange without delay. This took place at Warwick House on 16 June, when Charlotte announced flatly that in view of the way her mother was being treated she could not possibly go off to Holland leaving the Princess alone and unsupported. Quite apart from the considerations of duty and natural affection, it would be a most unpopular thing to do at a time when the tide of public opinion was flowing so strongly in Caroline's favour. Whenever Charlotte appeared out of doors, the crowds gathered round, urging her never to forsake her mother, and she was convinced that her own interests were 'materially connected' with those of her mother. It was therefore more than ever necessary that she should not leave England, 'as when she had a house of her own, it must be open to the Princess'. She must show her duty equally to both her parents 'without entering into their unfortunate differences'.

The Prince of Orange had been long enough in England to know that this was impossible. He seemed, says Cornelia Knight, 'greatly hurt' and embarrassed, muttering that he had always hoped Charlotte would agree to spend most of the year with him in Holland and that if she stuck to her latest determination 'he knew not how the affair could go on'. It could not, of course; and as far as Charlotte was concerned it was already over. To remove any possibility of misunderstanding, she wrote to Clifford Street that same evening that, after 'reconsidering' the morning's conversation, she was still of the opinion 'that the duties and affections that naturally bind us to our respective countries render our marriage incompatible, not only from motives of policy, but domestick happiness'. She therefore considered the engagement to be '*totally and for ever at an end*'. She asked William to explain matters to the Prince Regent 'in whatever manner is most agreeable to you', expressed her 'sincere concern' at being the cause of giving him pain, and ended with 'sincerest and best wishes' for his future happiness.

William waited two days before sending a rather huffy note refusing to break the news to the Regent, which he thought was Charlotte's business, and hoping she would never 'feel any cause to repent' the step she had taken. Slender Billy had not sought the marriage for himself in the first place, and there is no reason to suppose he had ever fallen in love, but nobody likes being jilted.

Charlotte now had to write to her father in a hurry – putting the blame for the delay on William's 'neglect'. His reply was prompt, and terse, expressing 'astonishment, grief and concern'. He was obviously furious but for the time being at least was holding his fire.

Charlotte had not mentioned her feelings about her mother as being the cause of her broken engagement when writing to her father, and few people believed this to be the true reason. Charlotte Bury certainly did not. 'I know too much of all parties', she wrote, 'to believe that Princess Charlotte, in her heart, quarrelled with her lover from any motive of real tenderness towards her mother.' Her ladyship thought that 'what the Princess of Wales told me some time ago is perfectly true, namely, that her daughter did not at all admire the Prince of Orange, and only wanted to be her own mistress; and now finding . . . that end would not be answered by marrying him, she has determined to break off the engagement'. The Opposition mischief-makers, of course, were exultant. 'By God! it is capital,' wrote that incorrigible old gossip Thomas Creevey to his wife. 'And now what do you suppose has produced this sudden attachment to her mother? It arises from the profound resources of old Brougham, and is, in truth, one of the most brilliant movements in his campaign.' 'Old Brougham' was less pleased when Caroline chose this moment of all others to accept what was in effect a government bribe of an increase in her allowance and declare her intention of going abroad. 'I suppose you have heard of Mother P. bungling the thing so compleatly – snapping eagerly at the cash, and concluding with a civil observation about unwillingness to "impair the Regent's tranquility!!"'

Sober Lord Grey thought Caroline's 'determination' understandable, considering the circumstances of her situation, but 'a most unfortunate measure both for the Princess herself and the Princess Charlotte'. Grey was also worried about the impression which might be created by Charlotte's breaking off her engagement, and in a letter to Mercer, who was a constant visitor at Warwick House at this time, he advised 'the most cautious conduct' and no public statements, at least until such time as 'explanation shall be rendered necessary'. 'I much fear', he went on, 'that the Princess's difficulties will now be greater than ever. The Prince's note evinces violent displeasure, and the Princess must prepare herself for its effects.'

The ominous silence from Carlton House continued while the Allied sovereigns were still in London – it is not easy to conduct a full-scale family row in front of visitors. But on 23 June the Regent escorted the Tsar and the King of Prussia to Portsmouth for a review of the fleet, and, after bidding them farewell at Petworth House, he returned to town ready to do battle with his rebellious daughter. The opening salvo was fired by the Bishop of Salisbury, who, in a private interview with Charlotte, warned her that unless she wrote a submissive letter to her father, expressing contrition for having offended him and holding out some hope that after a decent interval she might be persuaded to agree to renew her engagement to marry the Prince of Orange, 'arrangements very disagreeable to herself would take place'.

The Great U.P. was known to be in regular contact with the Prime Minister and with Charlotte's old enemy, Lord Chancellor Eldon, and his words therefore had a disagreeably authentic ring about them. Charlotte wrote on 9 July expressing her dismay at having incurred Papa's displeasure and asking to be given an opportunity to justify and explain her conduct in person. All the 'distresses' she had suffered recently were seriously affecting her health. She felt most unwell and begged to be restored to the tranquillity of Papa's favour and affection. She did not mention the Prince of Orange or give any hint that she might change her mind. Lord Grey thought she was quite right not to do so. Charlotte might, in the short term, have to bear the full weight of official displeasure – and he advised patience and submission as being her best, indeed her only weapons – but however unpleasant the next few months might prove, anything was better than risking her private happiness and the public interest by allowing herself to be intimidated into renewing her treaty with the Prince of Orange. She could not hope or expect 'that the feeling of mutual confidence and affection, which ought to attend such a union, could now be effectually restored'.

On Monday 11 July the Bishop of Salisbury called again at Warwick House and told an anxious Princess Charlotte and Cornelia Knight that something was about to be done, but 'he was not at liberty to mention *what*'. Shortly after five o'clock a message arrived from the Regent summoning Charlotte and Miss Knight to Carlton House. Charlotte's courage failed her. She was feeling too wretched and too ill to face a scene with her father and used the painful swollen knee which had been troubling her for some time as an excuse, so that Cornelia Knight had to enter the lion's den alone. She found the Regent 'very cold, very bitter and very silent'. Miss Knight rushed nervously into speech. She was afraid His Royal Highness might have heard gossip linking the Prince of Saxe-Coburg with Princess Charlotte and wished to contradict it. It was true that, since the dismissal of Slender Billy, Leopold had become quite attentive. When Charlotte went to the Pulteney Hotel to say goodbye to the Grand Duchess Catherine, he had been hovering ready to escort her through the crowds to her carriage, and when she drove out in the Park he would ride up to her and 'endeavour to be noticed'. He had called once only at Warwick House and had not been asked to drink tea with the princess. Although he had paid her many compliments Charlotte had given him no encouragement and had received him with no more than common civility. But it seemed the Regent was not concerned with Prince Leopold, a most honourable young man who had, in any case, written to him fully explaining his conduct. No, it was not Leopold but Prince Augustus of Prussia who had been frequenting Warwick House and making up to Charlotte. 'I justified Prince Augustus, as he well deserved,' recorded Miss Knight, denying that he had ever uttered a word 'tending to a proposal'. She thought the Regent seemed satisfied, but he still insisted on Charlotte's coming to see him. He would expect her the following afternoon, unless Dr Baillie could say she was physically incapable of walking.

When Cornelia returned to her anxious princess, Warwick House was full of rumours. The Duchess of Leeds had already been asked to send in her resignation, and Miss Knight fully expected her own dismissal at any moment. Charlotte told one of her pages 'that it was possible all the servants might be sent away, but that she would never forget them, and would take them again whenever it was in her power'. It looked very much as if the whole Warwick House ménage was to be broken up, and Charlotte wrote frantically to Mercer late that evening, begging her to come *as early* as possible in the morning. She was determined not to be inveigled into going to Carlton House.

> I *am lost* if I set my foot. The plan is to be a *sudden one*, when once there to *keep me*, and *not* to *allow* my return. . . . Whatever is to be done is to be *sudden*. Tomorrow may probably be my last day, God knows, in this house. . . . I feel myself likely to be parted, cruelly torn away from you. No letters perhaps will reach but opened first. We may not be permitted to meet. If we do, always with a witness. . . . I dread everything and I know not why I fancy horrors in every one and thing round me.

The following day, Tuesday the 12th, passed in a state of agonizing suspense. Although Dr Baillie pronounced Charlotte quite capable of walking round to Carlton House, and indeed advised her to go, she refused. She felt far to ill and too upset, and wrote instead to her father begging him to come to her. At about six o'clock he came, accompanied by the Bishop of Salisbury. His lordship was left downstairs with Miss Knight while father and daughter were shut up together for three-quarters of an hour. Then the Bishop was summoned to join them. Another fifteen minutes passed. The door then opened,' says Miss Knight, 'and she [Charlotte] came out in the greatest agony, saying she had but one instant to speak to me, for that the Prince asked for me.' They went together into Charlotte's dressing-room, and the princess told her faithful friend that 'all was over'. Cornelia was to be dismissed and the servants turned off. A new set of ladies was already waiting to take over. Charlotte was to be taken to Carlton House and from there to Cranbourne Lodge, 'in the midst of Windsor Forest', where she would see no one but the Queen once a week, If she did not agree to go immediately the Regent would himself sleep at Warwick House that night. 'I begged her to be calm', wrote Miss Knight 'and advised her to go over as soon as possible, assuring her that her friends would not forget her.' But Charlotte was in no mood for calm. She fell on her knees 'in the greatest agitation, exclaiming "God almighty grant me patience!"'

At this point Cornelia had to go to the Regent, who told her that he was sorry to have to put a lady to inconvenience but he needed her room that evening for the new ladies. Miss Knight asked how she had offended, 'but he said he made no complaint, and would make none; that he had a right to make any changes he pleased and that he was blamed for having let things go on as they had done'. He repeated his apology for putting her to inconvenience, and the Chevalier replied with dignity that, her father the Admiral having served the King for fifty years and sacrificed health and fortune in the process, it would be strange if she could not put up with the temporary annoyance of being turned out of her place at an hour's notice.

While this conversation was in progress, some dramatic developments were taking place. Forgetting all about patience and submission, Charlotte had hurried back to her bedroom, seized a bonnet from her astonished maid, and vanished. A few moments later one of the Warwick House footmen was saying in surprise to a fellow servant, 'Well, if ever I saw the Princess Charlotte in my life, I saw her run down the back stairs just now!'

EIGHT

The Flight of the Princess

I have just run off.

Princess Charlotte to Brougham

Charlotte had run away. Her bad knee forgotten, she rushed out into the summer twilight and on down the narrow lane which connected Warwick House with Pall Mall. The sight of a young lady alone and on foot was sufficiently unusual to attract attention – especially a young lady in an obvious state of agitation – and a gentleman looking out of the window of a Pall Mall picture dealer's premises came out into the street to offer his assistance to this damsel in distress. Charlotte asked him to call a hackney-carriage and told the driver to take her 'towards Oxford Street'. When they got there she asked to be taken to the Princess of Wales's house in Connaught Place and ordered the jarvey to drive faster. He had not recognized his passenger and thought, according to his later account, that she was probably a lady's maid going to spend the evening with the servants at Connaught House. No doubt he was suitably impressed when the 'lady's maid' was bowed through the front entrance and he was rewarded with three guineas for his trouble.

Charlotte had found a temporary sanctuary but found it disconcertingly empty. The Princess of Wales had gone to visit friends at Blackheath, and a groom had to be sent pelting off to find her and fetch her back. Charlotte's next act was to summon the useful Henry Brougham to her side, but

Brougham was also unfortunately dining out, and a further nerve-stretching wait ensued while he was tracked down. Nor was he particularly pleased to be found. He was tired out, having been up most of the previous night working on a case; and thinking the summons came from Caroline, who often sent for him quite unnecessarily, he at first refused to go. Only when the messenger insisted that he was wanted 'on most particular business' did he feel reluctantly obliged to comply, dozing off as soon as he stepped into the carriage which had been sent to fetch him. But when he stumbled, still half-asleep, into the drawing-room at Connaught House and found both his hands seized by Princess Charlotte, exclaiming how impatient she had been at the delay in reaching him, all desire for sleep abruptly departed – his sharp legal brain shifting rapidly into top gear as he enquired by what extraordinary accident he had the honour and pleasure of seeing her Royal Highness. 'Oh, it is a too long to tell now,' replied Charlotte airily, 'for I have ordered dinner and hope it will soon come up.' But she added that she had 'run off', leaving Warwick House alone and getting into the first hackney-coach she could see.

Caroline now arrived, accompanied by her lady-in-waiting Charlotte Lindsay, the same who had once acted as courier for Charlotte's unlicensed correspondence with Mercer and, more recently with Brougham. The party sat down to dinner. Charlotte was in tearing high spirits – 'seeming to enjoy herself like a bird set loose from its cage', commented Brougham in an unconscious echo of George Keppel's description of little Charlotte released from Warwick House all those years ago. Dinner proceeded 'very merrily', but Brougham felt the need for reinforcements in the battle to come. Lord Grey was out of town, and neither Whitbread nor Tierney were to be found. However, Brougham happened to know that the Duke of Sussex, a stalwart supporter of the radical Whigs, was dining nearby and wrote a hasty note begging his Royal Highness to step round to Connaught House without delay.

Meanwhile a number of other personages had begun converging on Bayswater from the general direction of Pall Mall. There had never been any doubt as to where Charlotte had gone. As soon as Cornelia Knight emerged from her confrontation with the Regent to find Charlotte missing and her devoted maid Mrs Louis in tears, Mercer, who had been changing in the Princess's bedroom, came out to say she had heard Charlotte say she was going to her mother and that she had disappeared before they could stop her. The Regent took the news very coolly and even, according to the indignant Miss Knight, 'seemed pleased, saying he was glad that everybody would now see what she (Charlotte) was, and that it would be known on the Continent and no one would marry her'.

Mercer and the Bishop of Salisbury now offered to go in search of the runaway and suggested that Miss Knight should accompany them. This she refused to do, 'for that I did not wish to be in *that house* – meaning the Princess of Wales' – but that if I went, and Princess Charlotte asked me to stay with her, I could not refuse remaining with her *there or in a prison*'.

Mercer and the Great U.P. arrived while the Connaught House party were still at the dinner table, but though Mercer was at once invited to join them, the BishUP was left to cool his heels below. Other representatives of officialdom – Lord Chancellor Eldon, Lord Ellenborough, the Lord Chief Justice, Mr Adam and another lawyer and supporter of the Prince Regent, John Leach – were now queueing up in a fleet of hackney-coaches. As each name was announced, Caroline and Charlotte, amid hoots of merriment, decided what was to be done with them. Eldon was to wait in his hackney, never the most comfortable of conveyances. Brougham tried to put in a word for Ellenborough, who was, after all, his chief, but in vain. It was decreed that he, too, should remain in the street with Old Bags. In his own account of the night's events, Old Bags says that he informed the princess that a carriage was at the door and he and his colleagues were waiting to attend her home. 'But home she would not go. She kicked and bounced but would not go . . . I told her I was sorry for it,' Eldon went on; 'for until she did go, she would be obliged to entertain us, as we could not leave her.' In fact, it seems that none of the law officers actually spoke to Charlotte, and no one sent from the Regent was allowed upstairs. Charlotte did, however, take advantage of the Great U.P.'s presence in the house to use him as a messenger, sending him with a letter to her father in which she set out her terms for returning home. These included the reinstatement of Cornelia Knight and a promise that she might keep her personal maid and receive visits from Mercer.

Cornelia Knight was still at Warwick House, awaiting developments. She had borrowed a carriage from her friend Lady Salisbury and, when she heard, about nine o'clock, that the Bishop had returned to Carlton House without Charlotte, decided to go herself to Connaught Place. There she was welcomed into the drawing-room but was not allowed to see Charlotte alone, Mercer Elphinstone rather officiously interposing to say she had promised the Regent not to leave the princess alone with anyone. Cornelia replied 'rather stiffly' that surely she might be considered safe, and finally Charlotte came with her to the further end of the room behind a pillar. Here the Chevalier handed over the princess's seals, a key and a letter which had arrived after her flight. We are not told who this letter was from or if it had been expected. Was it perhaps from F., and had Cornelia been waiting for it?

Amidst all these comings and goings, Henry Brougham was trying to get some sort of coherent statement from Charlotte as to what had caused her to run away. 'She said', he recalled, 'she could not bear any longer the treatment she met with.' All the familiar complaints were brought out again – her general lack of liberty, the changing of her ladies without consultation or consent, the unreasonable interference of her intercourse with her mother and with Mercer, her most intimate friend, and how it was now her 'fixed resolution' to throw herself on her mother's protection and live with her entirely. She also 'dwelt much' upon the Orange match, and it was clear that this was the principal cause of her distress. Brougham repeated his assurances that 'without her consent freely given it never could take place', but Charlotte was not impressed. It was all very well for Brougham to talk. He could not know the sort of pressure, day in, day out, which might be brought to bear on her – 'they may wear me out by ill-treatment, and may represent that I have changed my mind and consented'.

The Duke of Sussex had arrived by this time, and joined in a general wide-ranging discussion of Charlotte's grievances. At last she took Brougham aside and asked what, on the whole, he advised her to do. There was, of course, only one answer to this – 'return to Warwick House or Carlton House and on no account pass a night out of her own house'. Poor Charlotte was deeply disappointed. She cried, asking if Brougham, too, refused to stand by her. On the contrary, he replied, and as far as her marriage was concerned she should follow her own inclinations entirely, but 'her returning home was absolutely necessary'. Everyone else agreed: Mercer, Charlotte Lindsay and the Duke of Sussex. The Duke had asked Brougham if the Regent could legally force his daughter to return and on being told that he could had advised her to go 'with as much speed and as little noise as possible'. Even Caroline sided with the others. Charlotte's unexpected arrival on her doorstep had come as something of an embarrassment to Caroline. It was true that not so long ago she had envisaged her daughter and herself standing together, presenting a united front against husbandly and parental persecution. But now the situation looked different. With the war over and Europe open to travellers again, the Princess of Wales was bent on escape. She would leave the country where she had known nothing but disillusion, disappointment and humiliation and just be herself, 'Caroline, a happy, merry soul'. The fact that this would now also involve abandoning her only child in her hour of need was unfortunate, but could not be helped. Charlotte would have to resign herself to putting up with whatever unpleasantness might result from her escapade, knowing that in the long term her position was assured.

But Charlotte was not feeling in the least resigned and she was not giving up yet. The Bishop had still not returned with the reply to her letter, and Cornelia Knight offered to go and try to find out what was happening at Carlton House. She asked boldly to see the Regent and instead was offered the Prime Minister or the Lord Chancellor. In the end she saw both Lords Eldon and Ellenborough, who had long since abandoned their siege of Connaught Place. Eldon told her that Salisbury was already on his way back to Bayswater with the answer that her Royal Highness must 'submit unconditionally'. Then, said Miss Knight, there was nothing more for her to do but go back to the Princess and take her maid and night-things, as it seemed she might be obliged to spend the night at Connaught Place.

It was now well after midnight, and everyone was exhausted, but Charlotte was still fighting, although Brougham told her bluntly that 'the Prince had her wholly in his hands', adding 'in a very peremptory tone' that the only question was whether she went of her own free will or was taken by force by the habeas corpus which he knew Lord Ellenborough would grant. Charlotte was 'affected beyond description', stunned by the deliberate harshness of this warning. All the excitement and euphoria of the previous evening had, of course, evaporated hours before, but now, wrote Brougham, 'I have told many a client he was going to be convicted, but I never saw anything like her *stupefaction*.' Still she would not give in. She knew that no power in heaven or on earth would ever bring the Regent to Connaught House, and she seems still to have been hoping for a miracle.

Some time between two and three a.m. the Duke of York arrived, bringing him with the authority to take the princess by force if necessary. But it had not come to that – yet. The Duke was admitted to the downstairs dining-room, and Caroline went down to speak to him. Upstairs the weary argument went grinding on. Again and again, says Brougham, Charlotte begged him to consider her situation, 'and to think whether, looking to that, it was absolutely necessary she should return'. Dawn was now beginning to break, and, remembering there was to be a Parliamentary by-election in Westminster that day, Brougham had a sudden inspiration. He led Charlotte to the window. Connaught House overlooked the open space known as Tyburn, where until recently the gallows had stood, and beyond it Hyde Park, silent and deserted in the grey dawn light.

'Look there, Madam,' he said. 'In a few hours all the streets and the Park, now empty, will be crowded with tens of thousands. I have only to take you to that window, and show you to the multitude, and tell them your grievances, and they will all rise in your behalf.'

Charlotte said something like, 'And why should they not?'

'The commotion,' replied Brougham impressively, 'will be excessive. Carlton House will be attacked – perhaps pulled down; the soldiers will be ordered out; blood will be shed; and if your Royal Highness were to live a hundred years, it never would be forgotten that your running away from your father's house was the cause of the mischief: and you may depend upon it, such is the English people's horror of bloodshed, you never would get over it.'

This was unanswerable. Charlotte knew it and knew that she was beaten. Supported by Mercer, she went downstairs to see her uncle Frederick. She asked for his help. He said his orders were only to bring her back and make no terms. She asked for access to her friends, and he repeated that he had no power to negotiate. He did, however, promise 'to do what he could' and seemed to hold out at least a glimmer of hope that contact with Mercer would be maintained. Charlotte then stipulated that one of her father's carriages should be sent to fetch her and while this was being arranged she went back upstairs, where she asked Brougham 'to make a minute of her declaration that she was resolved not to marry the Prince of Orange, and that if ever there should be an announcement of such a match, it must be understood to be without her consent and against her will. She added', says Brougham, '"I desire Augustus [Duke of Sussex] and Mr Brougham would particularly take notice of this."' When the declaration had been drawn up it was solemnly read aloud and signed by everyone present, Charlotte signing first. Six copies were then made and signed and distributed – one for each person present, Charlotte saying that if every any of them heard the marriage announced, they were to make her disclaimer public.

Now it was time to go. Escorted by her mother, by her uncle Augustus, by Mercer and by Brougham, who had been very much impressed by her 'sensibility and good feeling', she went down to where the Duke of York and one of the royal carriages were waiting. Poor Miss Knight, faced with the end of her career in the royal service, had been 'too much affected' to go with the others but she heard afterwards that York had tried to leave Mrs Louis behind. It was Caroline, who had behaved with unwonted discretion throughout the proceedings and also earned words of praise from Mr Brougham, who insisted that her daughter's maid must be allowed to accompany her, and at the last moment Mrs Louis, still clutching Charlotte's overnight bag, was bundled up the steps into the carriage. It was five a.m. The bird was back in the cage after not quite twelve hours' freedom. She was taken straight back to Carlton House where, so the Duke of Sussex heard, she was kept waiting in the courtyard for half an hour while the Regent decided how she was to be received or, perhaps more likely, the ladies of her new establishment were being hurriedly assembled. Then the doors of her father's house closed behind her, and she disappeared from view.

The whole amazing story was already being 'buzzed over

town'. 'All are against the Prince,' reported Brougham, and the Opposition press naturally made the most of the predicament of the runaway Princess, driven by desperation to take refuge with her mother. In fact, the honours in the public relations battle came out about even, as the government propaganda machine was able to represent that the restrictions being imposed on Charlotte were the consequence rather than the occasion of her flight and 'unnatural rebellion' against legitimate parental authority. Father and daughter had had an emotional meeting at Carlton House on the thirteenth. Both were in tears as Charlotte heartily begged his pardon for her 'rash act'. He forgave her, and she thought he seemed frightened 'because he was for making the best of it, did not know what to do for me, but would try and not make my life miserable'.

Her life, though, *was* being made miserable, for she was now to all intents and purposes a prisoner. The new ladies – Lady Ilchester, Lady Rosslyn, Lady Rosslyn's nieces, and Mrs Campbell, her former sub-governess – were little more than gaolers under strict orders never to let the Princess out of their sight. Even at night one of them was obliged 'either to sleep in the room with her, or in the next with the door open'. When Mrs Louis went over to Warwick House to collect some of Charlotte's clothes, Lady Ilchester went too and 'followed her everywhere she went . . . and told her there must be no talking or messages with the servants'. All correspondence, of course, was heavily censored, but Charlotte still contrived to smuggle out two letters, written in pencil on paper she had *stolen*, one to the Duke of Sussex, the other to Mercer, dated Thursday morning, 14 July, which illustrates all too clearly her overwrought mental condition.

'Never can I express half I feel towards you, she wrote,

nor my deep sence [*sic*] of obligation. . . . What wretchedness to be parted from you at such a moment. My life, my everything, has long been at your disposal, but how doubly so, after the dreadful scene you went thro' for me. It is I who by my *mad conduct* brought all this upon you. Well, well, did I feel, when kneeling beside you, that we should be parted, and that moment, that dreadful one, when I pressed you to my burning lips, half distracted, broken hearted, at being forced from you absolutely that I could not utter one single word because you could not. Oh, how doubly were my pangs added to, when I knew I had occasioned that scene, that pale face, that suffering, and yet *you love me still*. I need not implore of you not to forget, to love me less for all I have caused you. Dearly am I ashamed of the precipitate steps I took, by my anguish and self-upbraidings, for having drawn you in. . . . For Heaven's sake make a *push* to *see me*; the P. promised you *his protection*; he cannot banish *you* therefore from me wholly surely.

Charlotte's letter to her uncle Sussex, which reached him by a circuitous route via her sympathetic French master and then Mercer and Cornelia Knight, contained such a melancholy description 'of the manner in which she was confined and watched day and night' that on 19 July the Duke, carefully coached by Henry Brougham, rose in the House of Lords to question the Prime Minister regarding his niece's welfare. His Royal Highness wanted to know whether, since her removal to Carlton House, Princess Charlotte was being allowed to see her friends as usual; whether she was able to write and receive letters and had pen, ink and paper. Was she under the restraints generally of actual imprisonment? Had not her doctors advised this year, as last, that sea-bathing and sea-air were imperative for her health? Lastly, now that she was past the age when the law recognized her as fit to govern without assistance, had any steps been taken towards providing her with an establishment suitable for her position and the part she might soon have to perform?

The Duke got a predictably dusty answer from Lord Liverpool. The Prince Regent was the father of his family and had a perfect right to regulate his daughter's education 'as he might think proper'. The Prince had done nothing, with respect to her Royal Highness, except what was for her benefit. He felt towards her as a father ought to feel, 'with the strongest and warmest affection', and was only anxious to perform those duties which God, nature and the laws of the land imposed upon him. The Prime Minister therefore trusted that their lordships 'would give his Royal Highness credit for having conducted himself on grounds the best calculated to promote her [Charlotte's] comfort, benefit and honour'. Sussex was not satisfied and said so, adding that he would bring forward a motion on the subject on the following Friday, 22 July.

Charlotte, meanwhile, had been moved to Cranbourne Lodge and was agreeably surprised to find 'the house is indeed very cheerful and very good, the view lovely'. There was one room in particular where she sat in the evenings, which she thought charming, and the garden was large and would have been a good one 'but for being very much neglected'. The place was, in short, 'an *honourable retreat*' and a distinct improvement on Lower Lodge. Although she still complained bitterly about lack of privacy, and all incoming mail was still being opened and 'rummaged' by the ladies-in-waiting, there had been some other improvements in her situation since leaving Carlton House. She was not, after all, to be entirely separated from Mercer – they were corresponding again, and a visit was promised in August. She was able to go riding, though this made her knee worse, very stiff and painful, and her phaeton and grey ponies were also to be allowed. She had received a visit from the Queen and three of her aunts, who were, she thought, '*put out*' at finding her on civil if not exactly friendly terms with her lady wardresses. These she had at first dismissed as 'stupider and duller than anything', but Mrs Campbell, she now admitted, 'behaves uncommonly well to me, with much diffidence and delicacy'. Lady Ilchester was good humoured enough, but Lady Rosslyn remained 'as detestable an old lump of bones as ever was, never seems good humored [*sic*] or pleased, and is always listening to what is going on'.

In addition to the ladies, General Thomas Garth had now been seconded to the Cranbourne Lodge establishment. The General was a cheerful old rascal, 'very vulgar in his conversation and language', but anxious to please and make things comfortable and pleasant. Nevertheless, Charlotte would, on the whole, rather not have had him, and he certainly seems an odd choice in the circumstances, for it was he who had once been her aunt Sophia's lover and was the father of the Princess's illegitimate child.

Charlotte had been kept informed by Mercer and the Bishop of Salisbury about the Duke of Sussex's efforts on her behalf in the House of Lords, but she was relieved when Sussex agreed to withdraw his motion. Lord Grey had felt that no useful purpose would be served at this point by a full debate on the subject of her affairs and that it might, on the contrary, do more harm than good, especially since it appeared that some of the restrictions on her liberty were being eased. Grey, though deeply sympathetic, still believed that Charlotte's best and only policy was calm submission, patience, and firmness, which he continued, somewhat apologetically, to urge through Mercer. Charlotte herself thought that perhaps it was as well that she should be quite '*out of the way*' just now and asked Mercer to throw cold water on any well-meaning but ill-judged attempts to champion her cause by people like Cornelia Knight. She was very depressed – 'my spirits are in a most deplorable state' – and while deriving some comfort from the knowledge that she had friends ready to protect her interests where they could, she saw little hope for the future and nothing but distrust and suspicion surrounding her. Her chief dread was that another attempt might be made to force 'that nasty, ugly spider-legged little Duchman [*sic*]' down her throat, and she wondered if she might write to 'the P.R. or any of them so as to *utterly destroy* any vague hopes they still retain'; for otherwise, she was convinced, they would try to 'launch him off again'. There seemed no end to the plague of Oranges. Slender Billy's younger brother, a thin young man who rode a fine prancing horse, was now in England. Worse, he was at Windsor and present at a review of the Horse Guards, the Blues, by the Duke of Wellington, actually within sight of Cranbourne Lodge. Charlotte was outraged at Wellington's indelicacy in bringing him so close to her house. 'The only effect this Orange siege will have upon me is that *I shall become very savage*.'

She had a visit from her father at the end of July. He came to tell her what he supposed she already knew – that her mother had applied, through Lord Liverpool, for permission to leave England, 'desiring to set sail at Worthing, not to go in a frigate but a man of war, and for it to go round as quiet as possible'. The Regent was obviously relieved, so much so that he was quite mellow. 'He could only wish her [the Princess] to be happy wherever she was, and if it made her more so travelling on the Continent, he could not but agree.' He appeared to be '*most perfectly satisfied*', and no doubt the farther Caroline travelled the better he would like it. Charlotte, however, was 'very unhappy' at the news of her mother's impending departure. In her present nervous, hag-ridden state the disappearance of any friendly face could only add to her general wretchedness: 'I am so hurt about it that I am very low.' She was allowed to pay a farewell visit to Connaught Place, heavily chaperoned by the wardresses-in-waiting, but was further wounded by Caroline's casual, '*indifferent*' manner of leave-taking, 'for God knows how long, or *what events* may occur before we meet again'.

Grieved though she was by her mother's desertion, Charlotte did not think there was anything she could usefully say or do to persuade her to change her mind. 'After all, if a *mother* has not *feeling* for her child, or children, are they to *teach it her* or can they expect to be listened to with any *hopes of success?*' Grey, Brougham, and Whitbread, who all deeply disapproved of the Princess of Wales's plans, *did* try to persuade her to stay in England. Lord Grey thought that 'the old Princess's conduct is unfeeling to the greatest degree, and most injurious, as I fear the event will prove, both to herself and her daughter'. Brougham wrote, 'solemnly warning' her of the risks she would be running. 'Depend upon it, Madam, there are many persons who now begin to see a chance of divorcing your Royal Highness from the Prince.' As long as Caroline and Charlotte remained on English soil, surrounded by their friends, and by Englishmen and Englishwomen, 'and having our laws to protect them', Brougham would answer for it that no plot could succeed against either of them. But it would be quite another matter if the 'old Princess' persisted in her intention of going to Italy. 'Never let your Royal Highness forget that in England spies and false witnesses can do nothing; abroad, everything may be apprehended from them.'

Brougham described this letter as 'a strong dose, but necessary'. Unfortunately it had no effect on Caroline. 'Nothing can stop her,' wrote Lady Charlotte Lindsay. 'I never saw so fixed a determination.' Caroline, in short, had had enough. The brutally insulting way in which she had been treated during a visit of the Allied sovereigns seems to have been the last straw, and the only concession her Whig friends had managed to extract was a promise to return at once if any 'inimical designs' were threatened. At the beginning of August she travelled down to Worthing and a few days later, accompanied by the ubiquitous Willikin, now a rather vacant-looking teenager, and a handful of attendants, she embarked at Lancing in the frigate *Jason*. A silent, rather puzzled crowd lined the beach to see her off, a stout, much rouged figure in a satin perlisse with large gold clasps and a tall, military-style hat of violet and green satin bedecked with a plume of green feathers. She had chosen to travel under the *nom de guerre* of Countess von Wolfenbüttel; but if anonymity was her objective, the conspicuous presence among her baggage of a large metal trunk painted with the words 'Her Royal Highness the Princess of Wales, to be always with her' rather spoilt the effect.

Nearly twenty years had passed since the young Caroline of Brunswick had bounced happily ashore at Gravesend, bursting with 'pleasant unaffected joy' at the prospect before her – marriage to the 'finest and handsomest prince in the world' and life in the 'most desirable country in Europe'. Now, as she set forth on her travels, we are told that she wept. Another account says she fainted as the *Jason*'s barge pulled away from the shore. Her daughter, immured at Cranbourne Lodge, was suffering from violent nervous spasms brought on by the worry and distress caused by her faithlessness. Charlotte had wondered if Caroline would ever return to England, but it naturally did not occur to her that when that day came she herself would have been nearly three years in her grave.

At the beginning of August the Londoners were treated to a monster firework display in the Royal Parks in honour of the peace and the centenary of the Hanoverian dynasty. There was a balloon ascent, a mock battle on the Serpentine, a seven-story gaslit pagoda in St James's Park and a Temple of Peace in Green Park. An enormous, good-humoured crowd flocked to enjoy all these wonders and to patronize the refreshment stalls and the gaming and drinking booths. A week later it was still there, resisting all the Home Secretary's efforts to dislodge it. Princess Charlotte, of course, saw none of the celebrations but on 16 August she was permitted to attend a fête at Frogmore and, towards the end of the month, 'a very seemly little musick party', also at Frogmore.

Living at Windsor, she was inevitably seeing a good deal of her grandmother and aunts – indeed, she saw hardly anyone else – but one result of her mother's departure was a distinct improvement in her relationship with her grandmother. With the dreaded figure of the Princess of Wales no longer standing between them, the two Charlottes began to draw together. 'The Queen has been remarkably good humored [*sic*] and gracious to me ever since I came here,' wrote young Charlotte on 26 August, and she was to find the old lady an increasingly valuable ally in her dealings with her father.

Just how valuable the Queen's support could be became apparent over the affair of Charlotte's seaside holiday. She was still not at all well, and her swollen painful knee was now so much worse that her daily rides had to be abandoned. The doctors continued to urge the therapeutic value of sea air and sea bathing, but Charlotte was convinced that her father did not mean to let her go – 'he never believes I am ill'. She had wanted to go to Brighton. The Pavilion would be vacant after 30 August, a royal residence, aired and ready and close to medical assistance – but no, it was to be lent to the Regent's friends the Duke and Duchess of Rutland. 'Garth says it is *only because I wished Brighton* that I *am not to go there*,' Charlotte wrote to an indignant Mercer. Lord Grey was also up in arms on Charlotte's behalf. 'The treatment of the Pss. is really too horrible. All the best season will be wasted before she gets to the sea-side.'

At last, on Wednesday 31 August, the Regent arrived at Cranbourne Lodge in high spirits and full of bonhomie, announcing that Charlotte was to leave immediately for Weymouth to stay at his mother's house, Gloucester Lodge, and brushing aside objections that nothing was ready and the house not aired. He had been plagued into letting her go to the sea, and by God she should go. He would not, however, allow Mercer to go with her as she had hoped. What with one thing and another, Charlotte was so distressed that she cried the whole way from Cranbourne Lodge to the Castle, where she was bidden to dine, and was ready to cry all through dinner, though the Queen and her aunt Mary both tried to cheer her up. The Queen, in fact, was really kind, would not hear of her setting out to an *unaired* house, and arranged instead that she should travel down in ten days' time. Money was also discussed between them. Her Majesty had been told by General Garth that he had no money and had been allocated none for expenses. She was equally shocked to discover that her granddaughter's allowance had not been paid since she had been removed from Warwick House. 'She asked me what it was,' wrote Charlotte. 'I told her. She quite clasped her hands together with astonishment and said severely, "I wish the P.R. was not gone. I would have spoken to him. It is no joke."' The Queen appears to have been ready to go into battle. Garth told Charlotte that steps were being taken to ensure that in future she should have a handsome sum of money always in her hands to dispose of as she pleased, and Her Majesty told the Regent that from now on she would refuse to act as his go-between. Charlotte was no longer a child, and he must deal with her direct. 'He said nothing to this but "Then I shall be plagued from morning noon and night with letters and questions." "Well, and pray who is to be if you are not?" was the Q.'s answer; and so ended the conference.'

Charlotte had asked if she was to be '*wholly excluded* from society at Weymouth' and was told not; anyone received at Windsor might visit her at Gloucester Lodge. This cheered her slightly, but only slightly, and she set out on 9 September with her entourage of 'nasty ugly women' in a mood of deep despondency. However, the journey, which she had expected to be 'detestable', went surprisingly well. The party proceeded at a brisk thirteen miles an hour and by four o'clock had reached Andover, where they stopped for dinner at a nice clean inn. 'Wherever I changed horses there were people assembled to see me, and they all looked good humored [*sic*] and took off their hats.' At Andover a crowd gathered to get a glimpse of the princess at her sitting-room window, 'and I of course remained at it to indulge them with *so fine a sight*'. At Salisbury her reception was even more enthusiastic. The streets leading to the Antelope Inn, where she spent the night, were lined with people carrying lights of all kinds 'and *one acclamation* the whole way. Charlotte could hardly get out of the carriage for the multitude pressing round her, 'and when I got upstairs . . . they called for me to appear at the window, which I did with a candle held behind that they might see me, and 2 [too] I was obliged to go and bow at an open window.' Next morning was the same, all through breakfast, 'and when I went away the house and stairs and all were filled with the most respectable people who were all anxious to see me and show their loyalty. . . . Blandford was equally loyal,' she told Mercer, 'and I must say wherever I have stopped or passed thro' I have been always well recvd, and cordially.' At Weymouth, which she rather unkindly called 'an odious place', the esplanade was full of people, and a band played the national anthem. 'They played for an hour or more very delightfully, and the prettiest waltz I have heard for some time. . . . The applause continued loud at different times. At last I went to the window, bowed, and quitted it for the evening, when the people went away too.'

Weymouth's reputation as a fashionable resort had been made when George III had first gone there to convalesce with his family in 1789, and the townsfolk were naturally delighted to have his granddaughter in their midst. Gloucester Lodge, built in 1780 by the Duke of Gloucester, father of Charlotte's recent 'suitor', was pleasantly situated on the sea front and her accommodation 'good and comfortable'. She had naturally been much heartened by all the evidence of popular warmth and sympathy she had encountered on what was her first journey into the country since childhood, and away from the stultifying atmosphere of Windsor she was gradually to find more liberty and less espionage within the household. After all the emotional upheavals of the summer she began to relax a little. 'Here I am quiet and tolerably free from worries and fidgets.' Some fidgets there were. Charlotte was embarrassed and annoyed by General Garth's tactless parading of his fourteen-year-old 'adopted' son and when she realized that young Tom Garth was, in fact, the fruit of the General's liaison with her aunt Sophia, she was 'so shockingly affected' that she felt quite ashamed. Lady Ilchester was horrified by old Garth's 'unfeeling and indelicate conduct' and understandably astonished at his being continued in the royal family's service at all, let alone appointed to be with Charlotte. It was a relief all round when young Tom went back to school, though Charlotte now had the doubtful pleasure of the Great U.P.'s company at dinner every day, the Bishop having come down to Weymouth with his family and taken a house nearby. Another vexation was the news that Captain Hesse had joined up with the Princess of Wales in her travels. In view of the fact that Mercer had still not succeeded in making him return Charlotte's letters, this was disquieting. It seemed more than ever necessary to retrieve 'the packet', but Charlotte did not see how this was to be managed. Could Mercer think of a solution to the problem? What would she think of consulting her father, Lord Keith, who already knew so much about it, and seeing what he thought could be done?

The autumn days slipped by. Charlotte obediently followed the doctors' instructions, bathing in tepid sea-water and then in the open sea. This had always agreed with her, and she had great faith in its doing her general health a great deal of good. Certainly she seemed better physically. Dr Baillie was pleased with her progress, and her knee was less swollen. She visited several local places of interest, such as Portland Bill, Lulworth, Abbotsbury, and Corfe Castle. She went sailing aboard the sloop HMS *Zephyr* and enjoyed the experience very much; went to church 'and heard the most extraordinary sermon preached by the oddest man that ever was . . . a Dr Dupré, who delivers his discourses entirely extemporary'. Charlotte got the giggles but was fortunately wearing a poke bonnet which concealed her 'dreadful risibility'. She heard of a smuggler selling 'most delightful French silks at 5 shillings a yard' and determined to track him down. There was quite a variety of French merchandise available in Weymouth, '*even Frenchwomen*, who sell prints, etc. . . . You never saw such odd looking people.' On the anniversary of the King's Jubilee she distributed a sum of money amongst the poor of the town and invited 'a select party' to Gloucester Lodge to witness 'an elegant display of fireworks'. One of the attractions of the evening was 'the celebrated Italian minstrel, Signor Rivolta'. This talented individual performed a concert on eight instruments at the same time, with which, we are told, 'her Royal Highness was highly gratified'.

To the Bishop of Salisbury, to Mrs Campbell, her ex-governess, Charlotte seemed 'tranquil', even happy. '*People* are so *little observant*', remarked the Princess, 'and have so *little penetration* that *I believe they say* what *they think* because they *see* or *know no better*.' Poor Charlotte, her real problems, of which she had plenty, were currently being rendered even more insoluble by her continuing, futile infatuation for the Prussian Prince 'F', and her letters to Mercer were full of '*this all powerful subject*' which was engaging her 'whole heart, soul and mind'. The day after her arrival at Weymouth she had been bitterly distressed by the loss of a little turquoise heart out of a ring which F. had given her and which she wore constantly – 'think only of my misery and horror'. It seemed a bad omen, and 'when one is out of spirits and nervous, anything . . . will add and make it worse.'

Charlotte fretted endlessly about 'the F. business'. 'I think and think about how it will be, and how it will all turn out, till my head quite gets bewildered. . . . Sometimes I am in very good spirits about it, and sometimes the reverse, and then I despair, and think it a hopeless attachment.' The trouble was the usual one in such cases. It would be difficult, if not impossible, for Charlotte to come into the open and 'confess my partiality or my sentiments for him'. Nor, of course, could she ever confess to the illicit correspondence which they had carried on by means of the sympathetic Cornelia Knight. No, it was up to F. to take the initiative, to return to England and 'in person offer himself' to the P.R.'. The Princess wanted him to come while Parliament was sitting, so that she could if necessary fly to Parliament and the country for support. But, sadly, F. showed no sign of proposing himself to the Prince Regent in person or on paper. Neither was he writing any more of those ardent letters which Charlotte could not even re-read for consolation. 'These letters are not in existence, for they are burnt.' She made all the usual excuses for his silence. He was 'testing' her. He did not like running the risk of a refusal, and for that reason was proceeding very cautiously. In fact, it seems all too probable that F. was doing his best to extricate himself from what had never been more than a little transient dalliance, which had become an embarrassment. Charlotte might be a great matrimonial prize, but he plainly had no ambitions in that direction. He was currently occupied with other matters, getting ready to accompany the King of Prussia to the conference of Heads of State being held at Vienna, and Charlotte heard a disquieting rumour that he was to be made Governor of Saxony. If this were true, she wrote to Mercer in November, 'it will be equivalent to a *decided abandonment of me* and of all my fondly cherished hopes'.

The report proved to be unfounded, as did an even more disquieting one that F. was contemplating another marriage, but Charlotte was now at last beginning to come to terms with the fact that her cherished 'romance' had little, if any, existence outside her imagination and that it was time to think realistically about the future. She knew that the nation wanted to see her married and settled, the sooner the better. She also knew that there was no chance of her ever being 'tolerably comfortable' with her own family unless she married. She loved and would always love F., but if her hopes of *real* happiness in matrimony were destined to be blighted she would have to accept the next best thing, 'a good tempered man with good sence', with whom she could have a 'reasonable hope of being *less unhappy and comfortless*' than she had been in her single state. She had still not given up all hope of F. and on 11 November was planning, with Mercer's help, a last desperate attempt to make contact with him and extract 'a decided answer of some kind'. After all, '*a man must mean something* by writing, and writing as he does', and in any case Charlotte now felt that anything would be better than the continued uncertainty preying on her health and spirits. But a month later, on the eve of her return to Windsor, she had still heard nothing. 'If grief is to be my only share', she wrote, 'then I will cherish, nourish, feed and love it, for nothing that comes from him can be otherwise than dear, tho' it may cut me to the soul.'

She was undoubtedly very miserable, poor Charlotte, but another name had now begun to appear in her letters to Mercer, that of the good-tempered man of sense who '*decidedly would be accepted*' as a second-best choice. This was Prince Leopold of Saxe-Coburg, and if she knew beyond doubt that F. was lost to her, or if some other name were proposed, she would not scruple to suggest him herself to the Regent. 'What odd mortals we are,' she remarked, 'That I should be as wholly occupied and devoted as I am to *one*, and yet think and talk and even provide for another would appear unnatural in the highest degree were it written in a novel, and yet it is *true*.'

She left Weymouth on 16 December, again spending the night at Salisbury. It was a 'sad, uncomfortable journey', and Lady Rosslyn, who sat opposite her in the carriage, nearly drove the princess distracted by 'her eternal fidgets and frights'. Back at Cranbourne Lodge nothing seemed to have changed, although Mrs Campbell had assured Charlotte that her father did not want to go on treating her like a child, shutting her up at 'Cranburn', and depriving her of agreeable society. His only wish, apparently, was to keep her from 'mischievous people'. Charlotte, still eating her heart out for F., remained unimpressed, but when the Regent dropped in unexpectedly to see her on 21 December he was in his most affable mood, and nothing could have been kinder or more affectionate than his general demeanour. Indeed, wrote Charlotte, 'it has been the most comfortable visit *to me and my feelings* that I have ever had yet'.

They met again at Windsor Castle on Christmas Day and after dinner had a long, confidential chat in Princess Mary's rooms. The Regent, who may well have had divorce on his mind, brought up the subject of the Princess of Wales and her conduct towards 'the boy who she took abroad with her'. This, of course, was Willikin. As long as he lived, said the Regent, this boy could be of no consequence, but after his death he might become 'a very serious misfortune' to Charlotte as well as to the country, and he hoped this 'would now make her *see*, upon what grounds he had acted for so many years past' and why he and the King had always 'so decidedly forbid her ever seeing that boy', who, from every point of view, was an improper companion for her. Charlotte replied that Willikin had always been 'greatly preferred before her'. She had never seen him in the drawing-room after the order that she was not to keep company with him was given, but her mother often spoke of him with the greatest affection, and he was always in the house, whether at Blackfriars, Kensington, or Connaught Place. She obviously believed that Willikin was Caroline's bastard, as did her uncle the Duke of Brunswick, and when the conversation moved on to 'the society which Princess Charlotte used to meet at her mother's' she appeared to be 'perfectly acquainted' with all Caroline's gentlemen friends as far back as the days of Sidney Smith and Captain Manby. She had never actually seen Sapio but knew that he had dined with her mother every day and told the Regent, unasked, that she thought Mr Craven, who had gone abroad with Caroline as her chamberlain, was the current lover. Charlotte also told her father all about Captain Hesse: how they had met at Kensington with Caroline's connivance and unknown to Lady de Clifford, and how her mother had left them together in her own bedroom. Upon the

Prince 'being horror struck', she went on: 'I can tell you what is more, that my mother carried on a correspondence for us, and all the letters backwards and forwards went through her hands.' This led on to the confession that her letters and presents had never been returned, and having heard that Captain Hesse had joined up with her mother abroad she had written that, if Caroline did not get him now to return all her letters, 'she should throw herself upon her father's mercy and acknowledge the whole to him'. Charlotte realized that she had had a narrow escape.

'God knows,' she exclaimed piously, 'God knows what would have become of me if he [Hesse] had not behaved with so much respect to me.'

'My dear child, it is Providence alone that has saved you,' responded the Regent. He wanted a firm assurance from Charlotte that she had never 'either in writing or by word of mouth' given a promise of marriage to Captain Hesse, and went on to represent 'the necessity of concealing nothing'. He would not reproach her, but must know the whole if he was to extricate her safely 'out of this difficulty', and ensure that such a thing could never happen again.

Whether Charlotte had actually intended to make a clean breast of the Hesse affair is not very clear, but it was probably a wise thing to have done and resulted in an apparently complete reconciliation with her father – that, plus the fact that she told her aunt Mary she was sure the only thing for her mother was to keep out of England, for after what had happened 'the Prince never can let me see her again or do I *now* wish it *myself*'. Caroline, she now supposed, had deliberately drawn her into the scrape with Captain Hesse in order 'to bring the boy forwards'. Charlotte was greatly relieved, she said, at having 'told *all* she had in her *mind*' to her father and happy at being once more on such cordial and affectionate terms with him; but Lord Grey, for one, was suspicious of the motives behind the Regent's 'new demonstrations of kindness.' Grey placed no credence in the stories about Billy Austin, which he thought had been invented to frighten Charlotte and make her more amenable. He agreed with Mercer Elphinstone that the Prince very likely had some point to carry. 'What it is remains to be seen,' he wrote; 'but my suspicion points to a renewal of the match with the Prince of Orange.'

Charlotte had her own misgivings and, in spite of the unaccustomed atmosphere of family goodwill at Windsor, approached the New Year with 'a sort of presentiment of evil'. 'I see there is some deep and desperate intrigue de coeur of wh. I am to be the first card to be played off. . . . When I think of all this mess my poor little head quite turns round, and I really don't know which way to look or turn myself. I shall soon fear really to utter a word for fear I am saying something wrong or that may be taken up against me.'

It is noticeable that her recent confessional urges had not included any mention of F., but this sad little affair was about to die of natural causes. On 18 January, Charlotte heard at last from Notte (another of her nicknames for Cornelia Knight) enclosing a letter from F. It was 'quite an easy, cool, familiar friendly letter' but it left no further room for doubt, or hope. Charlotte, of course, would not answer it. She was a good deal surprised at the cool way in which Notte had taken the ending of what had always been a favourite scheme of hers. However, she praised the Princess's conduct as 'wise and prudent', and Charlotte also felt satisfied that she had handled 'the F. business' well, 'and that is one step, and a great one, to getting comfortable if not happy again.' She could not forget her lost love all at once – had she not vowed to be faithful unto death? – and at the end of January felt less cured than ever of her 'unfortunate passion'. However, the process had been slightly hastened by the Duchess of York telling her that Prince Augustus (who was her cousin) suffered severely from halitosis, and adding that although she believed him to be an excellent officer, he was altogether too fond of the ladies.

Meanwhile, Charlotte's nineteenth birthday had come and gone, and still nothing was being done about giving her an 'establishment', a house of her own, or even an adequate income. She was thinking seriously now about Leopold of Saxe-Coburg and discussing him with the family. When Princess Mary brought his name into one of the regular confidential chats taking place these days between aunt and niece, Charlotte told her that, while she was 'not the least in the world' in love with 'the Prince of C.', she had a very good opinion of him, and for that reason would rather marry him than any other prince. Mary then 'launched forth vehemently in his praises, said no one's character stood higher, and that he was of a very old House'. Charlotte also spoke of 'the Prince of C.' to the Duchess of York, 'upon wh. she *colored* [*sic*] beyond anything and said, "I beg a favor [*sic*] you will never let it be known you mentioned it to me, for as I happen to be nearly related to him . . . like him very much, and am in *constant correspondence* with him, it would be directly said that I managed this match."' However, the Duchess fully agreed that Leopold was the *best* of all the princes who had been in England the previous year, and Charlotte was much heartened to know that she had the support of the Yorks, of Princess Mary, and, she believed, of the Duke of Kent and Princess Sophia. She was pleased, too, to hear from Mercer that the Prince Regent had spoken in general praise of Leopold, 'the Leo' as she was beginning to refer to him, and on 23 January informed Mercer that, having made up her mind to marry, the person she had 'decidedly fixed on' was Prince Leopold, believing that he would make her 'tolerably comfortable and happy'. She had to admit she was still pining for the unworthy F., and 'till that passion subsides it cannot be supposed the heart can receive another impression of that sort'. However, she believed friendship and liking would at least provide her with some consolation, 'and upon that, why should I not hope to be happy? At all events I know that *worse off*, more unhappy and wretched I *cannot* well be than I *am now*, and after all if I end by marrying Prince L. I marry the *best* of all those I *have seen*, and that is some satisfaction.'

Charlotte and Mercer were agreed that 'the Leo' ought to come over to England without waiting for an invitation, and Charlotte wondered if her ever useful friend thought she could 'by *any means send him a hint that his presence at this moment . . .* would be of service to *his views* if they were the same as 6 months ago'. If he were to appear now, his arrival would be sure to cause comment – 'the world would talk and fancy about it' – so much so that the Prince Regent would find it very difficult to reject the 'direct application' which Charlotte planned to make and from which she was only now being restrained by the Duke of York's advice to wait until after the Congress of Vienna.

All these hopeful and constructive plans received a check when the Regent confirmed Lord Grey's and Charlotte's worst fears by attempting to revive the bogy of the Orange match. Towards the end of January, Mercer had been summoned to Brighton and she told Brougham that 'the grand object at present is to bring about the Orange marriage'. For two hours she was harangued by the Prince, who used every argument to try and persuade her to urge Charlotte to agree to it, 'as the only means of saving her own reputation, getting out of her mother's hands, and making herself quite happy, whether she would or not'. Mercer was unmoved and finally told his Royal Highness bluntly that any attempt to renew the engagement would only be to risk 'a renewal of all the unpleasant scenes of last year to no purpose'.

Warned of what was in the wind, Charlotte herself wrote to her father. She was aware, she told him, that people in their station of life could not marry as the rest of the world did, but 'esteem and regard' she felt were still essential between husband and wife. The whole happiness of her future life was at stake, and she could not be too plain 'in humbly stating my strong and fixed aversion to a match with a man for whom I can never feel those sentiments'. She hoped that Papa would not love her the less for having thus opened her heart to him, and reminded him of his promise never to urge 'any union that would make me miserable'.

But it seemed that Papa did not mean to take no for an answer. Back came a strongly worded request to reconsider, coupled with a warning that, after 'the melancholy and frightful disclosures' of Christmas Day, a return to her engagement to marry the Prince of Orange, in whom 'youth, character, power, rank, consequence, national interests and actual national alliance' were all united, might well prove her only chance of retrieving her reputation and foiling further attempts to compromise her.

Charlotte was 'in a terrible bad state of nerves, spirits and everything', but in spite of nervous headaches and sleepless nights she remained unshaken in her resolve. No arguments, no threats, would ever induce her to marry the 'detested Dutchman', and she was sustained in that resolve by the knowledge that she now had the support of the whole royal family. The Queen had been especially affectionate and sympathetic, imploring her granddaughter not ever to marry a man she did not like. In the face of this united front of opposition, the Regent was reluctantly obliged to concede defeat, and no more was heard of the Orange marriage. In August came news that the 'detested Dutchman' had become engaged to a Russian bride, and so, wrote Henry Brougham, 'there's an end of the little Princess's annoyance from that quarter'.

The princess's annoyance from another quarter also came to an end, when it transpired that Captain Hesse had not, after all, kept her letters, and Charlotte did not really mind if he kept the few trinkets she had given him, since no one could prove they had come from her.

So, in the spring of her twentieth year, free at last of all entanglements, Charlotte could look forward with some optimism to a happier future.

NINE

Charlotte the Bride

And gracious Heaven thy chosen nuptials bless
With all a Wife's and all a Mother's happiness.

Robert Southey

I delight in Coburg because I am quite satisfied he is really, truly and
sincerely attached to me.

Princess Charlotte to Mercer Elphinstone, March 1816

Except when I went out to shoot, we were together always, and we
could be together, we did not tire.

Prince Leopold of Saxe-Coburg

I am so perfectly happy.

Princess Charlotte to Mercer Elphinstone, August 1816

In the early months of 1815 the government was preoccupied with the mounting popular agitation against the so-called Corn Laws – a protectionist measure intended to restrict the import of cheap foreign grain and which it was feared would have the effect of pushing up the price of a loaf of bread. There were violent demonstrations in London and other parts of the country, and Charlotte heard that 'the Ministers were very much shook, and that on the *walls* were written up, "Prince Regent, dissolve your Parliament directly or your head shall pay for it."' The PR himself '*could not laugh it off*' and was reported to be 'very low and half frightened'. Then, at the beginning of March, Europe was convulsed by the news that Napoleon had escaped from Elba.

'Bony being landed was a fine source of conversation', wrote Charlotte after a visit from the Queen and princesses on the 12th and again, on the 17th, 'all at the Castle are full of the affair on the Continent. All out of spirits. The Queen much affected visibly but trying to talk off danger and conceal its extent.' Charlotte had no doubt as to the extent of the danger threatened by this latest crisis. 'If we do not all unite to the extermination of this monster, we shall all be involved in one common ruin.'

The renewal of the war inevitably led to still further delay in the delicate process of negotiation with Prince Leopold. 'The Leo' held a commission in the Russian army, and, as he explained in a letter to Mercer written from Vienna at the end of April, his military duties would make it impossible for him to come to England that spring. A rumour that he was getting engaged to a Hungarian countess proved to be false, but Charlotte, already disappointed that he had not responded more eagerly to Mercer's discreet encouragement – 'I do not at all see why Leo could not take your hint . . . if he is really as anxious as he appeared to be' – knew some moments of deep despondency. 'The more I really wish and think of this marriage for me, the more I begin to be in despair and out of heart about it – and if I am disappointed in this too, I shall be quite broken hearted.'

She had returned to London in April and was back at Warwick House, but now sharing an entrance with Carlton House – the yard through which she had made her dramatic exit the previous summer being closed off. Her life continued to follow the old pattern of boredom and restriction, not far removed from house arrest. 'Nothing can be so wretchedly uncertain and uncomfortable as my situation; no changes for the better.' She saw nothing of her father, 'though *next door*', and was allowed to invite very few of the people she really liked to visit her. The ladies who remained her constant companions were 'not many of them agreeable to me, some far from it, but the evil one knows is better than what one does not'. In fact, the only bright spots in the general dreariness were her weekly visits to the theatre, her improved relations with her aunts and uncles – not that they could do very much to help her, but their support and affection were comforting – and, of course, her continuing treasured relationship with Mercer Elphinstone, who was fortunately still in favour with the Regent, despite her refusal to co-operate with him in trying to revive the Orange project. Charlotte was depending on Mercer to keep up an undercover correspondence with Leopold, although his letters remained tantalizingly few and far between. He seemed reluctant to commit himself, unsure of his welcome if he were to venture to come to England, unsure even of Charlotte's feelings; perhaps Mercer had been rather too discreet.

As the spring of 1815 advanced into summer, everyone's attention was increasingly focussed on the armies now massing on the Franco-Belgian frontier and on the forthcoming confrontation which must settle the fate of Europe. Charlotte had been following the progress of events with eager attention. As soon as she heard that the Allied forces were engaged, she instructed her equerry, Colonel Addenbrooke, to write to the War Office begging Lord Bathurst to send on any news from the battle-front as soon as it was received, no matter what hour of the day or night, 'the Princess being exceedingly anxious to receive tidings and particularly to know the fate of some of her friends'. Happily the cavalry regiment in which Leopold was serving did not reach Brussels in time to take part in the action at Waterloo, but Captain Hesse was wounded – he lost an arm – and the Duke of Brunswick, the uncle Charlotte had hero-worshipped as a little girl, was killed at Quatre Bras.

Brunswick's death revived the embarrassing question of the Princess of Wales. Since leaving England, Caroline had been traipsing restlessly round Europe. In October 1814 Charlotte Bury, who was also on a European tour, encountered Her Royal Highness in Geneva, where a ball was organized in her honour – not without difficulty, since 'so many of the English travellers wished to avoid knowing her', and the natives 'had no mind to be troubled with royalty'. Eventually, however, enough guests were scraped together, and the ball took place, but Lady Charlotte was horrified when the Princess appeared 'dressed *en Venus*, or rather not dressed, further than the waist'. Indeed, so mortified was Lady Charlotte to see the Princess making herself 'so utterly ridiculous' that she made up her mind to set off from Geneva directly rather than witness her old friend's degradation. However, Caroline saved her the trouble by terminating her career in Switzerland within a very few days and continuing on her journey 'without having an idea, in fact, where she was going to, or how she should be received at any of the courts where she purposed to reside. It was really as if, in leaving England, she had cast off all common sense and conduct and gone suddenly mad.'

Caroline went south, spending the winter at the Court of Naples, where she struck up one of her unsuitable friendships with the King, Napoleon's brother-in-law, Joachim Murat. In March 1815 there was a scare that she meant to go back to England. Princess Mary told Charlotte 'of the rage the PR put himself in when they told him *she* was certainly coming, for he *would not* believe it, and declared she *could* not come'. She did not. Instead she turned up in Genoa, where, in spite of everything, Charlotte Bury rejoined her for a few weeks. Communication between Caroline and her daughter had now virtually ceased, although Caroline boasted to Charlotte Lindsay that she wrote every week. In May, Charlotte promised the Regent that she would no longer write 'directly or indirectly' to her mother and would not attempt to see her if and when she came to England. But the Duke of Brunswick's death could not be passed over in silence. He was Caroline's brother and had died heroically defending the Allied cause. Charlotte therefore asked, and was permitted to write a letter of condolence.

Thus the social niceties were observed, but as the months passed Charlotte had to accept the fact that her mother was fast approaching, if she had not already crossed, the boundary which separates the licensed eccentric from the true outcast. Stories of her outlandish appearance and behaviour proliferated, and the fastidious Lady Bessborough did not attempt to conceal her revulsion when a short, very fat, elderly woman, with 'an extremely red face', dressed in a girl's white frock but cut quite low, 'disgustingly so' in fact, down to the middle of her stomach, and a black wig surmounted by a wreath of pale pink roses, was pointed out to her as the Princess of Wales. 'I could not bear the sort of whispering and talking all round about the Principessa d'Inghilterra [*sic*],' she commented.

By the end of 1815 the last of Caroline's respectable English entourage had left her; and in December, Charlotte Bury received 'some strange and unsatisfactory tidings' of the Princess from a friend of Florence. 'At a small place called Borgo St Domino, three days' journey from hence,' wrote this lady,

what was my surprise to come up to a whole rabble rout belonging to the Princess of Wales. This consisted of twenty-four persons in all – six carriages and a baggage waggon. I saw no face that I knew; many Italians and strange-looking persons of various nations. . . . My servants told me that some of these persons declared they were going to join their Mistress at Pisa; others said they were going to the sea coast to embark for America; others that her Royal Highness was at Rome; but they all differed in their statements, and were evidently a *low* set of people. Many of the women were dressed up *like itinerant* show players, and altogether looked quite unfit to be her attendants. I did not see any person that I *mistook* for a gentleman; but my maids told me that they saw several men dressed in uniforms and swords. . . . I cannot tell you how strange it seemed to me to fall in with all this motley crew; something of regret too, mingled with the feeling – something of kindness towards that unhappy woman.

By this time some very disturbing rumours about Caroline's relations with her courier, rapidly promoted to be her chamberlain, Bartolomeo Bergami or Pergami. This individual, formerly a soldier and of a respectable but impoverished family, was notably good-looking – six feet tall, with a magnificent head of black hair, pale complexion and luxuriant mustachios. He and his numerous relations became natural successors to the Sapio-Squallinis of Bayswater days. They were loaded with gifts and favours, mostly of a financial nature, which enabled Bergami to acquire a country estate near Milan, and soon Charlotte was hearing horrifying tales of her mother being completely in the power of 'a low common servant'. She was genuinely distressed – 'wretched and horror-struck' – and ready, she said, to run any risk to serve her poor mother '*if it would be of any avail*'. But there seemed nothing she could usefully do. Even if she broke her promise to her father and wrote to Caroline, she could not see that it would achieve anything but more wretchedness. 'Sacrificing *myself with her* [Caroline] can be of no use,' she observed; 'sacrificing myself *for her* still less' – and especially not at a time when her own affairs were reaching a critical state.

She was packed off to Weymouth at the end of July, lamenting: 'I cannot choose for myself; I am quite dependent; such is my hard fate.' She believed her departure was being hastened to get her out of the way of a great row currently brewing up over the Duke of Cumberland's marriage to the Princess of Solms, a divorcee whom the Queen flatly refused to receive. Charlotte, on the whole, supported her grandmother, but 'the discussions in the family are *grievous*, and the terms they are on very bad'.

Before leaving town Charlotte had formally applied to the

Regent through Lord Liverpool, asking for his consent to her marriage with Prince Leopold. The response had not been particularly encouraging. 'I have seen Liverpool,' she told Mercer on 22 July, 'who told me he had said and done all I desired, but that the PR's answer was: "This was a subject he could not now enter upon, from the state of the continent and the negotiations, therefore it was again *postponed* for his R.H.'s *further consideration.*"' Lord Liverpool felt he had done all he could, and Charlotte, on the advice of Mercer and the Duke and Duchess of York, resigned herself to waiting until after the end of her forthcoming three months' exile, when she intended to push the matter again with 'a *direct* and formal attack by letter to the P.R.'. But so much waiting and suspense was hard to endure. 'I am grown thin,' she wrote to Priscilla Burghersh, 'sleep ill, and eat but little. Baily says my complaints are all nervous and that bathing and sailing will brace me; but I say *oh no*! no good can be done whilst the mind and soul are on the rack.'

She was due to set out for Weymouth on 26 July, but a few days before had made a rare and interesting excursion, driving through the City to the docks. 'I did not get out but saw all I could of them in a carriage. It is a most curious and grand sight, and gives me a vast idea of our country's consequence. The scene is quite different to anything else one has ever seen, and the 1000 of people employed, and the *sort of people* got together, gives me an idea of what a *real mass* is composed of. The tars received me very well, for they gave me 3 cheers as I past.'

Arrived at Gloucester Lodge her thoughts reverted once more to the subject of Leopold, who must by now, she believed, be at Paris with his regiment of the Grand Duke Constantine's cuirassiers. She begged Mercer to write to him again. 'Pray make your letter a kind one, but preach up prudence. A false step now I feel would ruin all.' It hardly seemed necessary, on past form, to preach prudence to Leopold, and a fortnight later Charlotte was fretting over his continued inaction. Paris was so near and yet so far. 'Oh why should he not come over . . . it is but a run over of a few hours. I quite languish for his arrival. He is *really wrong in keeping back* as he does.' And again, on 21 August: 'I am surprised Leo has not answered you yet, I think he might be a little quicker in what he is about. . . . I sincerely trust when it comes to the push that he will act a spirited manly part. . . . Do make him write to you soon, and never forget to let me know when you hear.'

A few days earlier Charlotte had received some encouragement from an unexpected quarter. 'Now I will tell you an extraordinary thing,' she wrote to Mercer on the 13th, 'wh. is that I have reason to believe Garth *knows* what has passed between the P.R. and me and Lord Liverpool, for he *spoke to me unasked* about it yesterday.' It seemed that General Garth had hinted that if the Princess was patient and quiet for just a little longer, 'all would go well'. He went on to advise her not to approach her father's ministers, because that made him jealous and angry. She would do better always to apply direct to himself'. This was not the moment for anything to be settled, as there were too many things on the *tapis*. But she might call Garth an old fool if all was not arranged as she wished by Christmas. Charlotte had ungratefully called Garth a two-faced, cunning old dog on her arrival at Weymouth, but he was undoubtedly well informed – 'I do certainly think he knows more than he likes to say' – and he was to prove a useful friend.

Towards the end of August came the news of Slender Billy's betrothal to the Russian Grand Duchess Anne. 'He has none of my good wishes', wrote Charlotte nastily, 'except that of his being *made sufficiently* uneasy by his Grand Dss.' But as if the Orange Prince's removal from the matrimonial scene had been a signal, Mercer heard at last from Leopold, and on the night of Tuesday the 29th Charlotte was writing: 'I am *delighted*, not to say *charmed* and *flattered*, at what Leo writes about his sentiments and feelings for me, and the way in wh. he expresses himself is peculiarly pleasing.'

There was some talk of Leopold's coming over – to Brighton, of all places – and having a secret interview with Mercer. Charlotte was terrified that gossip about F. might reach him from the Prussians, or that her father would try to put him off by telling tales about 'Hesse's affair'. Mercer was therefore to 'clear all that up', leaving *no doubts, no tales* uncleared or undiscovered'. Charlotte could honestly say that she had 'quite entirely got the better' of the F. business, and only sometimes thought of him now 'a little with fear lest what *has passed* should come to light, and *spoil all* that I have *really* and *truly* set *my heart and mind* upon'. This was all the result of 'having been imprudent and done wrong', sighed Charlotte, brooding over her purple past; but, thank God, she had learned some wisdom at last and no longer felt any inclination to get into scrapes.

Meanwhile, the interminable autumn weeks of waiting dragged by. Leopold had retreated into another of his unaccountable silences, and Charlotte heard a whisper that he was not coming *this year* but *early in the next*. There were more foreign princes in London at the end of October, two Austrian archdukes – 'the infernal Arches' – and a Prince of Hesse Homburg. 'There will be so many proposed and thought of', grumbled Charlotte, 'that I think the best thing I can do to make *all easy and equally* pleased is to *marry them all at once in the lump*.'

On Sunday 12 November she was writing to tell Mercer 'of an *adventure* wh. has happened to me'. Two days before, looking out of her dressing-room window, she had seen a man with his arm in a sling, sauntering up and down the Esplanade. He looked exactly like Mr Hesse, and Charlotte, watching him through her 'teliscope', found that it was indeed 'identically him'. What to do was the next question. Certainly there was no time to be lost, for she dared not think of the consequences if the Regent were to learn of the 'little lieutenant's' presence in Weymouth.

Sensibly, she laid the problem before General Garth, who

would, in any case, quickly have found out about it, 'as he knows everything that is done in this place, and everybody that comes in and out of it'. The old General responded at once to this appeal to his chivalry – 'very reasonable, and really kind and good natured'. He sought out the intruder and, following Charlotte's instructions, urged him to leave town without delay, adding a warning that the repercussions, if his imprudent appearance came to the notice of 'higher powers', would be most serious. Hesse proved tractable, submissive even. He was, he said, on his way to Cornwall and, never having been to Weymouth, had stopped off for a few hours to see the place, 'but with no view at all of remaining'. He readily agreed to leave next day, and Charlotte actually saw him go, for he walked past Gloucester Lodge on his way to catch the noon coach for Exeter. Whether Mr Hesse had been entirely truthful about his reasons for coming to Weymouth, where he must have known the princess was in residence, remains somewhat questionable, but Charlotte was greatly relieved that the whole disturbing incident had ended so 'quietly and well'. Garth promised to say nothing about it, 'that it should remain between us'. However, as an extra safeguard, Charlotte decided to write and tell the Duke of York, so that 'in case it ever came out hereafter . . . he might be able to say he had heard it all from me immediately'.

She also seized the opportunity to ask her uncle Frederick *fairly for his advice* as to what action he thought she could, or should, now take 'on a certain subject'. She felt her claim to some further exertions being made on her behalf was reasonable, bearing in mind the length of time which had elapsed. Her twentieth birthday was fast approaching, and surely she had arrived at that time of life when she might be considered old enough to know her own mind. 'The fact is', she wrote to Mercer, 'I am resolved on the thing, and nothing shall prevent my following it up thro' thick and thin.' She had come to regard Frederick as her principal ally within the family and was bitterly disappointed when a letter came from him on 22 November in which 'the subject' was not even mentioned. For all her anxiety that things should be 'pushed with the P.R. and that he should come to some eclaircissement [sic] with me', there seemed to be nothing she could do. It was up to Leopold to make the next move, and, if only he would come, Charlotte felt all difficulties would be done away with. Meanwhile, she was completely in the dark, though there was 'evidently something behind the curtain' which was being kept from her. The Yorks '*must know more than* they chose [sic] to allow or to tell'.

Things were, in fact, beginning to move at last, and on 5 December the Princess received another letter from Frederick assuring her that, though absent, she was not forgotten, and her *real friends* were doing everything in their power to serve her. A number of influential persons were now urging the Regent to make a push to settle his daughter's future. The Duke of Kent, as well as the Duke and Duchess of York, spoke out in favour of Leopold. So did Lord Castlereagh. The Foreign Secretary had met the Coburg Prince in Vienna and formed a high opinion of his character and abilities. The Earl of Lauderdale, another peer who knew Leopold personally, was asked to supply a character reference by Lord Anglesey and 'came out strong' in the young man's favour, praising his 'good feeling and good sense'. Lauderdale also dismissed the Regent's fears that Leopold might show 'a propensity towards Russia'. On the contrary, he had 'a mania for England and English manners'. Anglesey was convinced and he and Lord Castlereagh between them appeared to have been largely instrumental in overcoming the Regent's prejudices, although he never did like Leopold. Indeed, Anglesey, a hero of Waterloo, later boasted to Queen Victoria that he had 'a great hand' in persuading the Prince to consent to the Coburg marriage.

Charlotte returned to Cranbourne Lodge on New Year's Day 1816 in better spirits than she had been for a long time. Lady Ilchester noticed a new air of happiness about her, and gossip had already begun to spread that she was to marry

Leopold of Saxe-Coburg 'at her own request'. Charlotte blamed Lady Castlereagh for this, but felt it was not entirely a bad thing that 'my liking Leo should be a little talked of'. On 6 January she travelled to Brighton with the Queen and the princesses Elizabeth and Mary to stay at the Pavilion, where her twentieth birthday was celebrated with the usual family dinner party. The visit lasted for two weeks, and during that time father and daughter had their long-awaited *éclaircissement* about her future. The Regent was in approachable mood and ready to listen, but Charlotte, as always when they came face to face, found herself tongue-tied and paralysed with nervous tension.

'You do not see Charlotte at all to advantage,' the Queen had once remarked revealingly to her eldest son. 'She is quite different with us, I assure you.'

'You always say so, I know,' he replied. 'It is very unfortunate, but she appears to me half in the sulks.'

Having once more failed to break the communication barrier, Charlotte was obliged to have recourse to writing what she had been unable to put into speech, confirming that she did indeed wish to marry the Prince of Coburg and promising that no one would be more steady and consistent in this present and last engagement than herself. So it was settled at last, and an official invitation was dispatched to Leopold.

Back at Cranbourne Lodge, Charlotte was soon happily discussing wedding plans with Mercer. The intention, it seems, was that she should be married from Carlton House as the Prince of Wales's daughter rather than the heiress presumptive to the Crown, and with as little fuss and delay as possible. By this time everyone was talking about the marriage, although Charlotte herself was still pledged to secrecy – a promise which she faithfully kept, except in her letters to Mercer. 'I should be as apt as you to suspect this silence and secrecy was *for no good*', she wrote on 18 February, 'but that so *much mystery* is always made in this house about every trifle.' It had been just the same over the Prince of Orange, and Charlotte suspected that her father knew of 'Leo having had *some Opposition friends* or correspondents', which would explain his urgent instructions, relayed through Lord Castlereagh, that Leopold was not to be allowed to make contact with anyone until he had been to Brighton.

In fact, no one of whatever political complexion had yet had the opportunity to make contact with Leopold. He had been on his way east and was at Berlin before the Foreign Office messenger finally caught up with him; but on 21 February, Charlotte could find *no reason* (except the bad roads) for his not being here now. As it happened he arrived that very day, checking in at the Clarendon Hotel in Bond Street in a dinstinctly travel-worn condition and suffering from an acute attack of neuralgia. 'He says he waits to see me to cure that and all other ailments,' wrote Charlotte happily. 'I find he is to be *naturalized*, wh. will take 3 weeks doing. Only think *how absurd*, I am still not *absolved* from my promise of secrecy.'

There had been rumours in the press 'of an intention to appoint Prince Leopold Viceroy of Hanover', or that he had asked for command of the troops in Hanover, and that Charlotte had refused to marry him 'as he would take her to Hanover'. Charlotte herself believed this was '*all a humbug*' and was inclined to blame the Duke of Cumberland for trying to make mischief. But 'thank God all fear of that is over . . . for I *own* I am a *bad intreaguer* [*sic*] and a *still worse* head at finding out intreagues [*sic*]. I do like a little plain sailing.'

And now, at last, it really seemed as if it would be plain sailing. On 26 February, Charlotte went again to Brighton with her grandmother and aunts and late that evening took the opportunity of a messenger going to town in the morning to scrawl one line to Mercer to announce the final arrival of the Prince of Coburg. He was all she had ever hoped he would be, and more. 'I find him quite charming, and I go to

bed happier than I have ever done yet in my life.' They had
had a delightful evening together discussing their future
plans, and 'as far as he is concerned I have not one anxious
wish left'. Charlotte was almost pathetically appreciative of
her good luck. 'I am certainly a most fortunate creature and
have to bless God. A Pss. never, I believe, set out in life (or
married) with such prospects of happiness, real domestic
ones like other people. I am so very grateful at my lot, I
cannot express it sufficiently to you.'

This sojourn in Brighton was a brief one, only four or five
days, but it was a period of unclouded and unusual goodwill
all round. The Regent, in 'high spirits, good looks and humor
[*sic*]', much better than Charlottte had expected, was
wheeling himself about in his 'merlin chair' to save his
swollen gouty legs, although these seemed 'considerably
reduced'. The old Queen actually did not play cards,
preferring to sit and talk instead. Charlotte had never seen
her grandmother 'so happy or so gracious as she is, delighted
at my marriage, and with him. . . . She has told the P.R. that
it is a *match* she *most highly approves* and had *long wished*.' As
for Charlotte, she continued to *delight* in Coburg because, she
told Mercer, she was '*quite satisfied he is really*, truly and
sincerely attached *to me*, and very much so desirous to the
greatest degree to do all in his power to make me happy. In
return, she was prepared *quite to give up* riding, as Leo
thought it too violent an exercise for ladies. He said they
would walk a great deal together and 'be a great deal
together', and if there were parties 'he could go to and that I
could not, why that he should decline them, preferring to
stay with me and not leave me alone'. She kept finding new
talents in her betrothed, who seemed to have a thousand
resources – 'musick, singing, drawing, agriculture, farming
and botany' – and besides all that he was a capital Italian
scholar, 'so I have *everything* almost I could *wish* and *desire
collected together in one*'. 'Everyone is pleased with him,' she
wrote on 1 March; 'certainly his manners and appearance

strike amazingly. The P.R. told me it would be my *own fault* if I was not happy, as from the little he had seen . . . he thought he had every qualification to make a woman happy' – and the P.R. should have been an authority on the subject.

Certainly Leopold was doing his very best to please, and Charlotte thought he was 'terribly afraid of anything offending or frightening the P.R.' and thus giving him an excuse for delaying or breaking off the marriage which 'in his heart he don't like', even at this late stage. Leopold had been advised by his friend Lauderdale 'to conciliate and keep as quiet as he could' until the knot was actually tied, though this was hardly necessary. The young Coburger had not waited so long and so patiently to run any foolish risks now that the prize was within his grasp. He was well aware that he was regarded in some quarters as a very poor match for the heiress to the British crown – the near penniless sixth child and youngest son of a minor German ducal family, he wielded no political influence, brought with him no great political or dynastic alliance. Admittedly this could have its advantages – at least there would be no conflict of interests and loyalties such as had contributed to the Orange fiasco – and at twenty-five Leopold's reputation was commendably unsullied by scandal of any kind; but these negative virtues apart, it could reasonably be postulated that he had little to offer beyond youth and, hopefully, virility, a serious, well-informed mind, undeniable good looks, and highly polished manners. Not that these last appealed to everyone. Lady Charlotte Bury, who had encountered the Prince on her travels, noticed that he never looked at the person he was speaking to. She thought him sly and was instinctively disinclined to trust him. The Prince Regent nicknamed him 'le Marquis *peu à peu*', while the more rough-hewn members of the family found him too smooth-spoken by half – 'a damned humbug' was the verdict of Lord Frederick Fitzclarence. But although there is no doubt that behind the suavely ingratiating façade lurked a shrewd, coldly calculating political brain and a driving ambition, Leopold, unlike many ambitious men, was prepared to be agreeable while elbowing his way upwards. He contrived to manage the Prince Regent without any of the unpleasantness and *tracasseries* so frequent inside the royal circle – 'Coburg says petit à petit, then we will go our own way.' He was wise enough to take great pains to cultivate the Queen and to avoid any exchange of confidences with the princesses.

On 2 March, Charlotte was packed off back to Cranbourne Lodge, leaving her betrothed at Brighton under the jealous eye of his prospective father-in-law. Leopold did not care for the heavy drinking at the Pavilion and found that the stifling overheated rooms made his neuralgia worse; but he thought it better to remain on the spot, reported Charlotte, as there was so much business to be got through. On the whole, the pre-marriage business went through very smoothly. The contract was being drafted, and Charlotte found to her relief that 'the article' – that is, the clause stipulating her right to remain in England – had been included 'without even my asking for it'. The formal announcements of the betrothal was sent to the House of Commons on 14 March and received with apparently unanimous acclaim – both government and opposition being pleased and relieved to see the princess's future settled at last. Financial matters were now debated, and it was agreed that the young people should be granted an annual income of £50,000 to enable them to maintain an establishment suitable to their rank and station. In addition, Charlotte was to have £10,000 a year 'pin-money', out of which she would pay her ladies, maids, and so on. The rest of the household was all in Leopold's department. 'I *see he will be master* of his own house too,' wrote his fiancée happily. It was further agreed that whichever died first, the survivor would continue to enjoy the same income, and Parliament proceeded to vote a capital sum of £60,000 to be spent on furniture, plate, jewellery, and other 'personal equipment' necessary for setting up house for the first time. Charlotte was delighted at the generosity shown to her. 'It will be my anxious wish and study' she told Lady Charlotte

Lindsay, 'to prove myself worthy, and grateful to my country and its representatives for all they have *said* and done for me, by setting a *moral* and *well-principled* example before them.' Her only concern was that the Regent, with his well-known insouciance over money, had very little idea of how far £50,000 a year would go and talked of 'tacking on to us a quantity of people wh. will be too much, and must be reduced afterwards'. Eight footmen, for example, would be unnecessarily ostentatious, nor did she think she needed as many as four ladies at the *enormous* salaries of £400 a year. However, as Coburg said again 'petit à petit'. Things would sort themselves out when they had felt their way a little, and Charlotte was very glad to find that 'no one can think more rightly than C. does upon the consequences of getting into debt'.

Houses were also being discussed. Cranbourne Lodge was to be given up by mutual consent and agreement. 'Neither Leo, myself *nor* the Regent are in favour of my keeping it.' The Queen, too, thought it was a mistake for any newly married couple to live too close to their family or be too intimate with them. Besides which, if Charlotte and Leopold had remained at Windsor, she would be sure to be accused of spying on them. Castle Hill, the Duke of Kent's villa at Ealing, was considered as a possible alternative. Charlotte thought it would have done very well as a first home – 'all ready to go into, a charming distance from town, quite within itself and a most complete house and place'. Lord Liverpool, however, opposed the idea *vehemently*, on what grounds the princess did not know, unless it was that he disliked the thought of obliging poor Edward by putting money into his pocket. In the end, Claremont House at Esher was decided on – 'the most beautiful house and place possible' – and, despite the rather mean-spirited objections of the Opposition MP George Tierney, Claremont and its 200-acre park were acquired by the government for the sum of £69,000.

In contrast to the splendours of their country home,

Camelford House, which had been leased as a town residence, was a cramped, depressing place situated at the north end of Park Lane with a frontage on Oxford Street. It was much too small, wrote Charlotte, after she had seen the plans; 'it will do for this season, but really for the next we must look out for another'. She was absorbed in plans for the future. She and Leo were thinking of making some trips round England and Scotland later in the summer, as Leo liked the idea of showing himself to the people at Charlotte's side. Nothing, though, could be said about this yet, for fear of rousing the Regent's jealousy. Leo talked of going abroad, perhaps next year, and paying a round of family visits – to Brunswick, to Stuttgart to see the former Princess Royal, to Hanover to the Duke of Cambridge, and then to Coburg. He seemed, Charlotte noted with an air of faint surprise, to be 'vastly fond of his family who are exceedingly united'. She herself would rather have liked to visit Europe for a few weeks *this* summer. 'Another year there is no saying what may happen or turn up, and I confess I should be very sorry were anything to prevent my being *once at least* on the *Continent* in my life.' However, Leo thought it would be tactless to leave England so soon after Parliament had granted them such a handsome income, and Charlotte had but one wish 'that of doing what is right and what will be liked by this country'.

During the two months which preceded her marriage she saw very little of her betrothed and never alone – the PR being determined that this engagement should be conducted on very different lines to the previous one – but her enthusiasm remained undimmed. Interspersed with details of houses and servants' wages – £40 a year for a footman was surely ample – her letters to Mercer are full of admiring references to Leo's many attributes, his amiability, kindness, consideration, and general thoughtfulness. He had 'a very good head and understanding, and temper, besides being affectionate and warm hearted, as well as much delicacy of feeling'. In fact, taken altogether, he was 'a very dear creature'.

Although the correspondence continued to flow throughout March and April, the relationship with Margaret Mercer Elphinstone was not quite what it had once been. The arrival of Leopold inevitably lessened Charlotte's dependence on the friend who had guided, supported, and to a large extent dominated her during the difficult, unhappy years of her adolescence, but the direction of Mercer's life was changing too. She had recently formed an attachment for a French diplomat, the Comte de Flahault, of whom Leopold disapproved. 'I must not forget to tell you', wrote Charlotte, 'that I am *desired by him* to *scold you* for your *intimacy* with Flahaud.' Mercer (who subsequently married the Comte) took offence, and despite Charlotte's anxious attempts to placate her – 'you know I must love you always just as much and just the same, independently of who you live with and what your society may be' – the friendship began to wither away, as no doubt Leopold had intended that it should.

Meanwhile, preparations for the wedding were well under way. On 10 April, Mr Phillips, Charlotte's new steward, moved into Camelford House to begin the daunting task of making it 'in every respect a suitable residence for the illustrious couple'. It was decreed that the illustrious couple's liveried servants should wear bottle-green coats ornamented with gold lace, and waistcoats and breeches of fine white cloth, but the ornaments and decorations for the carriages being built for them had not yet been finally settled. Charlotte's own trousseau was being made in the Mayfair workrooms of Mrs Triand and Mrs Bean – gowns of net over satin, embroidered in gold and bright and dead silver, and trimmed with lace; a gown of silver tissue trimmed with silver lace and Brussels point; gowns of fine Indian muslin all worked with embroidery and heavily decorated with flounces of Mechlin or Valenciennes; two dresses of Brussels point and two more of British blond net and lace to be worn over satin slips; several dresses of plain satin handsomely trimmed with lace and net, and so on and on. There were some thirty garments altogether, plus bonnets and caps, ruffs and cuffs, and capes. All these splendours had been ordered by the Queen. Charlotte seems to have taken very little interest in her clothes or her appearance.

The date of the wedding had been fixed for 2 May. Official notice of the event was sent to the diplomatic corps and cards of invitation issued. On 22 April, Leopold arrived at Windsor, and on the 25th there was a big family dinner party to celebrate Princess Mary's fortieth birthday. The Regent was in good form and spirits, but Charlotte was shocked by his appearance – 'he looks old and ugly, and is grown to an immense size'. Four days later the family began moving up to London for the wedding. Leopold was staying at Clarence House, where large crowds of well-wishers were waiting to see him. These crowds continued to gather in the Stable Yard in front of Clarence House, shouting, cheering, and 'huzzaing', until his Highness, 'in the most condescending and gentlemanlike manner', came out on to the first-floor balcony, bowing politely to the assembled multitude. And for the next two days he continued to appear at frequent intervals to be stared at, still patiently bowing and smiling. This 'ready and cheerful exhibition of himself' greatly endeared him to the Londoners, who quite took the handsome, unassuming young man to their hearts.

People were in holiday mood – glad perhaps of the excuse of a royal wedding to forget, however briefly, the general gloom of the post-war economic depression – and the comings and goings of the royal family during the pre-wedding period provided the crowds milling about in the Mall with plenty to stare and huzza at. On 30 April, Leopold, wearing his Russian dress uniform with 'a very brilliant Austrian order' on a light blue ribbon of watered silk, drove to Carlton House in one of the Regent's carriages to attend a formal reception; and shortly afterwards Charlotte, in purple silk and white feathers, was to be seen on her way to Buckingham House to a private Court. On 1 May, Leopold met his bride, with the Queen and Princess Mary, at Camelford House, which, on inspection, was found to be very poky and inconvenient. After this, the ladies went to look at the wedding dress while Leopold returned to Clarence House, where he resumed his balcony scenes with the constantly changing throng of spectators until it was time for a dinner attended by the foreign ambassadors and ministers.

The wedding itself, 'looked forward to by many with the most anxious wishes, and by the nation at large with the fondest hopes', dawned fine and sunny. By early morning the streets were crowded, and every inch of space from Charing Cross to Carlton House and along the Mall in St James's Park was fully occupied. At 10 a.m. a team of fine matched grey carriage horses, chosen 'from a taste of the Princess for horses of that colour', were brought to Clarence House for Leopold's approval before being trotted away to Oatlands, where the honeymoon was being spent. During the morning a guard of honour of the Grenadier guards with the band of the Coldstreams in full dress marched into Pall Mall to take up their station in the courtyard of Carlton House, and after them came the magistrates Sir Nathaniel Conant and Mr Birnie leading some fifty police officers and constables who were to keep order in the public streets. About two o'clock Leopold came out in a curricle and drove round to see Charlotte at Warwick House. When he returned at half-past three the crowds had increased so that there was nearly a nasty incident. A footman, letting him out of the carriage, was nearly crushed to death, and a number of women and children were forced into Clarence House by the press.

Charlotte had spent the morning sitting to the sculptor Turnerelli, who was doing a bust of her, and chatting to a party of friends. After Leopold had left her in the afternoon, she changed and drove to Buckingham House for a quiet dinner with her grandmother and aunts, while the groom entertained 'a select party of gentlemen' at Clarence House. The ceremony was to take place at 9 p.m. in the Crimson Saloon at Carlton House, and, as soon as dinner was over, Charlotte went upstairs to put on her wedding dress. This was a slip of white and silver with a border of bunches of flowers forming festoons round the hem. The sleeves and neck were trimmed with Brussels point lace, and the train, two and a half yards long, was in the same white and silver trimmed to match the dress, which it was said had cost more than £10,000. For her wedding Charlotte wore a wreath of diamond leaves and rosebuds, with a diamond necklace and large drop earrings given to her by her father and a diamond bracelet, the gift of Prince Leopold. A few minutes before eight o'clock she came down the grand staircase at Buckingham House in all her glittering finery and proceeded to the entrance of the grand hall, where she was met by the Queen and watched by those ladies and gentlemen privileged to stand inside the courtyard to see the various royal personages as they came out to their carriages. For the journey back to Carlton House, Charlotte rode in the first carriage with her grandmother and aunts Augusta and Elizabeth, followed by the princesses Mary and Sophia of Gloucester and escorted by a posse of Life Guards. 'Bless me, what a crowd!' exclaimed the bride as the procession emerged into the Mall to be greeted by a storm of cheering from the huge mass of people, who had been waiting patiently for this moment since early morning.

When Leopold appeared in the doorway of Clarence House to get into his carriage, he was received with equal enthusiasm, especially by the female spectators, 'whose hearty good wishes were not confined to the waving of handkerchiefs . . . but proceeded to the homely though sincere declaration of the interest they felt in his hopes and future felicity, by approaching him closely, patting him on the back, and invoking upon him blessings of every description'.

> *First came a crowd of fair beholders*
> *To bless and clap him on the shoulders,*
> *Giving him many hearty smacks*
> *And calling him a lad of wax,*
> *Desiring him to use her well,*
> *With other things I must not tell.*

Some of the more exuberent spirits in the crowd wanted to take the horses out of the traces and draw the Prince's carriage, 'in the accustomed spirit of English good-will', to Carlton House themselves. But they were tactfully dissuaded from this ungenteel proceeding, and the groom arrived in proper order within the colonnade of his father-in-law's palatial residence to the welcoming strains of the national anthem.

Charlotte's fears that she might be given a 'smuggled' wedding had proved groundless, and she had nothing to complain of in her father's stage-management of the occasion. The Grand Crimson Saloon had been fitted up with 'an elegant temporary altar', and the crimson velvet cushions, the prayer books, candlesticks, and other church plate had been brought over from the Chapel Royal. All the Cabinet ministers were there, except Lord Liverpool, who was indisposed; all the officers of the royal household and the diplomatic corps; nearly all the aunts; and three of the uncles. Not present was the bride's mother. In the spring of 1816 the Princess of Wales and her motley crew of companions were somewhere in the eastern Mediterranean *en route* to the Holy Land. Another, and rather more surprising, absentee was Margaret Mercer Elphinstone, also said to be unwell.

Charlotte was given away by her father, resplendent in Field Marshal's uniform and wearing all his orders. The Great U.P. was among the clergymen present, but the marriage service was taken by the Archbishop of Canterbury assisted by the Bishop of London. The bride, it was reported, 'advanced to the altar with steadiness, and went through the ceremony with a chastened joy, giving the responses with great clearness, so as to be heard distinctly by every person present'. The service was a short one, lasting no more than twenty-five minutes, and as it came to an end 'the brazen throats' of the guns on Horse Guards Parade and the Tower batteries barked in salute, announcing to the metropolis and the nation that Princess Charlotte of Wales and the Prince of Saxe-Coburg Saalfeld were man and wife. The newly-weds did not linger at Carlton House. Charlotte embraced her assembled relations, kissing her aunts and shaking hands – 'twanging hands' perhaps – with her uncles, before retiring to change into a going-away costume of white silk dress, white satin pelisse trimmed with ermine, and white feathered bonnet. She did not take leave of the company, but avoided 'all compliments and congratulations' by slipping away down the private stairs to the ground floor. Leopold was waiting to join her, but it is said that as they were about to drive away the Queen, in a sudden access of prudery, declared it would be improper for them to travel without a chaperone and ordered Mrs Campbell to sit between them. Mrs Campbell however, refused to put herself into such an embarrassing position, and before an argument could develop the carriage had sped off into the summer night, bearing Charlotte away to her new life, so long and so ardently desired.

Although Mercer had not been at the wedding, she was still very much in Charlotte's thoughts, and her last words as she drove away had been to her maid to go and tell Miss Elphinstone 'how I looked and was to the last'. 'I am calmer today altogether', she wrote on the second day of the honeymoon, 'but I cannot tell you how strange it all is and appears to me . . . for it all seems to be a dream. . . . You ask me about Leo. He is very amiable and very affectionate and kind to me, the perfection of a lover and a very agreeable and comfortable companion.' Before her marriage Charlotte had, at the Regent's behest, nerved herself 'with much difficulty' to tell Leopold all about Captain Hesse. He had taken it 'uncommonly well' and been very understanding, saying 'it was past and long gone by and should not be thought or talked of any more'. He had not, however, concealed how shocked he felt at Caroline's part in the affair and had told Charlotte bluntly that her mother's conduct 'was so notorious and so much talked of abroad that he was as well informed as everyone else was about her'. At the same time, he had seemed to feel for and pity her situation, as she was torn between her parents, and had assured her that 'his conduct would always be that of the utmost confidence and openness'.

On 4 May the honeymooners were honoured by 'a very *unexpected* and *undesired*' visit from the Prince Regent. To Charlotte's relief, no dangerous or disagreeable subject was touched on. Instead the Regent chose to hold forth on one of his favourite topics – 'the merits and demerits of such and such a uniform, the cut of such a coat, cape, sleeve, small clothes, etc. In short for 2 hours and more I think we had a most learned dissertation upon every regiment under the sun wh. is a *great mark* of the *most perfect good humor* [*sic*].' And, as his daughter later heard from both her aunt Mary and from Mrs Campbell, the PR had been 'delighted with his visit and with both of us'.

They stayed about ten days at Oatlands, and it was not, in fact, a period of unalloyed bliss. Charlotte was still a little shy of her husband, and not yet 'quite comfortable' in his society, although she expected this sort of awkwardness would soon wear off. Also they were neither of them feeling well. Charlotte blamed this in part on the weather, which after the usual fashion of an English May had turned damp and cold. And then, the air of the house was really quite unwholesome, impregnated as it was with 'the smell and breath of the Duchess of York's menagerie' of pet dogs, birds, and all sorts of animals. Another inconvenience was that hardly any of her elegant and expensive new clothes fitted her. 'Conceive what a *bore* . . . I have been obliged to get a girl from the village to help Louis to alter some of them, that I might have something to put on.' But there was the charming novelty of going to church at Weybridge on her husband's arm and helping him with his English – he was making very good progress considering how short a time had been learning the language. There had been a delightful excursion, too, over to Claremont, which was a real paradise. Charlotte was shown round the house and kitchen garden and found it *princely*, 'the *most fit royal residence* that can be found anywhere'.

By the middle of the month they were back in town, moving into Camelford House and taking their place in London society. The Queen held a grand Nuptial Drawing-Room on the 16th 'for the purpose of receiving publicly . . . the congratulations of the English nobility and gentry, as well as of the foreigners of distinction, upon the happy event of the marriage of her Royal Highness the Princess Charlotte'; and so great was the number of those wishing to attend that at one time the queue of carriages stretched as far as Oxford Street. On 23 May there was a Court at Carlton House when the Regent invested his son-in-law with the Garter and the Grand Cross of the Bath, and that evening Charlotte and Leopold held their first dinner party, at which the Regent was guest of honour.

They made several visits to the opera and to the theatre. They saw Edmund Kean at Drury Lane; Mrs Siddons as Queen Katherine in Shakespeare's *Henry VIII* at Covent Garden; *The Jealous Wife*, a comedy, also at Covent Garden; and a performance of Italian opera for which tickets were being sold at the extortionate price of ten guineas. Charlotte had always been an enthusiastic play- and opera-goer, but gone were the days when her father had insisted that she stay at the back of the box and leave inconspicuously before the end of the last act. Now, when she occupied the royal box with her husband beside her, the performance would be interrupted for 'God Save the King', and the audience clamoured noisily to see them, ignoring the unfortunate actors until they had stared and applauded their fill. But Charlotte was unable to attend a special performance of *Macbeth*, arranged for 9 June, at which the ageing Mrs Siddons was to recreate one of her most renowned tragic roles as Lady Macbeth. The princess was indisposed with a troublesome cold and cough. A month later she was again unwell – it was given out that she had caught a cold at the Opera House – and was obliged to cancel all her engagements, including a visit to the Guildhall to see Leopold and three of the royal dukes receive the freedom of the City of London. She was also unable to attend the wedding on 22 July of her favourite aunt Mary to the despised 'Slice' of Gloucester. Rumours were circulating that the real cause of Charlotte's repeated indisposition was 'more calculated to excite joy than fear throughout the nation', but by the end of July it had leaked out that she had miscarried and that 'the nations's hopes must for a time be considered annihilated'. It was not until 8 August that the Princess ventured out again, taking the air in an open barouche on the Harrow Road, followed by a short outing next day in the direction of Chelsea with Prince Leopold at her side. Leopold had not been well either. He had had a recurrence of the neuralgia and toothache which had afflicted him on his arrival in England and had been obliged to endure a painful extraction which kept him out of circulation for a week.

By this time they were both anxious to leave the gloom and cramped surroundings of Camelford House. There had been some talk of their taking over the vacant apartments in Kensington Palace as a temporary expedient, but the idea was abandoned, as the purchase of Claremont was now complete, and Charlotte wanted to move down to the country as soon as the house could be got ready. Preparations for the move were therefore pushed ahead. Furniture and household effects went off in daily convoys of army waggons, with the more valuable articles being dispatched separately, and on the day of the move itself, 24 August, a stage coach specially hired for the occasion set out from Camelford House laden with the domestic staff and their belongings, followed shortly afterwards by the officers of the household in a fleet of carriages. Charlotte and Leopold left together at half-past three to reach their destination in time for dinner. Crowds had gathered and waited all day on the road leading to Claremont House, and as soon as the royal carriage came into view the bells of the little town of Esher, which bordered the Claremont estate, 'struck up a joyous peal'. Charlotte went up the steps leading to the front door of her new home and turned to look at the view, exclaiming: 'Well, thank Heaven, I am here at last!'

Certainly Claremont was a charming spot for any young couple to being their married life. Designed by Capability Brown for Clive of India in the late 1760s, it was built in the Palladian style and set in grounds originally laid out by William Kent, the first English landscape gardener. The view from the library windows was especially picturesque, with lawns sloping away to a sheet of water populated by swans and further decorated by a little Gothic cottage. To Charlotte, used all her life to being arbitrarily shunted about from one characterless and unloved abode to another, to be mistress of Claremont seemed paradise indeed. 'I am so perfectly happy,' she wrote to Mercer on 26 August. The marriage which she had once coolly envisaged as no more than a means of escape from intolerable bondage, and the husband who had been chosen as the best of the uninspiring bunch – 'the *best* of all those I *have seen*' – were bringing her a serenity and fulfilment beyond anything she had dreamt of. 'What makes it the more delightful is that our mutual affection has grown by degrees, and with the more intimate acquaintance and knowledge of each other's dispositions and characters.' Charlotte, in short, was deep in love, with all her natural, warm-hearted generosity, for so long repressed and rejected, at last finding a legitimate outlet.

If Leopold sometimes felt a trifle overwhelmed, he did not

show it. On the contrary, he appeared from the first to be very much in control on the domestic front. He had told Charlotte before they were married that he would do everything in his power 'to soothe and calm' that nervous agitation of spirit induced by all the trauma of her early life – her parents' battles, her mother's indiscretions, her father's insensitive despotism – and he was as good as his word. From the beginning, too, he set himself the task of soothing the rough edges of his bride's still distressingly hoydenish deportment. His close friend and confidant, the young German doctor Christian Stockmar, who first met Charlotte at Claremont, commented that she was better looking than he had expected, but 'with most peculiar manners, her hands generally folded behind her, her body always pushed forward, never standing quiet, from time to time stamping her foot, laughing a great deal, and talking still more'. Charlotte and Stockmar had encountered one another unexpectedly at the breakfast table, and his first impression was not favourable – the princess staring him up and down with the unnerving, unselfconscious rudeness of a small child. But as he got to know her better he came to appreciate her 'good and noble' qualities, and she accepted him into the charmed circle at Claremont for Leopold's sake.

Stockmar, recalling the harmony, peace, and love which had reigned at Claremont, considered Leopold to have been 'the best of all husbands in all the four quarters of the globe', and Leopold did undoubtedly exert a calming and beneficient influence over the volatile Charlotte. 'Doucement, chérie, doucement,' he would murmur when her laughter grew too loud or her speech to voluble. Sometimes,too, he would utter words of gentle reproof when she seemed to make unkind fun of some acquaintance – he could not reconcile the habit of 'quizzing' to any rule of good breeding. This all makes him sound intolerably priggish, but Charlotte, always so self-willed, so stubborn and hot-tempered, accepted his criticisms and his rule of never letting the sun go down on *ein*

Missverständniss, however trifling, with almost embarrassing docility. The wiseacres who had prophesied with gloomy relish that she would certainly wear the breeches were confounded – and yet there was no mystery about it. For the first time since the far-off days of Eggy and Mr Nott, Charlotte had come into the hands of a mentor she could both love and respect, whose good opinion she was eager to earn. They were always together, the very picture of domestic felicity, reading, walking, driving, playing the piano, singing duets. Charlotte would comb and arrange her husband's thick, silky hair and fold his cravats, and was always to be seen in public leaning on his arm.

'Except when I went out to shoot, we were together always,' Leopold remembered, 'and we *could* be together, we did not tire.' It was during these quiet months – 'we lead a very quiet and retired life here, but a very *very* happy one' – that Leopold was unobtrusively laying the foundations of what he hoped would be a lifelong habit of deference to his judgement and authority. Charlotte, pathetically anxious to please, revelling in her new role of Mrs Coburg, the submissive and obedient wife, scarcely noticed that, with Leopold always present, making the decisions, choosing their friends, she had done little more than change one form of subjugation for another.

The Coburgs, as they were becoming known, did some entertaining that first autumn. The newly married Gloucesters came over from Bagshot and the Duchess of York from Oatlands. It was delightful having Oatlands so near. The Duchess was a dear, 'so kind and amiable, and the footing we are upon is just what could be desired when such near relations agree and mutually like one another'. The Prince Regent also paid a visit in October, riding over from Hampton Court and spending three hours walking round the Claremont estate. One good result of her marriage was the improvement in Charlotte's relationship with her father. Now that she no longer had to face him alone, she found she could be almost at ease with him.

At the beginning of December the Coburgs were persuaded to join a family house-party at the Pavilion. The Queen was there – but, thought her granddaughter, 'looking ill and sunk a good deal' – the princesses Augusta and Elizabeth, the Gloucesters, and the Duke of Clarence. 'All was good humour', and it appeared the Regent wanted to make everybody comfortable 'and as much at their ease as possible'. Charlotte, unfortunately was unwell again, but the visit passed off without any awkward or embarrassing incidents. The fact that everybody kept their own hours and did what they liked during the day, only meeting for dinner at six o'clock, helped to cut down the Regent's opportunities of being rude to the Duke of Gloucester. Charlotte and Leopold amused themselves by going for walks round Brighton. The first time they ventured out they were mobbed by enthusiastic crowds and had to be rescued by the police, so that, on subsequent occasions, it was thought prudent to have a carriage following them close behind in case they needed to extricate themselves from the over-friendly attentions of the multitude.

They were back at Claremont in time for Leopold's birthday on the 16th, which was celebrated by a large party, and next day there was a ball and supper for the servants. 'I never saw people enjoy themselves more or who eat, drank and danced to such a degree,' commented Charlotte. Christmas was a happy time. Christmas Eve was always a great day at Oatlands, when the Duchess of York kept open house for all the families in the neighbourhood.

> It was the gayest and prettiest sight . . . the numbers of children, their parents, and all the happy, merry faces, the noises they make with their toys and things. Everybody has their lot and share, great and small, both in and out of the house, by which means the Duchess contrives to please everybody and to do a great deal of good by distributing clothing etc. to the poor and needy of the village.'

After a disastrous harvest, there was a great deal of distress among the poor that winter, and Charlotte and Leopold ordered that a dole of bread, meat, and flannel petticoats should be distributed to every needy household in Esher to mark Leopold's birthday.

Charlotte's own birthday, on 7 January, her twenty-first, was the occasion of a grand ball hosted by the Prince Regent at the Pavilion, but Charlotte herself was not there. She preferred to celebrate her coming of age quietly at home with her husband. She had been married eight months now, and the only tiny cloud on the horizon was her failure so far to stay pregnant for more than a few weeks – she had had a second miscarriage in December.

At the beginning of February 1817 the artist Joseph Farington heard that the Princess 'suffered in her health' and there was no prospect of her being able to bear a child in the foreseeable future. Farington's information, however, was inaccurate. Charlotte conceived again in February, and, at the end of April, Leopold came to town especially to tell the Regent that she was in an interesting situation. This time there was no early mishap, and there seemed every prospect of her carrying the child to term.

TEN

That Good and Generous Charlotte

Daughter of England; for a Nation's sighs,
A Nation's heart, went with thine obsequies:
And oft shall time revert a look of grief,
On thine existence, beautiful and brief
Thomas Campbell, Monody

I am going to die, Mr Brougham; but it does not signify.
Queen Caroline

Peace, harmony and married bliss continued to prevail at Claremont throughout the spring and summer of 1817. The Coburgs paid a few brief visits to town, but Charlotte was always anxious to get back to Claremont where she and Leopold were full of schemes for improvements. Leopold had introduced his wife to the pleasures of gardening and together they planned new hothouses, a conservatory, and a Gothic temple or summer house to be built overlooking the lake. Some ill-natured persons complained that the nation was not paying the princess £60,000 a year to live in rural retreat, but neither criticism of her life-style, nor awareness of the hardships caused by continuing economic recession, could dim Charlotte's present happiness. After all, as she remarked reasonably enough, she could not alleviate the distresses of the people single-handed. She did, though, support a campaign to buy British started by the Regent, announcing that in future all her clothes would be of British materials and manufacture, and she and Leopold ordered a thousand pounds' worth of Spitalfields silk for the drawing-room at Claremont. They were also employing 'a vast many poor laboring people' who would otherwise be out of work and starving, and this, Charlotte thought, was 'the best charity of all'. 'We are in the middle now of rather an expensive piece of work but one exceedingly necessary . . .' she had told Mercer at the end of December, 'namely new pailing entirely round the Park, and when you see it again I flatter myself you will see considerable additions.'

Mercer was among the 'select party' of distinguished guests invited to Claremont in May, when the Coburgs' first wedding anniversary was celebrated by a dinner and musical entertainment, but the old affectionate intimacy had faded now; nor were matters improved by Mercer's refusal to return Charlotte's letters – those wildly indiscreet, emotional effusions in which the Princess had poured out all the frustrations and disappointments, the anxieties, fears and 'plagues' which had haunted her teenage years. Miss Elphinstone, about to become the Comtesse de Flahaut, offered to burn the purely personal letters (though she does not appear to have done so) and to have the rest of the correspondence deposited in a safe place in the presence of representatives of both parties, but she could not be persuaded to relinquish documents which might some day be needed as evidence to justify her past conduct – especially in connection with the breaking off of the Orange engagement.

The first date on which Charlotte could expect to be confined had been named as 19 October and in September her faithful friend and dresser Louisa Louis wrote that: 'the Princess is uncommonly well and I hope will do well'. Not everyone was quite so sanguine. Lady Holland, in a letter to Mrs Creevey also written in September, referred to 'some strange awkward symptoms' and old Queen Charlotte, who regarded herself as something of a connoisseur on the subject of childbirth, was beginning to have misgivings as she saw her granddaughter advance in her pregnancy. 'I had a bad opinion of her and named it to my daughters,' she said later, 'for her figure was so immense (to me not natural) that I could not help being uneasy to a considerable degree.' Some people, looking at Charlotte's immense figure, were moved to wonder rather nervously if she were carrying twins and whether she would be strong enough 'to go through with it'. Charlotte herself seems to have been looking forward to the approaching 'Event' with no more trepidation than was natural in a young woman awaiting the birth of her first child. 'I am not in bad spirits about it,' she told her friend Priscilla Burghersh, 'or frightened, yet I think it is a very anxious and awful moment to expect, and one that one cannot feel quite unconcerned about. Thank God! I am hitherto very well, and only hope to continue so.'

At the beginning of October the artist Thomas Lawrence spent a few days at Claremont painting a portrait of the Princess which was intended as a birthday present for her husband, and, like all their visitors, were greatly struck by the Coburgs' domestic happiness, the tranquillity and 'regularity' of their daily routine. Charlotte sat for him in the morning, with Leopold usually in attendance. In the afternoon she would go for an airing in her pony carriage, Leopold walking at her side, and then sit again for an hour or so. The household dined at about seven and afterwards there would be music, Charlotte and Leopold sitting together at the piano, often on the same long stool, or whist which Lawrence recalled, 'being played for shillings was not the most silent game I ever witnessed'. If he also recalled that occasion twenty years before, when he had painted Charlotte's mama in her tawdry tinsel palace at Blackheath, he must surely have reflected on the vast contrast between mother and daughter. Studying his present sitter with his painter's observant eye, Lawrence could not see anything of the hoyden or of that 'boisterous hilarity' said to be so characteristic of her. On the contrary, he was charmed by her simple, unaffected dignity. She seemed to him to have 'the plain honest mind of her grandfather the King' with 'no art about her'.

By this time, of course, everything was ready for the lying-in, which was to take place at Claremont. The wet nurse, the wife of a local yeoman, had been chosen and was standing by. The baby clothes, all 'in the plainest style and the finest quality', had been carefully laid out by Mrs Griffiths, the monthly nurse, 'a respectable woman in the habit of attending the first families in the country on similar occasions for the past thirty years', and Sir Richard Croft, the accoucheur, was already in residence.

Much odium has been heaped on the unfortunate Richard Croft, a fussy, pedantic individual who seems to have owed his favoured position in the medical hierarchy more to his family connections (his wife's sister was married to the royal physician Matthew Baillie) than to any outstanding professional skill or qualifications. A man of fixed ideas – among them a strong notion of his own infallibility – he nevertheless possessed the persuasive bedside manner essential for impressing and reassuring the aristocratic ladies he attended, and Charlotte, who christened him 'the old gentleman', liked and trusted him. She submitted uncomplainingly to the depressing regime of purging, blood-letting and reducing diet which he prescribed for her, and left off her stays in obedience to his dictum that since a cow did not wear stays, why should the Princess Charlotte?

Dr Baillie and another obstetrician, Dr John Sims, were on call as well as Sir Richard, but in spite of this formidable array of medical talent there were those who felt Charlotte ought to have had some female friend or relation with her, and the Queen was later criticized for having gone away to take the waters at Bath at this critical moment. No one, of course, was tactless enough to mention Charlotte's mother, or to regret the fact that she could not be at Claremont to support the princess through her ordeal. Charlotte, however, was thinking about Caroline. There had been another divorce scare the previous summer and a pamphlet entitled 'The attempt to divorce the Princess of Wales impartially considered' had been sent to Charlotte. Brougham, though, had assured her that any attempt to prove adultery with Bergami had had to be abandoned for lack of reliable evidence 'Thank God, my mind on that rubbish is now quite at rest.' But rumours about Caroline's disreputable lifestyle and the activities of the Regent's inquiry agents continued to circulate and occasionally to disturb the peace of Claremont, and at the end of October something prompted Charlotte to write to Lady Charlotte Bury asking for news. 'I have not heard from my mother for a long time. If you can give me any intelligence of her, I should be much obliged to you to do so. I am daily expecting to be confined, so you may imagine I am not very comfortable. If ever you think of me, do not imagine that *I am only a princess*, but remember me, with Leopold's kind compliments, as your sincere friend. . . .'

'Daily expecting to be confined. . . .' The autumn days passed uneventfully. Charlotte was said to be in excellent health, taking the 'moderate exercise' recommended by her physicians, walking or riding in a horse-drawn 'garden chair' in the Park or pleasure grounds, always of course escorted by her devoted consort. On 26 October they went as far as the home farm to inspect the alterations going on there and the following afternoon they walked in the shrubbery towards the grotto, or summer house, which was one of the princess's favourite projects. In the stables horses were kept ready saddled round the clock with grooms waiting to mount at a moment's notice and the nation – or at least that part of the nation which took an interest in such matters – waited eagerly for news of the first royal birth to take place since Charlotte's own. A boy would, it was estimated, send the stock market up by at least six points.

October turned into November and still the waiting went on. It was not until the small hours of Tuesday 4 November that the message at last went down to the stables sending the grooms on their way with the news that Her Royal Highness had started in labour. Dr Baillie came hurrying over from his home at Virginia Water and between the hours of five and seven on that Tuesday morning carriages bearing the Home Secretary, the Chancellor of the Exchequer, the Secretary for War, the Archbishop of Canterbury and the Bishop of London were setting their passengers down at the pillared and porticoed entrance of Claremont House. These distinguished personages had been summoned as witnesses to attest the birth, but it seemed that even now there was no particular urgency. At midday Sir Richard Croft announced that matters were 'in every way in as much forwardness as he would desire' but the Princess had still not been put to bed and was walking about her room on her husband's arm. At three o'clock another bulletin was issued, but that night Dr Sims, an expert in the use of instruments, was brought down from London, although he was not admitted to see the patient.

At a quarter past eight on the morning of Wednesday the fifth, when Charlotte had been in labour for more than thirty-six hours, the bishops and Cabinet ministers keeping their weary vigil in the breakfast room at Claremont were informed that considerable, though very gradual progress had been made during the night, and the doctors hoped that the child would be born without the need for artificial assistance. There was a strong prejudice against the use of forceps in the medical profession and, although in this case their use might conceivably have saved both mother and child, at a time when antiseptic precautions were still unknown there was always a frighteningly high morality rate when instruments *were* used.

Wednesday dragged slowly by. The village of Esher had filled up with journalists and sightseers and the Bear Inn was doing a roaring trade. At Claremont, the Princess seemed to be bearing up well under her long, exhausting, though apparently not especially painful travail. She was being devotedly supported by Leopold, who had scarcely left her side since her labour had first begun on Monday evening, walking her about her room, holding her hand and sometimes lying down on the bed beside her. At six o'clock Leopold's equerry, Sir Robert Gardner, despatched another report for transmission to the Prince Regent: 'I have heard no further fear expressed as to safety of her R. H. infant from the length of the labor – and H.R.H. I am most thankful to say has throughout preserved her spirit, and her strength continues quite equal to what the medical gentlemen expect.' Three hours later the infant was born at last. It was a boy, perfectly formed, unusually large, and dead.

Desperate efforts were made to revive it. It was slapped and shaken, plunged into hot water, rubbed with salt and mustard, even a primitive form of artificial respiration attempted; but it was no good, and at 10 p.m. a bulletin was issued over the names of all three doctors to the effect that H.R.H. the Princess Charlotte had been delivered of a still-born male child, adding that the Princess herself was 'doing extremely well'. And so indeed it seemed. Charlotte had accepted the loss of her baby with a stoicism bordering on indifference. She had been given some camphor julep as 'a cardiac stimulant' and now she was sitting up in bed eating toast and chicken broth, the first food she had been allowed to take for two days. Mrs Griffiths had gone away to change her dress and on her return the Princess exclaimed chattily, 'How smart you are, Griffiths. Why did you not put on the silk gown, my favourite?' The witnesses, having performed their gruesome duty of inspecting the baby's corpse – 'a noble infant it was, as like the Royal Family as possible' – had thankfully dispersed. Leopold, supported by Stockmar who had prudently refused to have anything to do with the proceedings in the birth chamber, went away to get some sleep. Drs Baillie and Sims also went to bed, and even Richard Croft thought it safe to leave his patient to rest.

Just after midnight Charlotte began to complain of nausea and ringing in her ears. Her pulse became rapid and although she had so far been able to keep her promise to Mrs Griffiths not to 'bawl or shriek', she was now obviously in great pain. Croft, hurriedly recalled by the nurse, found her very restless, breathing with difficulty and 'cold as any stone'. Frantically, the doctors tried to warm her, plying her with hot wine and brandy, and placing hot water bottles and hot flannels on the abdomen – this despite the fact that the recognized method of arresting *post partum* haemorrhage was to use cold compresses. The situation was now so grim that Croft himself went to Stockmar and begged him to call Leopold, but the prince was in a deep, probably sedated, sleep and before he could be roused sufficiently to take in what was happening another message came, this time from Dr Baillie, summoning Stockmar to come and see the princess. 'Here comes an old friend of yours!' cried Baillie, with the dreadful heartiness of the medico who knows that all is lost. Charlotte, 'in a state of great suffering', grasped Stockmar by the hand, pressing it 'vehemently'. The doctors were still urging her to drink. 'They have made me tipsy,' she whispered pathetically.

For the next quarter of an hour Stockmar flitted to and fro, still trying to wake Leopold, although oddly enough Charlotte does not appear to have asked for him. It was nearly half-past two when 'the rattle in the throat began'. Stockmar had just gone out of her room again, when the dying girl called out quite loudly 'Stocky! Stocky!' He went back to her. She was quieter now, but the rattling breath continued. She turned over on to her face and drew up her legs. Her hands grew cold. She was dead.

The news of the double tragedy at Claremont stunned the entire country which reacted with an unprecedented demonstration of public mourning. 'It is but little to say,' observed *The Times* newspaper in its leading article on 7 November, 'that we never recollect so strong and general an expression and indication of sorrow.' Even the poorest of the poor, it was said, tied a rag of black round their sleeves.

Henry Brougham would never forget the feelings of 'deepest sorrow and most bitter disappointment' which this melancholy event produced throughout the kingdom. 'It is scarcely possible to exaggerate, and it is difficult for persons not living at the time to believe, how universal and how genuine those feelings were' he wrote in his memoirs. 'It really was as if every household throughout Great Britain had lost a favourite child.'

Countess Granville, in a letter to her sister, felt 'quite unable to write upon any subject but one. We are all heart-sick at this terrible event. Poor Princess Charlotte. . . .' and Dorothea Lieven, the wife of the Russian ambassador, who had been a frequent visitor to Claremont, told her brother that the charming Princess Charlotte, 'so richly endowed with happiness, beauty, and splendid hopes', had been cut off from the love of a whole people. 'It is impossible to find in the history of nations or families an event which had evoked such heartfelt mourning,' she went on. 'One met in the streets people of every class in tears, the churches full at all hours, the shops shut for a fortnight (an eloquent testimony from a shop-keeping community), and everyone, from the highest to the lowest, in a state of despair which it is impossible to describe.' Up and down the country, in cathedrals, in parish churches, in chapels and in synagogues, memorial services were held and memorial sermons preached, while every public building wore a suit of black drapery. 'It certainly does not belong to us to repine at the visitations of Providence. . . .' boomed *The Times*; 'but as the Almighty sometimes, for the most benevolent purposes, deals severe chastisements on mankind, there is nothing impious in grieving for that as a calamity, which appears and is felt to be such.'

The Duke of Wellington's verdict on 'the melancholy event' was characteristically terse and to the point. He told his niece, Lady Burghersh, who had been Charlotte's friend, that he thought it probable that 'she would have behaved well,

and her death is one of the most serious misfortunes the country has ever met with'. 'She might have been great indeed,' wrote Cornelia Knight. 'She had a heart and a mind capable of rendering her so.' And Charlotte Bury, who heard the news in Italy, lamented the death of 'that kind-hearted princess', while dreading that this national calamity might be the forerunner of many future woes. 'There is now no object of great interest to the English people,' she wrote in her journal on 9 December, 'no one great rallying point, round which all parties are ready to join. . . . A greater public calamity could not have occurred to us; nor could it have happened at a more unfortunate moment.' And certainly at a time when the unemployed in the industrial towns were starving, when banks and businesses were failing at an alarming rate, and a spirit of revolution stalked the land, the death of the only member of the royal family who had seemed to offer any hope for the future of the monarchy might reasonably be regarded as calamitous by all those with an interest in the preservation of the status quo.

But if Charlotte's untimely end was a public calamity, to her husband it came as a personal disaster from which he never really recovered. To have been thus cruelly deprived of the career of power and influence which had lain before him and for which he considered himself uniquely suited was a bitter blow to a man of Leopold's energy and ambition; neither is there any reason to doubt the sincerity of his grief over the loss of the loving, passionate, sweet-natured girl who had given him eighteen months of unreserved and probably quite unexpected married bliss. He was to outlive her for nearly half a century. He became King of the Belgians. He married again and fathered a family. He saw his niece Victoria ascend the British throne and marry his nephew Albert, who was destined to fill the role he had once marked down for himself. But he never forgot 'that good and generous Charlotte' and never regained the feeling of happiness which had blessed their short life together.

To Charlotte's immediate family – her grandmother, her aunts and uncles – the news of her death brought shock and to some a genuine sadness. The old Queen covered her face and wept, while the Prince Regent was 'so deeply affected by the melancholy intelligence, that it became necessary to bleed him twice besides cupping him'. When the Princess Mary, now Duchess of Gloucester, went to him at Carlton House on 9 November, she was so distressed by the sight of 'the deep affliction which seemed almost to overwhelm her royal brother' that she was obliged to retire to another room to rest and recover her composure.

They buried Charlotte and 'her beautiful little boy' in the family vault at Windsor on the evening of 19 November with all the pompous ceremonial of a state funeral, the tolling bells, the mourning cloaks, the crape streamers, black plumes, black horses. The Great U.P. was there, and all the bishops, Old Bags and all the Cabinet Ministers – Liverpool and Castlereagh, Canning, Bathurst and Sidmouth. The doctors were there, Richard Croft (who was to kill himself three months later), Baillie and Sims and dear 'Stocky'. All the ladies and gentlemen of the various royal households were there, all the pages and equerries and chaplains, the heralds and pursuivants and kings of arms. The coffin, covered with a black velvet pall and adorned with eight escutcheons of the arms of the Princess Charlotte Augusta of Wales, was carried by eight Yeomen of the Guard under a black velvet canopy. Behind it, in the flickering light of the flambeaux held by every fourth man in the single files of Foot Guards who lined the route to St George's Chapel, walked Leopold as Chief Mourner and with him came the princes of the blood, York and Clarence, Sussex, Cumberland and Gloucester. Leopold, who had kept vigil all the previous night while Charlotte lay in state at Lower Lodge, was openly in tears and hurried away immediately after the service. The Queen and the princesses remained out of sight inside the Castle, but princess Augusta slipped out in time to hear 'the last bell for poor dear Charlotte' to have the comfort of repeating while it was sounding, 'God rest Her Soul in Peace.'

The Prince Regent was still prostrated at Carlton House and did not attend his daughter's obsequies. As for Caroline, who was living now in a villa on Lake Como, it appears that no one had troubled even to inform her of Charlotte's death and Charlotte Bury was shocked to hear that the Princess had been left to learn the news 'through the medium of a common newspaper!' Lady Charlotte hastened to write and offer her Royal Highness sincere sympathy 'in this her greatest affliction' and presently received in return a 'strangely worded but heartfelt expression of the poor mother's grief'. 'I have not only to lament an ever-beloved child', wrote Caroline, 'but one most warmly attached friend, and the only one I have had in England! But she is only gone before . . . and now I trust we shall soon meet in a much better world than the present one.'

Now that Charlotte was dead, it was generally believed that the Regent would renew his efforts to get a divorce, and in the summer of 1818 a three-man commission was despached to Italy to conduct yet another investigation into the manners and morals of the Princess of Wales. The so-called Milan Commission spent the best part of a year, and £10,000 of public money, examining no fewer than eighty-five witnesses and amassing a 'great body of evidence' to prove the existence of 'a continued adulterous intercourse' between Caroline and Bartolomeo Bergami – something which everyone who knew anything about the matter had never doubted for a moment. The Cabinet was however, extremely reluctant to sanction proceedings which would inevitably result in yet another unsavoury and possibly explosive royal scandal. The evidence brought back by the Milan Commission might look conclusive, but it was almost entirely the evidence of foreigners of the servant class, who spoke no English, and its credibility might well be destroyed in an English court. Caroline would not lack defenders only too glad of an opportunity to use her as a weapon to embarrass her husband and his government – and when it came to matters of adultery the Regent could scarcely be said to be standing on solid ground himself. There was also the little matter of bigamy, if his marriage to Mrs Fitzherbert were raised. Negotiations were, therefore, begun to try and reach a settlement. Caroline had repeatedly declared that she had no wish ever to return to England and Henry Brougham, who remained her legal adviser, thought she could be persuaded to renounce her right to the title of Queen – in other words, to a form of amicable separation – in return for a guaranteed financial settlement. Brougham strongly recommended this sensible solution as the best method of saving everyone's face. But, of course, it was not as simple as that. For one thing, it appeared that Parliament could not ratify such a settlement without proof or confession of adultery, and in any case neither side would agree to a separation by mutual consent – their bitterness and distrust went far too deep.

Matters remained in this state of suspended animation until the end of January 1820 when George III, the old, mad, blind ghost king in Windsor Castle, died at last and the Regent succeeded as George IV. But no sooner had the Proclamation been read than the new King succumbed to an acute inflammation of the lungs and for a few tense days it looked very much as if his reign might end almost before it had begun. 'Heavens, if he should die!' exclaimed Dorothea Lieven. 'Shakespeare's tragedies pale before such a catastrophe. Father and son, in the past, have been buried together. But two kings!' Catastrophe was, however, averted. The King's amazing constitution triumphed again, though as Henry Brougham told Mr Creevey, he had been 'as near death as any man . . . ever was before' and only a hundred and fifty ounces of blood let had saved his '*precious* life'.

One of the King's first acts on his recovery was to insist that his wife's name should be excluded from the Liturgy – he was immovably determined that no English congregation would ever pray for Queen Caroline, and equally determined that she should never be crowned or recognized as Queen. He was, in short, set on a divorce, no matter what he had to go through in order to get one. Caroline, for her part, was now determined to return to England to claim her undoubted legal rights. Brougham, envisaging 'every sort of mischief' and 'the risk of clamour and violence which no one can hope to estimate, far less to direct', tried his best to stop her, or at least to stop her coming further than, say, Paris or Calais. But Caroline had been listening to other advice, notably from one Alderman Matthew Wood, former Lord Mayor of London, a publicity hungry MP of extreme radical opinions and sworn enemy of the King and all he represented. The Queen, therefore, landed at Dover on 5 June to a tumultuous welcome, organized by Wood, and the scene was set for the final battle in the war which had begun just over a quarter of a century before.

An 'immense multitude' of cheering, waving people surrounded the Queen's carriage as she approached the capital. Charles Greville, who had ridden out to see the fun, found the roads thronged all the way from Westminster to Greenwich, and reported that she was everywhere received 'with the greatest enthusiasm'. Caroline, plus Willikin, was putting up at Alderman Wood's house in South Audley Street and for several days, until she moved out to the comparative tranquility of Brandenburg House at Hammersmith, London was in an uproar. Disorderly crowds roamed the West End yelling for 'Queen Caroline and her son King Austin', forcing passers-by to shout 'God Save the Queen!', demanding illuminations in her honour, smashing windows, and 'pelting those who would not take off their hats as they passed Wood's door'. Pro-Caroline demonstrations spread to the provinces and the slogan 'No Queen, no King' became the battle-cry of her supporters, who were by no means confined to the usual rioting classes. The mob screamed 'Nero!' under the windows of Carlton House, until the King, very gouty and in 'a terrible temper', retreated to Windsor, no doubt to brood on the enviable freedom enjoyed by some of his predecessors when it came to disposing of unwanted wives. An especially alarming feature of the crisis was the fact that the army, still the only effective law enforcement body, was showing ominous signs of becoming infected with the prevailing Queen-fever. A battalion of the Guards mutinied, leading one wit to observe that the extinguisher was taking fire and prompting the Duke of Wellington to reflect seriously on the need to provide some form of properly constituted, centralized civilian police force.

Greatly encouraged by the apparent strength of public sympathy for her cause, and egged on by Alderman Wood and his like, Caroline continued to refuse to consider any compromise settlement, while the King let it be known that he would abdicate rather than accept her as his Queen. The government, whose emissaries had been stoned on their visits to South Audley Street and who saw red revolution staring it in the face, was consequently obliged to bring before Parliament a Bill of Pains and Penalties, designed to prove Caroline's adultery, dissolve her marriage and deprive her of her title.

There was to be nothing in the least delicate about this investigation, which came as the climax to years of innuendo, gossip and scandal, and the so-called 'trial' of the Queen, a distasteful episode which reflected no credit on anybody, opened in the House of Lords on 17 August against a background of intense popular excitement.

The Queen arrived dressed in black sarsenet – mourning for the Duchess of York – with a white veil over her startling black wig and partially concealing her now regrettably coarse looking over-rouged complexion. She reminded Thomas Creevey of a doll called Fanny Royds – a Dutch toy with a round bottom weighted with lead so that it always jumped upright in whatever posistion it was laid. The first witness to be called was Teodoro Majocchi, who had been employed by Caroline during her travels as a livery servant. Described as a well-dressed man of decent appearance, his appearance nevertheless caused his former employer an unpleasant shock for she fixed her eyes upon him and then uttered a piercing cry of 'Teodoro, Teodoro, oh no! no!' Some people thought she had actually said 'Traditore, Traditore'. Whatever the truth, she was led away to her retiring room, looking, according to one of those present, more like fury than a woman.

Examined via an interpreter by the Attorney General, Sir Robert Gifford, Majocchi proceeded to give details of the sleeping arrangements of Caroline and Bartolomeo Bergami, her *courier de cabinet* as she described him. It appeared that it was always possible for them to move unobserved from one bedroom to the other and Majocchi, who often made the beds, could see that Bergami's had not always been slept in. During their sea voyage from the Holy Land in 1816 Caroline had had a tent pitched on deck with a sofa and travelling bed and when asked if anybody else slept in the same tent, he replied 'Bartolomeo Bergami.' He went on to say that he himself slept immediately below the deck where the tent was sited and agreed that he had heard noises 'like the creaking of a bench'. During cross-examination by Henry Brougham for Caroline, Majocchi's memory began to fail him, and his plaintive,constantly repeated cry of 'non mi ricordo' was to pass into the language as an instantly recognisable catch-phrase for anything it was not convenient to remember. Brougham was, though, able to establish that after leaving Caroline's service Majocchi had been employed by the British ambassador in Vienna where he had been interviewed by a member of the Milan Commission and hinted strongly that he was being well paid for his trouble.

The next witness was Gaetano Paturzo, who had been mate on borad the vessel which had taken the Queen and her entourage to Africa and the Holy Land and who testified that he had seen her sitting on Bergami's lap, or with their arms round each other. The ship's captain agreed that Bergami had gone below with Caroline when she was to take a bath and that he had seen her royal highness sitting and stomping on Bergami's bed. And so it went on. Two naval officers who had entertained

Caroline on her travels round the Mediterranean spoke with distaste of the liberties allowed to Bergami and an inn servant at Trieste could swear that Bergami's bed had not been slept in and that both chamber pots in the Queen's bedroom had been used – 'there was a good deal in each'. Louise Demont, Caroline's *femme de chambre* remembered an occasion at Naples when she had left her mistress undressed in her bedroom and had seen Bergami, in only his shirt and slippers, coming along the passage 'towards the bedroom of her royal highness', and Giuseppe Sacchi, courier and equerry, described finding Caroline and Bergami after a night time journey, asleep together in their carriage, with their respective hands one upon another: 'her royal highness held her hand upon the private part of Mr Bergami, and Bergami held his own upon that of her royal highness.'

Even allowing for the unreliable character of some of the evidence and the fact that some of the witnesses may well have received some financial inducement, by the time the prosecution case closed at the end of the sixteenth day, there really could be no reasonable room for doubt in anyone's mind that Caroline had indeed been guilty of 'a most unbecoming and degarding intimacy', even a 'licentious, disgraceful and adulterous intercourse' with Bartolomeo Bergami.

But the affair roused the most extraordinary passions – 'no other subject is ever talked of' – and had, of course, far more to do with the burning political and social issues of the day than with the immorality or otherwise of the unfortunate Caroline. The infamous 'Green Bag', which had contained some of the most incriminating of the affidavits collected by the Milan Commission, became a favourite subject for cartoonists as a symbol of government tyranny and corruption, while the trial itself was also a gift to the cartoonists, the lampoonists, satirists and anyone who could turn a witty phrase. Bartolomeo Bergami was a favourite butt:

> The Grand Master of St Caroline
> has found promotion's path.
> He is made both Night Companion
> and Commander of the Bath.

(This last was a reference to their shared bathing arrangements on board ship during that much discussed voyage to the Holy Land.) Caroline herself, who was inclined to snooze during the more boring bits of the proceedings in the House of Lords, inspired an epigram by Lord Holland:

> Her conduct at present no censure affords.
> She sins not with couriters, but sleeps with the Lords.

But all the jokes made at the expense of the Queen were as nothing to the flood of grossly offensive material libelling the King and his friends which was being openly hawked on the streets. This positive 'tempest of abuse' continued unchecked for months, while organized popular support for the Queen if anything increased. As the case drew towards its close, almost daily processions of sober, well-drilled citizens, many thousands strong, marching 'in a regular lock step, four or five abreast – banners flying – music playing . . .' were to be seen on their way to pay their respects to her Majesty. On 30 October Thomas Creevey recorded that he had never seen such a beautiful sight in his life as the Brass Founders' procession to the Queen that day. 'I had no notion there had been so many beautiful brass ornaments in all the world. Their men in armour, both horse and foot, were capital; nor was their humour amiss. The procession closed with a very handsome crown borne in state as a present to the Queen, preceded by a flag with the words – "The Queen's Guard are Men of *Metal*"'. Creevey estimated that there must have been 100,000 people in Piccadilly, 'all in the most perfect order'. And just as well. 'I should like any one to tell me what is to come next if this organised army loses its temper. . . .'

Thomas Creevey was by no means the only person to reflect on the all too probably consequences of such an eventuality. On 10 November the Bill of Pains and Penalties was given its third reading and passed – by a majority of nine; but the government, realizing that there was little or no chance of getting it through the Commons and terrified, not only of the counter-disclosures which might result from a debate in the Lower House, but also of the likelihood of uncontrollable mob violence breaking out if the matter was allowed to drag on any longer, decided to withdraw the whole measure. 'The Bill is gone, thank God! to the devil.'

The Opposition and all those who chose to regard the establishment's tactical retreat as a famous victory for innocence and liberty, celebrated with a three day debauch. 'The state of the town is beyond everything' wrote that sturdy Whig Thomas Creevey, who marked the occasion by drinking an extra bottle of claret with his cronies at Brook's Club, but thereafter the general hysteria began to subside and an inevitable reaction to set in.

> Most gracious Queen, we thee implore
> To go away and sin no more;
> Or if that effort be too great,
> To go away at any rate.

The following February Parliament made no difficulty about voting to exclude the Queen both from the Liturgy and the forthcoming Coronation, and when the King ventured to appear in public again at the theatre there were only some isolated shouts of 'Where's your wife, Georgy?'

It was widely expected, and certainly hoped, that Caroline would now go abroad again, but the Coronation was to take place in July 'and till that was over she could not quit London'. Her claim to be crowned had been referred to the Privy Council which ruled that 'as the Queen was living separate from the King, she had no right to be crowned; and thus it was left to the King to refuse it.' This, declared Brougham, was 'manifestly a political judgment', but he argued in vain that there was no precedent for a queen consort not being crowned 'when she was within the realm, of the same religion with the king, and willing to be crowned.'

Caroline was still living out at Brandenburg House, with a small retinue, but she was largely ostracized by society. 'Carlton House' according to Brougham, 'now took the course of filling the press with libels to deter all ladies from visiting the Queen.' Any woman of rank who accepted her invitation was liable to scurrilous attack, while at the same time the Court was thrown open to all those who were known to have shunned her. These tactics were predictably successful, not merely with the ladies but also with their male relations, who were both unwilling 'to expose their wives and sisters to a slanderous press, and averse to losing for them the balls at Carlton House.'

Caroline herself bore this spiteful campaign of persecution by the Carlton House set with 'great patience and even good humour', saying 'Oh, it is all in the common course. People go to different inns: one goes to the King's Head, another to the Angel.' She still had a few faithful supporters. The Duke of Sussex still came to see her and so did Alderman Wood and his wife. Caroline had developed one of her extraordinary violent fancies for Wood's little granddaughter, 'which amounted almost to a craze.' 'She would have it brought to play with her', wrote Brougham, 'not only at all hours of the day, but even of the night, as she often sat up till a very late hour.' This was another instance of her strange paedophilic tendencies. Brougham told Creevey that she was 'a *child-fancier*' and that in his opinion Pergami had owed his elevation in the first place to Caroline's attachment to his daughter, the Petite Victorine, who slept in her bed and to whom she left a bequest of jewellery in her will.

As the day of the coronation approached, the Queen's well-wishers tried to persuade her not to lay herself open to fresh humiliation by trying to force an entry to the Abbey, warning her 'that the public feeling would not go along with her.' The King was known to be 'beyond measure alarmed' that his bitch-queen might succeed in disrupting the extravagant ceremony of which he intended to be the undisputed star, and he ordered the Prime Minister to write and tell her that she would quite definitely not be welcome.

It was, and was meant to be, the final snub. But in spite of, or perhaps because of the efforts to dissuade her, Caroline clung to her determination to go to the Abbey and Brougham believed the authorities would let her pass if she persisted. But when she arrived in Dean's Yard at about six o'clock in the morning of 19 July 'the refusal was peremptory at all the doors of the Abbey when she tried, and one was banged in her face'. Her Chamberlain, Lord Hood, attempted to argue with one of the door-keepers who had refused to admit her without a peer's ticket. 'I present to you your Queen. Surely it is not necessary for her to have a ticket.' But orders were orders. They were specific and the door-keeper stood his ground. Caroline, however, did not. On the contrary, 'she flinched', Brougham reported, 'I verily believe, for the first time in her life; and instead of insisting on admission at the great gate, she drew back on the refusal . . . and she was entirely defeated.' It was 6.30 a.m. by the time she had finished 'her walks and calls at the doors' and got back into her carriage to return the way she had come, by Whitehall, Pall Mall and Piccadilly. There was some cheering. A section of the crowd followed her hooting and cursing the King and 'huzzaing' the Queen. But there was none of the wild enthusiasm of the previous summer and there was some unkind laughter, some hissing and shouts of 'Shame!' and 'Go away!' and 'Back to Bergami!'

It was the end of the road for Caroline. She was now a very sick woman, suffering great pain from an inflammation or obstruction of the bowels – presumably cancer – for which she dosed herself with enough calomel and castor oil to 'turn the stomach of a horse'. When Brougham saw her for the last time at the beginning of August, she told him with great firmness – 'I am going to die, Mr Brougham; but it does not signify.' Brougham said – 'Your Majesty's physicians are quite of a different opinion.' – 'Ah', she said, 'I know better than them. I tell you I shall die, but I don't mind it.' And die she did, at twenty-five minutes past ten o'clock on the evening of 8 August 1821.

The King had just arrived at the beginning of a state visit to Ireland when the news of his wife's death reached him and the government was greatly relieved when it was discovered that Caroline had asked to be buried in her family's vault at Brunswick. This, at least, avoided the embarrassment of a funeral at Windsor, but there remained the problem of transporting the coffin out of the country. Efforts to prevent the cortege from travelling through the City were frustrated by the mob – the chief Bow Street magistrate fearing that lives would be lost 'if it was persisted in not to go through the City' – and the procession went on its way through the town of Chelmsford to Harwich, where everything was ready for immediate embarkation. The scene was one which Henry Brougham could never forget 'or reflect upon without emotion. The multitudes assembled from all parts of the country were immense, and the pier crowded with them, as the sea was covered with boats of every size and kind, and the colours of the vessels were half-mast high, as on days of mourning. The contrast of a bright sun with the gloom on every face was striking, and the guns firing at intervals made a solemn impression . . . The crimson coffin slowly descended from the pier, and the barge that conveyed it bore the flag of England, floating over "Caroline of Brunswick, the injured Queen of England" . . .' Thomas Creevey wished he could have been there to see what, according to Brougham's account, was 'the most touching spectacle that can be imagined . . . soldiers and sailors all behaving themselves with the most touching solemnity – the yards of the four ships of war all manned – the Royal Standard drooping over the coffin . . . and thousands of people on the beach sobbing out loud . . . It was as it should be – and the only thing that was so during the six and twenty years' connection of this unhappy woman with this country.'

Charlotte Bury thought Caroline's fate 'must excite compassion in the sternest hearts . . . Divested by the King of the pomps and pleasures of royalty, she was at the same time debarred from the enjoyments of private life.' She had no relatives who cared for her and being a warm-hearted, affectionate creature would surely have pined without some object to love and be loved by. So, concluded Lady Charlotte, the Queen's death came as a 'happy release from loneliness and persecution'. Charlotte Bury had often in the past had cause to deprecate Caroline's reckless indiscretion, her lapses from good taste, her eccentricities and uncouth habits, but felt it must be left to posterity to decide 'how far her virtues were her own, and how far her follies were occasioned by force of circumstances, and the cruel treatment she received.' At the moment of her death one feeling alone could predominate, 'that of pity for her sufferings.'

Against all expectations King George IV lived on for another nine years and his death, in the early hours of Friday, 26 June 1830 marked the end of an era. There was little pretence at public mourning. 'King George had not been dead three days', observed Charles Greville, 'before everybody discovered that he was no loss.' There never was an individual less regretted by his fellow creatures than this deceased King', added *The Times* which did not even wait until the deceased King was in his grave before attacking his 'reckless, unceasing and unbounded prodigality', his 'indifference to the feelings of others' and his course of life, 'the character of which rose little higher than that of animal indulgence'. A few people, remembering past glories and past kindnesses received from that 'most extraordinary compound of talent, wit, buffoonery, obstinacy, and good feeling', did genuinely grieve for 'poor Prinney'. But the country in general was unmoved, except by relief. The usual decencies were perfunctorily observed, though on the day of the funeral *The Times* noticed 'no solemn expression of feeling nor much decorum of behaviour' and all Windsor was said to have been drunk that night. Bells tolled and minute guns fired from the Tower and St James's Park, but in London the streets gave 'more the appearance of rejoicing than mourning'. It seemed, in fact, 'more as if some good news had arrived than anything else.'

Although it was true he had 'never sincerely inspired anyone with attachment', that he was 'full of vanity and could be flattered at will', Dorothea Lieven, herself a highly polished and sophisticated cosmopolitan, had admired the King, finding him an amusing, well educated companion and conversationalist. Indeed, she had never known a person like him, 'who was also affectionate, sympathetic and gallant.' Charles Greville, on the other hand considered that, taken one with another, kings generally were of an inferior character and George IV 'one of the worst of the kind . . . with vices and weaknesses of the lowest and most contemptible order'. But let the last word on the subject to go that intelligent Frenchman Prince Talleyrand, who remarked that 'King George IV was *un roi grand seigneur*. There are no others left.' Perhaps it was just as well.

A Note on Sources

There is a great deal of material in print on both Caroline and Charlotte and the following should be regarded as no more than a general indication of the sources I found most valuable in writing this book.

First and foremost and indispensable were the collections of royal correspondence compiled and edited by the late Professor A. Aspinall, C.V.O., M.A., D. Litt. *The Correspondence of George, Prince of Wales*, 1770–1812, 8 vols. Cassell, 1963–71, *The Letters of King George IV*, 1812–1830, 3 vols., Cambridge University Press, 1938, *Letters of the Princess Charlotte*, 1811–1817, Home & Van Thal, 1949 (Fortunately for posterity, Mercer Elphinstone continued to resist the efforts of the royal family to persuade her to return Charlotte's letters. They later passed into the hands of her daughter, who married the 4th Marquess of Lansdowne, and were deposited in the Lansdowne family archives at Bowood.)

Among the contemporary diaries, memoirs and collections of correspondence, the most helpful for my purposes were: *The Diaries and Correspondence of James Harris first Earl of Malmesbury* (the Malmesbury Diaries) ed. 3rd Earl of Malmesbury, 4 vols. 1844, which provide a vivid and detailed picture of Caroline prior to her marriage and of her journey to England in 1795. *The Diary of a Lady in Waiting by Lady Charlotte Bury: Being the Diary Illustrative of the Times of George IV* (Bury Diary), ed. A.F. Steuart, 2 vols. 1908. Lady Charlotte, the younger daughter of the 5th Duke of Argyll, joined the Princess of Wales's 'family' in 1810 and remained with her on and off for the next five years. Although often disapproving, she felt 'a genuine compassion and a real though contemptuous affection' for the Princess and her

Diary provides a rich vein of first-hand description and reminiscence. *Fifty Years of my Life* by George Thomas (Keppel), Earl of Albermarle, 2 vols., 1876 is another valuable primary source. George Keppel was the grandson of Princess Charlotte's governess, Lady de Clifford and from 1808 to about 1810 the two were regular playmates. Also indispensable for Charlotte during the critical period 1812–1814 is Cornelia Knight's *Autobiography*, 2 vols., 1861. A one volume edition, edited by Roger Fulford was published by William Kimber in 1960. *The Life and Times of Henry, Lord Brougham* written by himself, 3 vols., 1871 contains Brougham's recollections of his dealings with both Caroline and Charlotte, with special reference to Charlotte's flight from Warwick House in 1814 and Caroline's 'trial' before the House of Lords in 1820. Other contemporary sources containing more occasional references include: *Extracts of the Journals and Correspondence of Miss (Mary) Berry from the year 1783–1852*, ed. Theresa Lewis, 3 vols., 1865; *The Creevey Papers*, Selected and edited by John Gore, John Murray, 1948; *Diaries of Sylvester Douglas* (Lord Glenbervie), ed. Francis Bickley 1928. *Granville Correspondence*, 1781–1921, ed. Leveson-Gower, 2 vols., 1916; Greville Memoirs, 1814–1860, ed. Lytton Strachey and Roger Fulford, Macmillan, 1938; and *The Private Letters of Princess Lieven to Prince Meternich*, ed. Peter Quennell and Dilys Powell, John Murray, 1948.

For material covering The Delicate Investigation of 1805/6, see *The Book, or the Proceedings and Correspondence upon the Subject of the Inquiry into the Conduct of the Princess of Wales*, printed by Richard Edwards, 1813. For the 'trial' of 1820, see the contemporary press reports, Brougham, Greville, Creevey and, for a modern account, *The Trial of Queen Caroline*, Roger Fulford, Batsford, 1967.

There are numerous contemporary or near contemporary biographies of both Caroline and Charlotte. The most useful are: *Memoirs of Caroline, Queen of Great Britain*, Robert Huish, 2 vols., 1821; *Lives of the Hanoverian Queens of England*, Alice

Greenwood, 2 vols., 1909–11; *Memoirs of Charlotte, Princess of Wales*, Robert Huish, 1818, and *A Brief Memoir of the Princess Charlotte of Wales* by Lady Rose Weigall, 1874, which contains the letters written by Princess Charlotte, the Princess Royal and Duchess of Würtemberg to Lady Elgin on the subject of little Charlotte's upbringing.

Modern biographies include: *Caroline*, Thea Holme, Hamish Hamilton, 1979; *The Regent and His Daughter*, Dormer Creston, Eyre & Spottiswoode, 1932; *Daughter of England*, D.M. Stuart, Macmillan, 1951; *Prinny's Daughter*, Thea Holme, Hamish Hamilton, 1976. See also *George, Prince of Wales*, Christopher Hibbert, Longmans, 1972 and *George IV, Regent and King*, Christopher Hibbert, Allen Lane, 1973; *The Disastrous Marriage*, Joanna Richardson, Cape, 1960; *The Royal Dukes*, Roger Fulford, Duckworth, 1933; *The Daughters of George III*, D.M. Stuart, Macmillan, 1939, and *Unruly Queen*, Flora Fraser, John Murray, 1996.

Index